ART AND THE TRANSITIONAL OBJECT IN VERNON LEE'S SUPERNATURAL TALES

For
Catherine and Terry

Art and the Transitional Object in Vernon Lee's Supernatural Tales

PATRICIA PULHAM
University of Portsmouth, UK

ASHGATE

Published by
Ashgate Publishing Limited
Gower House
Croft Road
Aldershot
Hampshire GU11 3HR
England

Ashgate Publishing Company
Suite 420
101 Cherry Street
Burlington, VT 05401-4405
USA

Ashgate website: http://www.ashgate.com

British Library Cataloguing in Publication Data
Pulham, Patricia, 1959–
   Art and the transitional object in Vernon Lee's supernatural tales
   1. Lee, Vernon, 1856–1935 – Criticism and interpretation 2. Fantasy fiction, English – History and criticism 3. Sex in literature 4. Aesthetics in literature 5. Voice in literature 6. Transitional objects (Psychology)
   I. Title
   823.8

Library of Congress Cataloging-in-Publication Data
Pulham, Patricia, 1959–
   Art and the transitional object in Vernon Lee's supernatural tales / by Patricia Pulham.
      p. cm.
   Includes bibliographical references and index.
   ISBN 978-0-7546-5096-6 (alk. paper)
   1. Lee, Vernon, 1856–1935—Criticism and interpretation. 2. Fantasy fiction, English—History and criticism. I. Title.

   PR5115.P2Z84 2007
   824'.8—dc22

2007023678

ISBN 978-0-7546-5096-6

Printed and bound in Great Britain by MPG Books Ltd, Bodmin, Cornwall.

Contents

List of Figures

Acknowledgements

Many people, including friends and family members, have provided invaluable support during the writing of this book which emerged from a doctoral dissertation completed at Queen Mary, University of London in 2001, financed by the Stopford Brooke Studentship Award, and a grant from the British Federation of Women Graduates. I am very grateful to all those who contributed to my success in gaining these awards, including Markman Ellis and Cornelia Cook, and especially to my D.Phil. supervisor, Catherine Maxwell, who introduced me to Vernon Lee, and whose infectious enthusiasm for her work has been a source of unfailing intellectual pleasure. I am also indebted to the University of London for funding my research at Colby College, Maine, U.S.A., and at the British Institute in Florence. My thanks to Nancy Reinhardt, Patricia Burdick, Mark Roberts and Alyson Price for their assistance with queries regarding the special collections at these institutions. I would also like to acknowledge the Centre for European and International Studies Research at the University of Portsmouth for funding the teaching relief that allowed me to bring this project to completion.

In its transformation from thesis to book, the manuscript has undergone a number of revisions based on the constructive comments of those who have taken the time to read through various versions and I wish to thank my examiners, Sally Ledger and Angela Leighton, for their initial observations, and the anonymous reader at Ashgate Press who had faith in my work. In particular, I am grateful to Carol Barker and Bran Nicol for their pertinent suggestions and continual encouragement. I should also like to express my gratitude to Susan Coffey, Franca Basta and Carlotta Farese for their help with translations and the acquisition of illustrations, and to Martin Bennett and colleagues at the University of Portsmouth for their practical advice. Finally, my special thanks to Terry, Joe and Sam Pulham for their love and their patience.

Part of Chapter One was originally published as 'The Castrato and the Cry in Vernon Lee's Wicked Voices' in *Victorian Literature and Culture*, Vol. 30, no. 2, (2002). Thanks to Abigail Bloom, Cambridge University Press, and the editors of *Victorian Literature and Culture* for granting me permission to reproduce this material and to the Harry Ransom Humanities Research Center, University of Texas at Austin for permitting quotations from Lee's letters to her publisher John Lane.

Introduction

In her preface to *Hauntings: Fantastic Stories* (1890), Vernon Lee questions the definition of a 'genuine ghost' (2006, 39). For Lee, this figure is not to be found in the annals of the Society for Psychical Research, but in one's own psyche: she asks, 'is not this he, or she, this one born of ourselves, of the weird places we have seen, the strange stories we have heard?' (2006, 39).[1] And the spirit's home is the Past, in which 'a legion of ghosts, very vague and changeful, are perpetually to and fro, fetching and carrying for us between it and the Present' (2006, 39). By the time Peter Gunn wrote his 1964 biography, *Vernon Lee: Violet Paget, 1856–1935*, Lee, now remembered only vaguely by the older generation, had become a similarly 'shadowy figure' who had performed a comparable function, writing for a late-Victorian audience about people, places, and events from the past (Gunn 1964, ix). Since then, she has entered the academic consciousness from time to time, but it is not until the 1980s that one sees a stronger resurgence of interest in her work, prompted perhaps by the reclamation of neglected women writers initiated by feminist critics. Subsequently, critical attention has been maintained, resulting in a range of journal articles, book chapters and three new full-length studies: Vineta Colby's *Vernon Lee: A Literary Biography* (2003); Christa Zorn's *Vernon Lee: Aesthetics, History, and the Victorian Female Intellectual* (2003); and Mary Patricia Kane's *Spurious Ghosts: The Fantastic Tales of Vernon Lee* (2004). More recently, two collections of critical essays, *Vernon Lee: Decadence, Ethics, Aesthetics* (2006), and *Vernon Lee e Firenze settant'anni dopo* (2006), as well as the first annotated edition of selected supernatural stories, *Hauntings and Other Fantastic Tales* (2006) have been published.[2]

In the last twenty years of the nineteenth century, however, Lee was recognized by educated readers as a significant writer, thinker and intellectual who contributed to important literary, cultural, and political debates. Having achieved prominence in 1880 with a critical work on Italian culture, *Studies of the Eighteenth Century in Italy*, she began to move in artistic circles that included significant literary figures such as Robert Browning, Walter Pater, Henry James, and Oscar Wilde. Between her professional debut in 1880 and the publication of her final major work, *Music and Its Lovers* in 1932, she wrote prodigiously, achieving international recognition and producing a wide range of works that covered fiction, history, aesthetics, philosophy and travel writing. The decline in her literary status as the twentieth century progressed was due to a number of factors: her work was not disseminated wisely; she became increasingly interested in obscure philosophical issues; the traditional essay style she favoured gradually grew unfashionable; and her strong pacifist views during World War One won her few friends in England. The arrival of modernism sealed her fate for, though her fiction often displayed that psychological and narrative complexity which features in modernist literature, and critical works such as *The Handling of Words and Other Studies in Literary Psychology* (1923) anticipated close-reading methods developed in I. A. Richards's *Principles of*

Literary Criticism (1926) and *Practical Criticism* (1929), her successors were eager to distance themselves from their Victorian precursors and often dismissed the latter's valuable contribution to their own intellectual development.[3] Despite this reluctance to recognize their literary predecessors, many modernists were evidently influenced by them. In *The Myth of the Modern*, Perry Meisel explores the fact that, at times, 'modernism' appears to be 'prisoner to the regime from which it claims to depart' and traces 'genealogical' relations between writers such as Arnold and Pater, Eliot and Joyce (1987, 9). Similarly, Woolf, in her reviews of Lee's works, admonishes what she calls Lee's 'slipshod thinking', but nevertheless admits that 'although we may doubt her conclusions … her exposition is full of ingenuity, and has often the suggestive power of brilliant talk', demonstrating her passion for the topics she discusses and infecting 'others with the same desire' (McNeillie, 1986, 158; 279).[4] Furthermore, in the penultimate chapter of *A Room of One's Own* (1929), Woolf tacitly acknowledges Lee's standing among female intellectuals, listing her 'books on aesthetics' alongside 'Jane Harrison's books on Greek archaeology' and 'Gertrude Bell's books on Persia' (1965, 79). Trapped between the Victorians and the modernists, Lee existed in a literary borderland, inhabiting an in-betweenness that also characterized her life and informed her work.

Born in Boulogne-sur-Mer, France, in 1856, Lee spent her early years in France, Switzerland, and Germany, before finally settling in Italy. She was a truly cosmopolitan figure, fluent in English, French, Italian, and German. As Christa Zorn notes, her 'extensive knowledge' of European literature and thought also 'brought her the attention of a more international community than most of her British contemporaries enjoyed', and this intellectual influence is evident in those 'references to European art and literature, to myth, history, and geography' that abound in her work (Zorn 2003, 2; Lee 2006, 10). In his review of *Satan the Waster* (1920), Lee's polemic on World War One, George Bernard Shaw applauded her 'cosmopolitan intellectualism', claiming that she had 'the whole European situation in the hollow of her hand', and when she died, Maurice Baring wrote in *The Times* that her death would 'make a gap in the world of European culture' (quoted in Gardner 1987, 44, 30). Whereas the in-between nature of Lee's national status sometimes proved profitable, other forms of liminality appeared less advantageous. While the modern reader may align her with that late-Victorian phenomenon, the 'New Woman', and admire her confidence, independence and refreshing lack of concern for public opinion, some of her male contemporaries were less enamoured:

> Lee's strong personality and strongly held opinions seem to have aroused the hostility of a number of male writers and thinkers: the historian John Addington Symonds (1840– 1893) resented her failure to accept his corrections, the philosopher Bertrand Russell (1872–1970) appeared jealous of her sway over younger women, the cartoonist Max Beerbohm (1872–1956) nastily caricatured her as a busybody who picked fights with male luminaries, and the art historian and critic Bernard Berenson (1865–1959) accused her of plagiarising his ideas (Maxwell and Pulham 2006, 10).

Such open disapproval stemmed perhaps from their own intellectual anxieties and it is clear that Berenson, at least, reluctantly admired her essay writing, noting that it had 'a lyrical form' and claimed of his early encounters with Lee's work:

'I didn't read her for the facts—it was for the vision, the inspiration she gave me' quoted in Gardner 1987, 61). In her discussion of Lee's critical reception, Zorn observes that her early critics 'share a language that splices the idiom of difference and classification with gender' 2003, 14). Some see her as 'a new type of female writer, who "possesses a vigorous pen ... unafraid to grapple with subjects women usually avoid"' while others, such as James Jackson Jarvis, 'a reviewer for the *New York Times* in 1879' reinforce sexual stereotypes, maintaining that Lee displays '"much careless thinking, not unusual in her sex in serious writing"' Zorn 2003, 14–15). Given that critiques of her work were often informed by considerations of gender, it is hardly surprising that, by 1878, Violet Paget had already assumed the 'masculine pen name' and 'male persona' – 'Vernon Lee'(Colby 2003, 52).

The assumption of a 'masculine' or, perhaps more accurately, androgynous, identity in her literary endeavours was coupled by the adoption of 'mannish attire— dark, severely tailored dresses, high starched collars, stiff bowler or boater hats' in everyday life (Colby 2003, 52). As a 'mannish woman' Lee contravened the expectations of conventional femininity, and raised the spectre of a fluid sexuality that complicates readings of her passionate friendships with women. Although, as Zorn remarks, Lee 'was not a self-identified lesbian', she engaged in a number of intimate relationships with women, including Annie Meyer, the poet Mary Robinson, and Clementina Anstruther-Thomson with whom she worked on the subject of physiological and psychological aesthetics (Zorn 2003, 98).[5] Vernon Lee's sexuality has long been a topic of discussion: in consultation with his friend, the sexologist Havelock Ellis, John Addington Symonds considered that she and Mary Robinson 'might serve as a possible case-history for the section on Lesbianism' in *Sexual Inversion* (1896); in her memoir, *As Time Went On* (1936), Ethel Smyth suggested that Lee's 'lesbian tendencies were repressed'; her executor, Irene Cooper Willis, argued that 'Vernon was homosexual but she never faced up to sexual facts'; and in a doctoral dissertation written in 1954, later published in book form as *The Lesbian Imagination (Victorian Style): A Psychological and Critical Study of 'Vernon Lee'* (1987), Burdett Gardner produced a full-length analysis of Lee's sexuality (quoted in Colby 2003, 51, 176; quoted in Gardner 1987, 85).[6] Gardner's negative, but informative, study examines Lee's sexual proclivities from a Freudian perspective in order to analyse the effect of what he calls her 'neurosis' on her writings and has influenced a number of later critical discussions of her work (Gardner 1987, 28).[7]

As Sally Newman observes, the descriptions of Lee afforded by Smyth and Cooper Willis and, one might add, Gardner, construct her 'as a "failed lesbian"' (2005, 55). Others, however, suggest a more direct lesbian identification by referring to Vernon Lee as Anstruther-Thomson's 'lover' (Maltz 1999, 21). Yet, as Newman points out, the term 'lesbian'itself requires interrogation. She argues that these representations of Lee's sexuality 'still circulate without any examination of the foundational assumptions upon which they rest' and suggests that we should ask 'What constitutes a lesbian? What is this lesbian desire everyone is talking about? And what does physical expression have to do with it?' (2005, 57). But, as Newman herself admits, these questions are difficult to answer and are continually debated for precisely that reason. While critics such as Newman, Martha Vicinus, Kathy Alexis Psomiades, and Christa Zorn have shown that it is possible to write sensitively and creatively about Lee's close friendships with women, it is notably difficult to discuss sexualities that, in Lee's own lifetime, sexologists had only recently begun to define, and using the term 'lesbian' in relation to Vernon Lee, and/or describing her relationships as 'romantic friendships' seem decidedly unsatisfactory.

As Sylvia Martin notes, the 'problem of the body underpins the division between romantic friends and lesbians as well as the dimensions of the debate. "Romantic friendship" tries to erase the body, emphasizing love and friendship' while '"lesbianism" foregrounds it, stressing sexual desire and practice' (quoted in Newman 2005, 59). Vicinus, in her history of same-sex partnerships published in 2004 attempts to negotiate these complications: the title of her book, refers to both 'intimate friends' and to 'women who loved women', while Colby, in her literary biography of Lee, calls her friendship with Mary Robinson a 'Boston Marriage', and stresses that 'their relationship was and remained nonsexual in the physical sense' (Colby 2003, 58).[8] Meanwhile, Zorn struggles to find a term that is sufficiently inclusive of Lee's passions for women, yet not reductive, and settles finally on Terry Castle's phrase 'lesbian worldliness', which positions the lesbian writer 'in "the very fabric of cultural life"' informed by 'an "expansive, outward-looking, and multifaceted humanity" as a function of difference' (2003, 99). Zorn argues that this term is useful when analysing *fin-de-siècle* literature like Lee's, 'since the homoerotic configurations in Lee's texts are large metaphorical spaces' which are available to 'mainstream audiences' while simultaneously 'inscribing a minority discourse that becomes a controlling center as soon as it is recognized' (2003, 99). My own discussion of Vernon Lee's short stories is informed by such concerns, and aims at a similar kind of cultural 'double-vision'. It focuses on questions of gender and sexuality, but examines these through the art object which fuels a conflict between its representation in Lee's writings on aesthetics and its, often homoerotic, role in her richly decadent fiction. However, my study centres not on Vernon Lee as biographical entity, but on 'Vernon Lee' as literary construction, although the tensions between these identities necessarily result in occasional slippages in the process of analysis.

So who is 'Vernon Lee'? In a letter to her friend, Mrs Jenkin, of 6 April 1875, in which she discusses her planned pseudonym, Lee writes 'The name I have chosen as containing part of my brother's and my father's and my own initials is H. P. Vernon-Lee. It has the advantage of leaving it undecided whether the writer be a man or a woman' (1937, 49), and eventually settles on the more familiar, shortened, version of this name. Lee, it seems, chose deliberately an androgynous *nom de plume* for her literary persona which, Newman claims, appears to be 'much more' than simply a pseudonym, being 'her chosen name and identification' (2005, 51, n. 1). Irene Cooper Willis, in a letter of the 22 August 1952 written to Professor Carl Weber at Colby College, Maine, where the majority of the Lee archive is now housed, states:

I must ask you to call [the catalog] the Vernon Lee issue. Except to mere acquaintances she was never known as Miss Paget: and she would have objected strongly to being referred to as Violet Paget in connection with her writings and papers. She was always known and thought of by her friends and readers as Vernon Lee (quoted in Newman 2005, 51).

This partially adopted 'masculinity' also informs certain aspects of her writing. Zorn notes that her 'theoretical texts deliver their messages in an interesting overlay of individual and general voice using the common "we" or "one," by which she could pass as a male writer', and speaking of her own artistic development in *The Handling of Words*, Lee observes, 'I can recognize long preliminary stages of being *not oneself*; of being; *being* not merely *trying* to be, an adulterated Ruskin, Pater, Michelet, Henry James, or a highly watered-down mixture of these and others, with only a late, rather sudden, curdling and emergence of something one recognizes … *as oneself*' (2003, 76; 1923, 296). The predominance of masculine names in this list suggests that, at the start of her writing career, Lee saw herself as competing mainly with men in the literary marketplace. Although, in a recent article, Emily Harrington (2006) argues that Lee was influenced by intellectual exchanges with women, in particular Mary Robinson, it is clear, as explained in the introduction to *Vernon Lee: Decadence, Ethics, Aesthetics*, that 'with the important exception of her mother' – who wished Lee to become another Mme de Staël – her 'creative relationships' and 'primary influences were male' (Maxwell and Pulham 2006, 6).[9] Nevertheless, as Zorn points out, in her fantastic tales Lee appears to search for other identities, particularly 'alternative forms of female subjectivity' that are 'embedded in the uncanny dimensions of these stories which recreate the contemporary social and psychological climates in which "otherness" is evoked in images of strange beauty' (2003, xxx–xxxi). I suggest that these 'images of strange beauty' emerge in two key figures that inhabit Lee's supernatural tales: the castrato and the *femme fatale*. In deploying these characters in order to explore not only alternative subjectivities, but also transgressive desires, Lee prefigures modernist women writers. Cassandra Laity explains that:

> Unable or unwilling to recognize a tradition of women poets in the nineteenth century, H.D. and others used the Decadents to fashion a modernist poetic of female desire. In the next generation of male poets, theories of modern poetry authored by Eliot, Pound, Yeats, and others repeatedly raise the spectres of the femme fatale and the Aesthete to warn against the 'hedonism' they believed had plunged Romanticism into decadence and decay. Women modernists such as H.D., however, responded differently to the powerful feminine subjectivities of their early reading that were presently driving their male contemporaries toward a foreboding masculinization of poetry. The ready agents of a sexually transgressive poetic – the fatal woman and the Aesthete androgyne – therefore articulated a fluid range of forbidden sexualities, including androgyny, homoeroticism, and role reversal, not available in the modernist poetic of male desire, which … prompted the twentieth-century woman writer to evolve alternative modernisms (1996, xi–xii).

While in Lee's works, the 'Aesthete androgyne' mentioned by Laity is transformed into the castrato, it is evident that this figure, along with the fatal woman or *femme fatale*, allows her to play with a sexual fluidity and eroticism that is denied by the moral, artistic 'masculinity' that she adopts in the role defined by Zorn as an honorary 'Victorian "man-of-letters"' (2003, xvi).[10] Her short fiction is set in a space that is itself characterized by ambiguity; the stories are often described as 'fantastic'. Tzvetan Todorov's explanation of the fantastic can certainly be applied to the majority of Lee's supernatural tales:

> In a world which is indeed our world, the one we know, a world without devils, sylphides, or vampires, there occurs an event which cannot be explained by the laws of this same familiar world. The person who experiences the event must opt for one of two possible solutions: either he is the victim of an illusion of the senses, of a product of the imagination – and the laws of the world then remain what they are; or else the event has indeed taken place, it is an integral part of reality – but then this reality is controlled by laws unknown to us … . The fantastic occupies the duration of this uncertainty … . The fantastic is that hesitation experienced by a person who knows only the laws of nature, confronting an apparently supernatural event (1975, 25).

In particular, the tales in *Hauntings*, dealing with ghosts that may or may not be the product of their unstable narrators' imaginations, clearly fall into the category of the fantastic. The 'hesitation' that marks the fantastic suggests a momentary suspension of activity, a limbo in which both potentialities can exist, and I contend that it is this particular aspect of the fantastic that offers Lee an interesting literary, but also psychic, space.

When one looks at the 'ghosts' which manifest themselves in Lee's fantastic tales, one is struck by their aesthetic properties. They often appear in the guise of ghostly singers, metamorphic sculptures, strange, uncanny dolls, or as portraits that come to life. This is perhaps only to be expected in the writings of a mind that is itself haunted by art, and their earthly relations can be found in the artworks and singers discussed in theoretical works such as *Belcaro: Being Essays on Sundry Aesthetical Questions* (1881), *Althea: A Second Book of Dialogues on Aspirations and Duties* (1894), *Renaissance Fancies and Studies* (1895), and in her numerous treatises on musical aesthetics. These physical counterparts lend Lee's 'ghosts' a solidity: they become 'art objects' in their own right. In 'Christkindchen', an essay in *Juvenilia: Being a Second Series of Essays on Sundry Aesthetical Questions* (1887), Lee likens the art object to the childhood toy:

> We grown-ups have our toys: the Venus of Milo, Raphael's Madonnas, the music of Mozart or of Wagner, the whole poetry of the world, from the Vedic hymns to Austin Dobson; heroes and heroines, great men and beautiful women of the Past and the Present; all so much toy-shop stuff, made on purpose to banish weariness and trouble (1887, 185).[11]

This identification between the art object and the toy resonates interestingly with Donald Winnicott's psychoanalytic theory of the 'transitional object'.[12] According to Winnicott, a child's subjectivity is formed through creative play in a 'holding environment' provided by the simultaneous absence and presence of the mother: the mother remains within the child's reach or call, but does not directly interact with him/her. Instead, the child interacts with a toy, or other item which, at this stage, it conceives as a part of itself. In this 'safe' space, which in *Playing and Reality* (1971), Winnicott calls a 'potential space', the child plays and gradually begins to separate the 'me' from the 'not-me', to develop its subjectivity (41, 107). Winnicott goes on to argue that, in adulthood, one's childhood engagement with 'toys' or 'transitional objects' is transferred to art, and cultural objects (1971, 106). In *Laurus Nobilis: Chapters on Art and Life* (1909), Vernon Lee anticipates and agrees with this hypothesis, seemingly formulated earlier by Herbert Spencer. She writes:

Whether or not Mr Herbert Spencer be correct in deducing all artistic activities from our primæval instinct of play, it seems to me that those artistic activities have for us adults much the same importance as the play activities have for a child. They represent the only perfectly free exercise, and therefore, free development, of our preferences (1909, 128–129).[13]

Spencer's theory, which appears in *The Principles of Psychology* (1855), is itself prompted by the work of another. He states:

Many years ago I met with a quotation from a German author to the effect that the aesthetic sentiments originate from the play-impulse. I do not remember the name of the author; and if any reasons were given for this statement or any inferences drawn from it, I cannot recall them. But the statement itself has remained with me, as being one which, if not literally true, is yet an adumbration of a truth (1872, 627).

The 'German author' whose name Spencer cannot remember is Friedrich Schiller who, in his treatise, *On the Aesthetic Education of Man in a Series of Letters* (1794–95), (*Über die ästhetische Erziehung des Menschen in einer Reihe von Briefen*), identified the existence of the 'play-drive', and suggested that play, as a 'primary instinct … finds its highest manifestation in aesthetic phenomena' (Wilkinson and Willoughby 1967, clxxxv). Given Lee's abiding interest in aesthetics, it is unlikely that she would not have read Schiller's treatise or at least been familiar with its concerns. As Angela Leighton remarks, Lee's recognition of the 'play instinct' in her own recovery of historical art and culture resonates with Schiller's theory of the play-drive which he believed 'essential to all artistic work' (2000, 4).

It appears that 'play' is at the heart of Lee's engagement with aesthetics, and the striking parallel between the thoughts of Winnicott and Lee on this subject, together with the centrality of the art object in Lee's supernatural fiction, inspire a reconsideration of these works in the light of Winnicott's theories. In this context, Lee's supernatural becomes a form of 'potential space' in which she 'plays' with cultural objects in order to explore alternative subjectivities. Viewed within Winnicott's theoretical framework, the predominance of the 'Past' in Lee's works, suggests not only an historical past, but also a psychic past that is grounded in childhood, and those art objects which inhabit the past become 'transitional objects' or 'toys'. Moreover, this world is one which is haunted by the 'absent' presence of the mother for, as Diana Basham observes, in her writing, 'Vernon Lee is committed to keeping [her] ... dead mother supernaturally alive' (1992, 174).

Lee's focus on the art object, both in her theoretical works and in her fiction, compels examination. In her writings on aesthetics, she expresses a strong concern with form and formlessness that she associates with Friedrich Nietzsche's definitions of 'Apolline' and 'Dionysiac' art.[14] For Nietzsche, in ancient Greek culture, 'the two gods of art, Apollo and Dionysus' and their respective qualities inform the opposition between the visual 'Apolline art of the sculptor and the non-visual, Dionysiac art of music' (2003, 14). In *The Birth of Tragedy* (1872), he argues:

These two very different tendencies walk side by side, usually in violent opposition to one another, inciting one another to ever more powerful births, perpetuating the struggle of the opposition only apparently bridged by the word 'art'; until, finally ... the two seem to be coupled, and in this coupling they seem at last to beget the work of art that is as Dionysiac as it is Apolline – Attic tragedy (2003, 14).

The Apollonian strand of art is concerned with vision, with illusion, beauty, restraint, and clarity and finds its aesthetic model in the clear lines and physical forms of sculpture. In contrast, the Dionysian element is characterized by chaos, cruelty, sexual abandon, and excess and expresses itself in music. According to Nietzsche, certain types of music may also be considered 'Apolline', but the 'music of Apollo' is simply 'Doric architecture transmuted into sounds'; 'Dionysiac music', on the other hand, consists of 'the overwhelming power of sound, the unified flow of melody and the utterly incomparable world of harmony' (2003, 20–21).[15]

The conflict between the Apollonian and Dionysian strands of art spans Lee's oeuvre, appearing in early writings such as *Belcaro*, and reappearing in late works such as *The Handling of Words*. In the latter, she is at pains to make a distinction between the Dionysian nature of the 'word' (which for Lee, in this context, means 'literature') as expressed by Nietzsche, and her own understanding of the term. She argues that, for Nietzsche, 'the word—and he was apt to feel it rather as the spoken than the written word—was essentially the response, almost the reflex, the impatient, violent, contemptuous and often self-contemptuous venting and easing of his inner distress, of his instability, soreness and frenzy' (1923, 314). Lee goes on to suggest that for both Nietzsche and 'all mankind in its Dionysiac moods', the word 'is a cry, sometimes a curse, at best an invocation of the unattainable' (1923, 314). In comparison, the works of writers 'like Goethe or Browning' enable 'both them and us to take up position to what is not ourself and to whatever in ourself had better not be' (1923, 315). In such literature, the word is 'no longer what Nietzsche called Dionysiac' but 'Apollinian: an instrument of lucid truthful vision, of healing joy, and perchance even of such prophecy as makes itself come true' (1927, 315). The division which Lee makes between the 'Dionysiac' and the 'Apollinian' word expresses that tension which is played out in the contrasts between her aesthetic writing and her supernatural fiction. In the former, she is concerned with form, with order: true art is conceived as something external to the self, untouched by the vagaries of the artist's unruly personality, existing only to give pleasure in the perfection of a musical composition, the clarity of a sculptural plane. Whilst appropriating the Apollonian principle in her discussions of sculpture, she rejected the Dionysian element in the orderly perfection of eighteenth-century music, and argued for its existence only in the melodramatic turmoil of 'modern' compositions, epitomized by the works of the composer Richard Wagner.

Yet Lee's own work is itself marked by the Dionysian. It haunts her writings on aesthetics, and manifests itself in force in her supernatural tales. It is perhaps inevitable that this should be so for, as Gardner observes, in Lee's fantastic stories, her style displays those lilting cadences, and rhythmic refrains that are features of musical compositions.[16] Moreover, this Dionysian trait produces a side-effect which is of particular importance in the exploration of identity. It allows the dissolution of boundaries: between the past and the present, between illusion and reality, between self and Other. It lures us into those borderlands which we keep at bay in our everyday existence and, for Lee, I would argue, it provides an elemental space in which to 'play' and cross the barriers between her public and private identities.

This fascinating struggle between the Apollonian and the Dionysian principles in her work is at its height in Lee's supernatural world that is peopled by revenants, exiles from the world of Greek myth, by Christian effigies, and by 'historical' ghosts who return from more recent periods: the Renaissance, Jacobean times, or the eighteenth century. These have mythic qualities of their own, and find their counterparts in the pagan figures of Athena, Medusa, Marsyas, Venus, and the Sphinx, all of whom are associated with forms of hybridity. I suggest that these characters, whether of ancient or recent origin, perform a crucial role. Through these mythic, metamorphic beings, embodied in 'objets d'art' which function as transitional objects, Lee explores her sexual and social personae in a 'safe' space: a space removed from the concerns and constraints of contemporary expectations.

The importance of myth in the literary expression of inadmissible desires has been usefully exploited by critics such as Vicinus, Zorn, and Camille Paglia whose works indicate that, in the literature of the *fin de siècle*, reworkings of myths often serve to codify decadent disclosures of homoerotic love.[17] Zorn notes, for example, that for 'the initiated reader', the 'lesbian text' offered 'alternative versions of common mythical figures' that provided 'new models of identification' and that 'Pan, Apollo, Athena, and other figures associated with nature, youth, and freedom in Greek mythology became particularly popular as carriers of encoded messages' (2003, 98). However, existing monographs on Lee do not centre on this aspect of her work. Vineta Colby's book is a literary biography; Christa Zorn focuses on Lee's intellectual standing, claiming her importance as a writer who bridges the gap between 'Victorian sage' and 'modern critic' (2003, xxiii); and, while engaging, like myself, in an analysis of Lee's fantastic tales, Mary Patricia Kane looks, at 'art, and the aesthetic experience' in these writings in order to foreground 'the political resonance of art' (2004, 17, 96). In contrast, my book focuses on the psychological value of the art object in Lee's works, not simply to 'decode' its sexual subtext, but also to suggest that such 'decodings' serve to highlight her negotiation of a fluid literary, as well as sexual, identity – manifested in the figures of the castrato and the *femme fatale* – within the rapidly-changing social and intellectual landscapes of the Victorian and early-modernist periods. In order to demonstrate the particularity of the role played by the art object in Lee's tales, I read her work alongside that of male contemporaries such as Walter Pater, Henry James, Thomas Hardy, Oscar Wilde, and Villiers de L'Isle Adam. Her stories are also juxtaposed with those of her precursors, Hoffmann, Balzac, and Mérimée, which were undoubtedly known to Lee, and whose echoes can be traced in her own. Along with Villiers's novel, these act as representations of that European literature which influenced Lee's literary sensibilities.

The book is divided into four chapters, each examining a key art object in Vernon Lee's works: the voice-object (represented by the operatic voice), the statue, the doll, and the portrait. Chapter One focuses on the castrato voice and traces its significance in her aesthetic philosophy; in her supernatural tales: 'A Culture Ghost, or Winthrop's Adventure' and 'A Wicked Voice'; and in her drama, *Ariadne in Mantua*. Having linked this androgynous voice to the turn-of-the-century 'mannish woman', and to the mythological figures, Athena and Medusa, I demonstrate that the castrato becomes simultaneously an alternative subjectivity and a maternal substitute that provides a Winnicottian 'holding environment' in which Lee 'plays' and explores hybrid identities that complicate her 'unsexed' artistic persona. Chapter Two tracks the continuing importance of the castrato voice in Lee's aesthetics, and shows that her writings on sculpture are influenced by those concerns that characterize her appreciation of music. I then examine three of her short stories: 'Marsyas in Flanders', 'St Eudaemon and His Orange Tree' and 'The Featureless Wisdom', in order to show how the metamorphic nature of the mythic figures which inform those tales that feature statues, represent a negotiation of sexuality and subjectivity. Chapter Three returns to the sculptural figure and shows the correlation between the statue and the doll in Lee's works, focusing briefly on her novel, *Miss Brown*, and at length on four stories: 'A Wedding Chest', 'Sister Benvenuta and the Christ Child', 'The Virgin of the Seven Daggers', and 'The Image', while examining the role played by colour and Marian imagery in the expression of desire. Subsequently, I argue that the doll-object provides a surface for the projection of Lee's transgressive sexuality, as well as figuring as a form of 'phallic mother': a potent feminine entity that challenges her artistic 'masculinity'. Chapter Four revisits Lee's tale, 'The Image', in which the figure of the doll, the copy of a dead beloved, functions as a *memento mori*, before exploring Lee's own thoughts on commemorative portraiture, and examining the treatment of the portrait in 'Amour Dure', 'Dionea', and 'Oke of Okehurst'. Highlighting the Medusan properties of the women in Lee's portrait-tales, I argue that, as *femmes fatales*, they are intimately related to the 'phallic mother' and represent the expression of a powerful and sexually ambiguous subjectivity that is allied to both the figure of the New Woman and the mannish woman writer. My interdisciplinary approach, which combines literature, psychology, aesthetics, mythology, religion, and social history, reflects not only Lee's own wide-ranging interests, but also the complex network of associations that posit her work as a rich source for debate in the analysis of gender and sexuality on the threshold of modernity.

Notes

[1]   Founded in 1882 by a group of Cambridge scholars, the Society for Psychical Research (SPR) examined paranormal activity in a scientific context.
[2]   For a more comprehensive discussion of critical works on Lee, see Lee 2006, 22–24. The collections of critical essays published in 2006 were the result of two international conferences held on Lee's work: 'Vernon Lee: Literary Revenant' at the Institute of English Studies, University of London June 2003, and 'Vernon Lee e Firenze settant'anni dopo' at the British Institute in Florence (organized in collaboration with Trento University) in May 2005 respectively.
[3]   The essays collected in *The Handling of Words* were formerly published in various journals between 1894 and 1904. For full details see Colby 2003, 352, note 10.
[4]   Woolf's reviews of Lee's *The Sentimental Traveller: Notes on Places* (1908) and of *Laurus Nobilis: Chapters on Art and Life* (1909) from which these quotations are taken appeared in the *Times Literary Supplement* on 9 January 1908 and 5 August 1909 respectively.

[5]   The word 'intimate' is used here to indicate emotional closeness rather than to specifically suggest sexual activity. Lee and Anstruther-Thomson worked on two articles: 'Beauty and Ugliness', Parts I and II published in the *Contemporary Review* in October and November 1897, later collected together in book form in *Beauty and Ugliness* (1912). They also collaborated on *Art and Man: Essays and Fragments* (1924).

[6]   Vernon Lee's friendships with women, and their homoerotic implications are also discussed in Gunn, 1964; Mannocchi 1986; Psomiadies, *Beauty's Body* 1997, and 'Still Burning' 1997; Vicinus 1994, 2004; Maltz, 1999; Colby 2003; Zorn 2003; Pulham 2006; Maxwell and Pulham 2006. Despite its reductive nature, Gardner's study is comprehensive and includes a wide range of interesting information, as well as interviews with a number of Lee's friends and acquaintances.

[7]   See in particular Hotchkiss 1996, and Maltz 1999.

[8]   The full title of Vicinus's book is *Intimate Friends: Women Who Loved Women*. Colby argues that it is 'beyond doubt' that Lee's relationship with Mary Robinson did not have a physical dimension. Yet, in a letter to Mary of 27 February 1881, Lee refers to being 'kissed' by Mary, and recalls having held her in her arms (quoted in Vicinus 2004, 272, note 78). See also, the discussion of the Lee/Robinson relationship in Newman 2005.

[9]   Vernon Lee pays tribute to her intelligent, intellectual and eccentric mother in *The Handling of Words*. Matilda Paget and her son, Lee's half-brother, Eugene Lee-Hamilton, oversaw Lee's education, hoping to produce 'another Mme de Staël' (Gunn 1964, 48). Anne-Louise Germaine Necker, Baroness de Staël-Holstein (1766–1817), French-Swiss woman of letters and early advocate of women's rights. Openly critical of Napoleon, de Staël spent much of her life in exile. *Corinne: ou L'Italie* (1807) is her most famous novel and tells the story of a celebrated female poet.

[10]   See Evangelista, 2006, and Wiley, 2006 for excellent discussions of the tensions between morality and immorality in Lee's writings.

[11]   The association of the art object with the toy is not exclusive to Lee. In 'Morale du Joujou' (1853), Charles Baudelaire described the toy as 'the child's earliest initiation into art' (1963, 525).

[12]   Donald Woods Winnicott (1896–1971), paediatrician and psychoanalyst whose work with disturbed children and their mothers led him to develop the concept of the 'transitional object', his significant contribution to object relations theory.

[13]   Herbert Spencer (1820–1903), English philosopher who contributed to contemporary thought on a wide range of subjects including ethics, metaphysics, biology and psychology.

[14]   Although the terms 'Apolline' and 'Dionysiac' are used in translated versions of Nietzsche, and Lee refers to the 'Apollinian' and 'Dionysiac', I will employ the more commonly-used terms, 'Apollonian' and 'Dionysian' throughout my discussion. Lee's fascination with Nietzsche finds expression in works ranging from essays such as 'Nietzsche and the Will to Power' in *Gospels of Anarchy and Other Contemporary Studies* (1908) to treatises such as *The Handling of Words* (1923). Annotated copies of *Beyond Good and Evil* and *Der Fall Wagner und Nietzsche contra Wagner* can be found in her book collection, held at the Harold Acton Library at the British Institute in Florence. See Gardner 1987, Caballero 1992, and Colby 2003 for earlier discussions of the tensions between the Apollonian and the Dionysian in Lee's works.

[15]   The Doric order of architecture was the earliest of three systems of Classical architecture (beginning in 7thC B.C.E.) – the others being Ionic and Corinthian – characterized by the clean, simple lines of its columns. The Dorians, a Hellenic tribe, also reputedly formalized the practice of pederasty in ancient Greece.

[16]   See Gardner 1987, especially Chapter 1.

[17]   See Vicinus 1994, and Paglia 1990.

Chapter 1

Castrato Cries and Wicked Voices

O dream of poet passing every bound!
My thoughts have built a fancy of thy form,
Till it is molten into silver sound,
And boy and girl are one in cadence warm.
Théophile Gautier (1849)[1]

In the opening chapter to a collection of essays entitled *Belcaro* (1881), Vernon Lee describes her sensations on completing her first published work, *Studies of the Eighteenth Century in Italy* (1880):

> When, two summers since, I wrote the last pages of my first book, it was, in a way, as if I had been working out the plans of another dead individual. The myself who had, almost as a child, been insanely bewitched by the composers and singers, the mask actors and pedants, and fine ladies and fops, ... this myself, thus smitten with the Italian 18th century, had already ceased to exist (1881, 3–4).

This eighteenth-century world, the subject of her literary debut, for which she had acquired a love 'at an age ... where some of us are still creatures of an unconscious play-instinct' functioned as a 'remote lumber-room full of discarded mysteries and of lurking ghosts, where a half-grown young prig might satisfy, in unsuspicious gravity mere childlike instincts of make-believe and romance' (Lee 1907, xvi). For Lee, the child that played in this world had been replaced by 'Another myself': a more discerning and discursive self who saw 'what the original collector had never guessed: illustrations, partial explanations', and 'questions of artistic genesis and evolution, of artistic right and wrong' and 'This new myself', she writes, 'is the myself by whom has been written this present book' (1881, 4). The passage implies a system of development and individuation that is played out through Lee's responses to Italian art and culture in the earlier text. Lee's words suggest not only the discovery of the self, but an anxiety to present herself as a mature writer who has surfaced from the chrysalis of childhood fantasy and engaged in the adult language of philosophy and aesthetics. Yet, her other self, the 'bewitched' child, continues to haunt the pages of *Belcaro*.

In an essay entitled 'The Child in the Vatican', Lee invents what she calls 'a fairy tale' in which a young child becomes the toy of the 'Statue-demons' that line the palace corridors who determine 'to cast a spell upon it which would make it theirs' (1881, 24). The child continues to live its ordinary life, but slowly begins to experience some inexplicable changes when it sees a beautiful landscape or hears a stray bar of music: 'little by little, into its everyday life, stole strange symptoms; sometimes there would come like a sudden stop, as of a boat caught in the rushes, a consciousness of immobility in the midst of swirling, flowing movement, a giddy brain-swimming feeling' (1881, 26). Eventually the child becomes aware that it is no longer a child and realizes that it had been learning something which others did not know. This esoteric knowledge is conveyed through music:

> For it heard one day a few pages of a symphony of Mozart's; the first it had ever heard save much more modern music; and those bars of symphony were intelligible words, conveyed to the child a secret. And the secret was: 'we are the brethern [*sic*], the sounding ones of the statues: and all we who are brethern [*sic*], whether in stone, or sound, or colour, or written word, shall to thee speak in such a way that thou recognise us, and distinguish us from others; and thou shalt love and believe only in us and those of our kin' (Lee 1881, 27).

That the child in the Vatican is Lee herself, there is little doubt. In his biography of Vernon Lee, Peter Gunn quotes her description of an early visit to St Peter's in Rome during which she is enthralled by 'the quavering notes of singers', the 'shrill blasts of trumpets' and the 'white splendour of the pontifical robes and jewels'. Lee writes:

> From that moment everything seemed changed ... I was wild to be taken into those dark, damp little churches ... full of long, sweet, tearful, almost infantine notes of voices, whose strange sweetness seemed to cut into your soul, only to pour into the wound some mysterious narcotic balm. I was wild to be taken to the chilly galleries ... [where] all those gods, all those goddesses, and nymphs, and heroes, all that nude and white and ice-cold world seemed to seek me with their blank, white glance, smiling with the faint and ironical smile which means – 'This creature is ours' (quoted in Gunn 1964, 38).

It seems suggestive that, in both the fictional and the factual text, Lee's initiation into this world of art and culture from which she emerges as an adult writer is marked primarily by a response to music and the voice, for both were to play an important part in her supernatural tales and in her work on aesthetics, as well as being a propelling force in her drama, *Ariadne in Mantua* (1903).

In her added introduction to the 1907 edition of *Studies of the Eighteenth Century in Italy*, Lee acknowledges the role played by music in her artistic development and she describes the mixed feelings of pleasure and pain she experienced as an adolescent whilst listening to her mother singing and playing a selection of airs from transcriptions of eighteenth-century songs newly received from Bologna. The first piece her mother plays is *Pallido il Sole*, 'one of the three legendary airs ... with which the madness of Saul-Philip of Spain had been soothed by virtuous David-Farinelli', the Italian castrato (1907, xlviii).[2] Lee states:

> I could not remain in the presence ... of what, I really do not know: I felt shy of those unknown, much longed-for songs, and had to escape into the garden ... . I can still feel the sickening fear, mingled with shame, *lest the piece should turn out to be hideous*. For if *Pallido il Sole* should turn out to be hideous, why ... . It is impossible to put into reasonable words the overwhelming sense that on that piece hung the fate of a world, the only one which mattered – the world of my fancies and longings (1907, xlviii).

For Lee, the fate of her imaginative world, 'the only one which mattered', depends on this song, indicating the importance of music to her creativity. It is music that first 'speaks' to her and that empowers her aesthetic appreciation and her subsequent literary production (1907, xvi).

Music and the word then are intertwined in Lee's artistic formation and it seems fitting that much of her musical philosophy addresses that fusion of word and music – the operatic voice: a voice that also dominates two of her short stories, 'A Culture Ghost: Winthrop's Adventure' (1881) and 'A Wicked Voice' (1889). In these tales the traumatic sensations elicited in Lee as she listens to her mother singing eighteenth-century arias, are evoked by the castrato voice which first makes its appearance in the 'enchanted garret' of her childhood imagination. Here, in this magical, illusory realm, where she is often held in thrall by her mother's voice, Lee 'plays', and finds her creative self in a pattern that suggests Winnicott's theoretical process of individuation that occurs in the potential space between child and mother, an intermediate space in which the child must develop from 'a state of being merged with the mother' to 'a stage of separating out the mother from the self' (1971, 107).[3] According to Winnicott, in this 'resting-place' the individual is 'engaged in the perpetual human task of keeping inner and outer reality separate yet interrelated', an area of illusion which, he explains, emerges in adult life in art and culture. In *Belcaro*, as we have seen, Lee marks her artistic development by rejecting the fancies and longings of childhood. Yet these fantasies return forcefully in her fiction, often 'haunted' both literally and figuratively by the maternal voice. In the following discussion I intend to examine the ways in which this voice functions in Lee's fictional texts, but before I do so I would like to look at the definition of the word 'voice' and its particular implications for Lee as a woman writer at the *fin de siècle*.

'Hens that Crow': the Maternal Song and the Vocal Object

Voice is defined as the 'sound formed in the human larynx' that expresses itself in speaking, shouting, and singing, but it also means to express an opinion, to have the 'right or privilege of speaking or voting in a legislative assembly, or of taking part in, or exercising control over some particular matter', for example in political decisions (*O.E.D.*). The latter definition of 'voice' increased in importance for women in the late nineteenth century. With the advent of a more militant commitment to women's suffrage, the female orator became not only increasingly visible but intensely disturbing. Elaine Showalter observes that 'The 1880s and the 1890s, in the words of the novelist George Gissing, were decades of "sexual anarchy", when all the laws that governed sexual identity and behaviour seemed to be breaking down' (1992, 3). She goes on to point out that the woman speaker was considered particularly deviant for 'To claim the pulpit or the podium was in itself ... a transgression of "womanly" modesty' (1992, 24). The mannish woman orator was an object of ridicule, and during this period anti-feminist literature in the form of cartoons, sermons, and caricatures proliferated (Kahane 1995, 6). This transgressive female orator was mirrored by her literary counterpart. By the 1870s and 1880s women writers had become a force to be reckoned with even at large publishing houses like Bentley's where more than forty percent of the authors were female, and many of them challenged the social and sexual limitations traditionally imposed on women (Showalter 1995, vi).

Despite being critical of women 'who saw the future for their sex in an aping of purely masculine behaviour', Lee, although 'no suffragette', certainly 'wanted a vote' and sympathized with their cause, recognizing discrimination against women as one of the 'long-organized social evils' (Hotchkiss 1996, 26). Moreover, as a female writer whose work constantly encroached on the predominantly masculine fields of art, history, and aesthetics, and who was herself often referred to as 'trenchant' and 'outspoken', Lee cannot avoid being associated with the powerful speaking woman (Gunn 1964, 3). Her essay 'The Economic Parasitism of Women' in *Gospels of Anarchy* (1908), which discusses, amongst other things, the inequalities of the female condition in society, attracted the hostile attention of Max Beerbohm who, on the fly-leaf of his copy of the essays, wrote:

> Oh dear! Poor dear dreadful little lady! Always having a crow to pick, ever so coyly, with Nietzsche, or a wee lance to break with Mr. Carlyle, or a sweet but sharp little warning to whisper in the ear of Mr. H.G. Wells, or Strindberg or Darwin or D'Annunzio! How artfully at this moment she must be button-holing Einstein! And Signor Croce – and Mr. James Joyce! (quoted in Gunn 1964, 3).[4]

Beerbohm's satiric diminution of Lee is perhaps a manifestation of masculine anxiety. As Gunn observes, 'what an impressive string of celebrities he needs to hang the "poor, dear, dreadful little lady"' (1964, 3). What is significant, however, is that Beerbohm's passage highlights an important factor in this anxiety: her 'voice'.[5] Moreover, whether spoken or written, this voice is judged in relation to Lee's sex and its attendant social limitations, a constraint which is exacerbated by the language in which her thoughts must be expressed, for as Cora Kaplan explains:

> Social entry into patriarchal culture is made in language, through speech. Our individual speech does not, therefore, free us in any simple way from the ideological constraints of our culture since it is through the forms that articulate those constraints that we speak in the first place (1992, 312).

Adopting a male pseudonym, Lee was certainly aware of the need to masquerade as male in order to be taken seriously in the male literary world. In December 1878, two years before her first critical success, she writes, 'I don't care that Vernon Lee should be known to be myself or any other young woman, as I am sure that no one reads a woman's writing on art, history or aesthetics with anything but unmitigated contempt' (quoted in Gunn 1964, 66). These 'mannish women' who violated the codes of acceptable female behaviour were labelled 'hens that crow' by the *New York Herald* (Sept. 1852), a comparison that unquestionably highlights the double-bind which fettered the female orator and the female writer: to speak was to be unsexed, and the language in which one spoke remained indubitably male (quoted in Kahane 1995, 6).

The problematic nature of this voice as it manifests itself in female writing has been extensively discussed, most prominently by French feminists such as Hélène Cixous and Luce Irigaray, both of whom ground their debates in a valorization of the maternal voice. Cixous, for example, writes that, 'The voice is the uterus'; it is '[the] song before the law, before ... the symbolic'; it can 'make the text gasp or fill it with suspense or silences, anaphorize it or tear it apart with cries' (quoted in Stanton 1986, 167). Cixous and Irigaray also often employ 'the age-old association of mother and water': Cixous favours 'topoi of the continuity and variety of the rhythms and songs of "our women's waters"', while for Irigaray this feminine fluidity is 'both the amniotic waters' and 'the movement of the sea' (Stanton 1986, 169; quoted in Stanton 1986, 169). Moreover, this fluidity is particularly discernible in the female voice for when 'that woman-thing speaks ... it speaks fluid' (Irigaray 1993, 111).

Critics such as Domna Stanton, Claire Kahane, and Felicia Miller Frank rightly challenge the validity of arguments that unavoidably reinforce 'the binary logic of opposition that produced them', but whatever the arguments for or against, the maternal models posited by French feminists in relation to female writing do provide an interesting parallel to psychoanalytic theories of the maternal voice, for both are said to play their role in the development of subjectivity (Frank 1995, 42). Guy Rosolato, for example, has called the maternal voice a 'blanket of sound', a 'sonorous envelope'; for Didier Anzieu it is 'a bath of sounds', a phrase which associates the voice with feminine fluidity; while Claude Bailblé describes it simply as 'music' (quoted in Silverman 1988, 72). 'These tropes of the voice', as Kahane observes, 'are analogous to Winnicott's "holding environment" or intermediate space in which the child's process of individuation takes place' (1995, 17). Here, the child is both surrounded and nurtured in an external mirror of the conditions in the mother's womb. Within the safety of this space, the child plays with transitional objects, exploring and discovering the separate identity of objects that it has hitherto understood as part of itself, thus allowing it to acknowledge its separation from the mother and to form its subjectivity. Yet, as Lacan suggests, the mother's voice itself must also function as a transitional object (an object like the breast, the faeces, a loved blanket or doll) from which the child must separate itself in order to become an independent subject.[6] In this scenario, the maternal voice can function as a metaphor of nightmarish entrapment. In *La Voix au Cinema*, which posits the importance of sound in the study of film, Michel Chion highlights this aspect of the mother's voice:

> In the beginning, in the uterine night, was the voice, that of the Mother. For the child after birth, the Mother is more an olfactory and vocal continuum than an image. One can imagine the voice of the Mother, which is woven around the child, and which originates from all points in space as her form enters and leaves the visual field, as a matrix of places to which we are tempted to give the name 'umbilical net'. A horrifying expression, since it evokes a cobweb – and in fact, this original vocal tie will remain ambivalent (quoted in Silverman 1988, 74).

In her reading of Chion's work, Kaja Silverman claims that the biblical resonance of Chion's words opposes 'the maternal voice to the paternal word' thus identifying 'the mother with sound and the father with meaning' (1988, 75). This gendered opposition between sound and meaning seems to have particular significance in relation to the operatic voice. In his now famous article, '"The Blue Note" and "The Objectified Voice and the Vocal Object"', Michel Poizat writes of the common disruption inevitably experienced by the music lover – constructed here as male

– who attempts to follow the text in the libretto whilst listening to a recording of a favourite opera. Certain musical passages are found to wrest his attention from the printed matter and he loses himself in listening, becoming increasingly oblivious to the written text. However, as Poizat notes, the listener feels what he describes as 'a radical antagonism' between letting himself be swept away by the emotion and applying himself to the meaning of each word as it is sung (1991, 199). Interestingly, this disturbing voice is characterized as feminine. It is woman's song which presents itself as 'pure music free of all ties to speech; singing which literally destroys speech in pursuit of a purely musical melody, a melody that develops little by little until it verges on the cry' (Poizat 1991, 199). Poizat suggests that:

> In instants such as these, when language disappears and is gradually superseded by the cry, an emotion arises which is expressible only by the irruption of something that signals the feeling of absolute loss, by the sob; finally a point is reached where the listener himself is stripped of all possibility of speech (1991, 199).

In *Belcaro*, in an essay entitled 'Chapelmaster Kreisler', Vernon Lee, too, acknowledges this contraposition between song and speech. She writes:

> We are apt to think of music as a sort of speech until, on examination, we find it has no defined meaning either for the speaker or for the listener ... as long as both exist only in embryo in the confused cries and rude imitations of the child ... they cannot be distinguished; but as soon as they can be called either speech or music, they become unlike and increase in dissimilarity in proportion as they develop (1881, 114–115).

Lee further delineates the division: the cry becomes on the one hand 'the word' which, 'as it develops, acquires a more precise and abstract signification, becomes more and more of a symbol', and on the other, 'the song' which becomes 'more and more a complete unsymbolical form' (1881, 115). The word, Lee argues, turns into 'a written sign', whilst the song, 'having become an object of mere pleasure, requires more and more musical development, and is transported from the lips of man to the strings of an instrument' (1881, 116).

I will say more about Lee's transposition of the voice onto the musical instrument in due course as I believe it has interesting implications for the manifestations of voice in her fiction. Aside from this development, however, Lee's theory of the voice can be clearly related to Julia Kristeva's formulation of the 'semiotic' and the 'symbolic'. Kristeva claims that the semiotic 'precedes the symbolic order, which is identified with the paternal law of the father', thus linking the semiotic to the 'preverbal period during which the child is bound to and depends on the mother's body and rhythms' (Frank 1995, 44). This relationship with the mother's body is suppressed as the child enters into language and subjectivity, yet the semiotic continues to exist within the symbolic, sometimes threatening the symbolic's monopoly of language particularly in poetic language which, according to Felicia Miller Frank, Kristeva defines as 'the semiotization of the symbolic' (1995, 44). This 'semiotic network gives "music" to literature', as well as 'melody, harmony, rhythm', thus creating 'pleasing sounds' (Kristeva 1986, 113; Kristeva 1977, 73). One might argue, then, that the symbolic is never more at risk from the semiotic than in opera where, according to Poizat, not only is the written word overwhelmed by the song, but the listener himself is 'stripped of all possibility of speech' (1991, 199). For Poizat, this paralysis of the symbolic seems inescapably linked to the 'cry'. Lee, too, appears to connect strong emotional effects with this phenomenon. In *Belcaro* she remarks:

> The most emotional thing ever written by Mozart is the exclamation of Donna Elvira, when, after leaving Don Giovanni at his ill-omened supper, she is met on the staircase by the statue of the commander; this exclamation is but one high, detached note, formless, meaningless, which pierces the nerves like a blade (1881, 123).

Lee calls this exclamation a 'cry', a moment during which art has been subverted, the result of 'a momentary suspension of artistic activity', a transient return to formlessness and meaninglessness which has inevitable associations with feminine fluidity and the infantile dependence and fusion that characterizes the preverbal relationship with the Mother and its attendant sensations of bliss and paranoia, of release and entrapment (1881, 122–123).

Dangerous Cries: The Medusa and the Castrato

Woman's song then is both beautiful and dangerous, pleasurable yet disturbing, descriptions which link the female voice irrevocably with its mythological embodiments. As Charles Segal observes:

> In its aural appeal and its power to dispel cares by its 'charm' ... the female voice also exercises magical power and seduction. The songs of the Sirens and of Circe in the *Odyssey* are the earliest and most famous examples. The Sirens would lure Odysseus off his course, end his voyage and leave him immobilized for death on an island full of the rotting bones and skins of those who succumbed to the magic ... . It is by the beauty of her song, too, that Circe lures the companions of Odysseus into her house before changing them into animals by the magic of her drugs (1994, 17–18).

That the Sirens' song results in 'immobilization', and that Circe's is the cause of a return to an animalistic form of life appears to dramatize both the death-like paralysis indicated by Poizat and Lee, and a reversion to the pre-Oedipal life of the dependent child, responses which, in their texts, are evoked by the cry. Interestingly the word 'cry', that in both Poizat's and Lee's texts forms the culmination of the feminine voice and its disruptive power, is itself linked to that terrifying image of motherhood, Medusa, for, as Segal explains, the name 'Gorgon' comes from the Indo-European root *garj*, meaning 'a fearful shriek, roar, or shout', combining a 'terrifying vocality with a demonic femaleness' (1994, 18–19). The word 'cry' also seems of distinct significance to our 'hens that crow' for 'to crow' is also 'to cry', suggesting that the savage reaction prompted by the figure of the vocal woman at the turn of the nineteenth century is deeply embedded in the mythological representation of a masculine fear (*O.E.D.*).

Like these transgressive females who violate the codes of feminine behaviour and suffer from social exclusion, Medusa lives in 'the shadowy border territory' situated 'at the extreme limit of Night', recalling also Chion's ambivalent maternal voice and its location in the 'uterine night' (Segal 1994, 20). Decapitated by Perseus, Medusa gives birth to Pegasus from her headless trunk. This scene offers a nightmare image of maternity, an image which associates her with 'night, immobility, serpentine monstrosity, and violent, bloody birth' (Segal 1994, 19–20). In his essay 'Medusa's Head' (1922), Freud develops the following analysis and formulation:

> To decapitate: to castrate. The terror of the Medusa is thus a terror of castration that is linked to the sight of something. Numerous analyses have made us familiar with the occasion for this: it occurs when a boy, who has hitherto been unwilling to believe the threat of castration, catches sight of the female genitals, probably those of an adult surrounded by hair, and essentially those of his mother (Freud, 1955, XVIII, 273).

In his critique of Freud's essay, Phillip Slater suggests that rather than symbolizing a fear of castration at the sight of female genitalia, Medusa is more likely to represent a 'fear of maternal envelopment' (quoted in Segal 1994, 20). It is of course possible that she may symbolize both, for the comparability between the gorgonian cry and the voice of the powerful speaking woman raises the spectre of emasculation, and the identification of Medusa with immobilization and maternal engulfment has interesting implications for the disruptive quality of the feminine operatic voice posited by Poizat, and for Chion's psychoanalytic model of the mother's voice as a site of nightmarish entrapment.

Segal traces the antitheses between Medusa and Athena, locating them in an opposition between the feminine and the masculine order of existence. Medusa, born of the primordial sea-divinities Phorkys and Keto, 'embodies flux, process, and animality', whereas Athena, 'sprung from the head of Zeus', is 'the most committed of the gods to the male-dominated order of Olympus' and ensures the 'invincibility of Zeus's patriarchal rule' (1994, 21). Grounding his argument in Pindar's Twelfth Pythian Ode (490 B.C.E.), Segal notes the transmutation of 'the surviving Gorgons' wail of mourning' at their sister Medusa's death into 'the flute-song', a deed which 'is a cultural act that controls and aestheticizes': the 'cry' which issues from the gorgonian mouth is here transformed into 'a pleasing sound' that emanates from 'an artificial channel, the constricted passage of which produces the "many-headed melody" at all-male contests of art and athletics' (1994, 23). However, the formidable female power of the Gorgon is perhaps not so easily suppressed. As Freud and others have noted, Athena wears the head of Medusa upon her dress and the flute is in itself no guarantee against the feminine chaos and disorder that the Gorgon embodies. As Segal points out:

> the flute's transformation from the Gorgons' wild, death-laden, liquid, and monstrous cry to an instrument of Athena's artistry is a figure for the incorporation of the otherness of female creative energy into the polis. Yet the flute's music, like the female in Greek myth, retains a certain mysterious power in its vacillation between the wild and the city, nature and culture (1994, 31).

Furthermore, the ambiguity of flute music, 'emanating differently from each of the double reeds and stirring unruly emotions', suggests that the seductive and dangerous aspects of the female voice cannot be completely erased and thus threaten to disrupt Apollonian order through Dionysian excess (Segal 1994, 31).

In her essay 'The Riddle of Music' Vernon Lee acknowledges that this disturbing duality exists in music: she writes 'why, from time immemorial, music has been considered sometimes as an art which enervates and demoralises, sometimes as one which disciplines, restrains and purifies' (1906, 226). In *Belcaro* she expresses a preference for its latter qualities which manifest themselves where music 'exists as an art' and the very first step in the formation of that art is 'the subjection of the emotional cry or the spontaneous imitation to a process of acoustic mensuration' (1881, 117). For Lee, musical art is a process of regulation, an imposition of form on the unruly sounds of nature, 'for art begins', she observes, 'only where the physical elements are subjected to an intellectual process, and it exists completely only where they abdicate their independence and become subservient to an intellectual design' (1881, 117). This insistence on regulation is perhaps best examined in the context of music's effect on the 'hearer' and the 'listener'. Lee argues that 'hearing' leads to a dangerous passivity and demoralization, implying corruption in contrast to 'listening' which imposes 'lucidity and order' through its active resistance (1906, 227). Listening then becomes an intellectual discipline on the natural process of hearing; a triumph of art over nature that is comparable to the imposition of form on music which emerges from the primordial 'cry'. During this process:

> the physical elements, inasmuch as they are subdued and regulated and neutralized by one another in the intellectual form, are inevitably deprived of the full vigour of their emotional power; the artistic form has tamed and curbed them, has forbidden their freely influencing the nerves, while at the same time it – the form – has exerted its full sway over the mind. The mountains have been hewn into terraces, the forests have been clipped into gardens, the waves have been constrained into fountains ... nature has submitted to man, and has abdicated her power into his hands (Lee 1881, 122).

Like the Gorgons' chthonian cry, emotion is here aestheticized via a man-made form, forcing and constraining the power of nature's voice through the regulated channels of Apollonian order.

Amongst the various treatises concerning what she refers to as the 'art of singing' is Lee's essay, 'An Eighteenth-Century Singer: An Imaginary Portrait'. Here, the voice has been stripped of its disorderly qualities and has become an art object in itself; 'The notes of the voice were the material, the paint or clay, in which the mind's conception must be embodied', and the breath the tool, the artist's brush or the sculptor's fingers, which controls and shapes the final product:

> It was by husbanding the breath, and employing it in a hundred different ways, that the singer shaped the component notes into a song ... . And, when he had thus modelled his song as the sculptor models, or as the painter prepares his cartoon in mere light and shade, it was with the breath again, now no longer a modelling tool, but rather a brush, that by varying and combining the various registers, movable differences in vocal quality, and the various timbres of his voice, and by giving different and infinite degrees of loudness and softness, that he put on the highlights, deepened the shadows, and varied the colouring of his marvellous pattern (1891, 855).

Vernon Lee's partiality for eighteenth-century singing is well documented. In 'The Art of Singing, Past and Present' she claims that 'by the end of the first quarter of the eighteenth century ... it had attained a degree of perfection absolutely analogous to the perfection of sculpture among the Greeks, and of painting in the Renaissance', and compares this to the contemporary trend of composers like Wagner who have made 'a clean sweep of all musical perfection in singing in order to replace it by emotional declamation' (1880, 323, 339). Wagner's operatic song comes too close to the 'cry', it lacks the aesthetic orderliness of eighteenth-century music which 'aims mainly at exquisite delicacy of form' (1880, 325).

It seems fitting that the singers who epitomized this art were themselves of 'man-made' construction for in the eighteenth century the castrato reigned supreme. Nicholas Clapton describes them as 'machines made for singing' and notes that, although the first records of castrati in a Western context appear in Byzantium in the fourth century A.D., the first documentary record of castrati in Europe does not appear until the sixteenth century (2006, 1–3). As the new opera form developed in the seventeenth century, castrati began to appear on the stage and by the eighteenth century, 'almost all the lead roles, male and female, were for high voices, and something like 70 percent of all male opera singers were castrati' (Reynolds 1995, 135). The operation was normally carried out on boys between the ages of eight and ten, officially by hospitals for 'medical' reasons, unofficially by a variety of unscrupulous practitioners, including barbers. Castrati often came from modest backgrounds and were taken from willing parents who saw the musical conservatories as a step on the road to fame and fortune that also brought the welcome relief of having one less mouth to feed at home (Barbier 1996, 11–21). Not all castrated boys were able to fulfil their potential but, for those that did, the reward was a potent castrato voice that was higher, lighter and more flexible than a man's, more brilliant and powerful than a woman's, and superior to the child's in its technique and expressivity (Barbier 1996, 17).

Through this 'manufactured' body came a voice that formed a trinity of voices: man, woman, and child, connoting the 'many-headed melody' that emerges from the 'artificial channel' of the Athenian flute; the castrato's asexual sound defamiliarizing the voice until it becomes 'more a musical instrument than a voice at all' (Reynolds 1995, 137). Given Lee's apparent need to aestheticize the cry in the relative safety of the musical instrument, it is hardly surprising that the operatic voice, which so precariously verges on the cry, should be especially acceptable when secured within the castrato.[7] Yet the figure of the castrato, like the flute, is laden with ambiguity. The larynx that produces his voice bears a feminine physiology; 'Modern scientific photographs of the singing larynx and glottis show us ... a lipped opening', and voice commentators 'describe the larynx as labial': an opening that mirrors both the vaginal wound of the 'castrated' female and the genital severance that marks the castrato (Koestenbaum 1994, 160).[8] Moreover, this sexual ambiguity extends to the roles acted by castrati on the operatic stage. Although often playing females, castrati were nevertheless for the most part 'assigned to eminently virile roles, like those of Caesar, Xerxes, and many other figures of masculine power' (Poizat 1991, 197). However, these powerful male figures are emasculated by the castrato's body, for masculinity is here represented as artifice or castration.

The castrati's decline dates from the 1790s; 'by the 1810s and 1820s there was a dearth of singers, and by 1844 ... they were all but extinct' (Reynolds 1995, 139). The chronological specificity of their ebbing popularity seems highly significant:

This puts their demise at the same time as the period of the French Revolutionary and the Napoleonic wars ... . During the intense European upheaval of this time, one of the things that increasingly worried contemporary arbiters of morals was that men were no longer men and women were no longer women. Strong women in the public eye (Mary Wollstonecraft, Madame de Staël) were demanding reforms and an equality of sex in the light of the new democracies ... . And where there are strong women it follows that they must be emasculating their men (Reynolds 1995, 139).

Confronting masculine order with its ultimate castration nightmare the castrato embodies not only the threat represented by the powerful speaking woman, but also her Medusan cry in his song with all its connotations of immobilization and entrapment. Paradoxically, the castrato represents a figure of that disorder which Lee is so anxious to avoid in her writings on aesthetic musicality. In her supernatural fiction, however, the castrato's ambiguity and the disruptive quality of his song become a source of power. Carlo Caballero notes this discrepancy and argues that Lee's theoretical writing 'allowed her partially to neutralize the power of music by taking stock of it, disciplining its dangerous unreason with the intellectual word', whilst her fiction, and particularly her 'ghost stories ... play out these powerful effects or put them on display' (1992, 403). According to Caballero, here, the 'vivid musical fantasies at play in her fiction speak for the concerns lurking in the rifts of her nonfiction, which willfully excluded anything that threatened to undermine her closed system "of differences"' (1992, 403). It is arguably this tension in Lee's writing that manifests itself through the voice in her supernatural tales, 'Winthrop's Adventure' and 'A Wicked Voice', and in her drama, *Ariadne in Mantua*.

In her introduction to *For Maurice: Five Unlikely Stories* (1927), Vernon Lee explains her inspiration for these works. Exploring the Accademia Filarmonica in Bologna, Lee and her friend John Singer Sargent came upon a portrait of Carlo Broschi, known as 'Farinelli' (1705–1782), one of the great castrati of the eighteenth century (fig. 1.1).[9] The portrait appears to have exerted a strange fascination over the young and impressionable pair. Lee writes:

'mysterious, uncanny, a wizard, serpent, sphinx; strange, weird, *curious.*' Such ... were the adjectives, the comparisons, with which we capped each other, my friend John and I, as we lingered and fantasticated in front of that smoky canvas in an ill-lit lumber room, ... in the Bologna music-school, at closing-hour on autumn afternoons of the year 1872 (1927, xxx–xxxi).

A year or two later Lee wrote the initial version of 'A Culture Ghost, or Winthrop's Adventure' which proved to be the founding narrative for other texts, 'the various transformations of a single leitmotiv, the harmonic changes and altered instrumentation thereof' that developed into 'A Wicked Voice' and *Ariadne in Mantua* (1927, xxxii).

Fig. 1.1   Corrado Giaquinto, *Carlo Broschi, il Farinelli, c.* 1753–55. Oil.

'Winthrop's Adventure'

'Winthrop's Adventure' concerns the experiences of an aspiring artist, Julian Winthrop, whose ominous reaction to an operatic air sung by his hostess at a social gathering excites curiosity, and prompts him to relate the bizarre events which surrounded his first encounter with this disturbing piece of music. Told in flashback, Winthrop's tale traces the sequence of events which lead from first seeing the titled manuscript for the air in a portrait of the fictitious singer Rinaldi, to hearing the aria sung by Rinaldi's ghost in the now damp and dilapidated villa in which the singer was brutally murdered. In the third-person narrative that frames his story, Winthrop's artistic talent is debated. Everyone agrees that his talent 'would never come to anything' (1927, 143). His endeavours are a series of seemingly unassociated images that merge into one another: 'acanthus leaves uncurling into sirens' tails, satyrs growing out of passion flowers [and] little Dutch manikins in tail coats and pigtails peeping out of tulip leaves under his whimsical pencil' (1927, 145). This unproductive style appears to have followed Winthrop's ghostly encounter for, prior to that, during a tour of an old palace which held a collection of musical memorabilia (including the fateful portrait), his artistic prowess encourages his cousin and companion to ask him for a water-colour sketch of a picture of Palestrina that adorned its walls.[10] It is in this palace, in a small lumber-room at the end of a narrow corridor 'somewhere in the heart of the building' that Winthrop first sees Rinaldi's portrait (1927, 158):

> It was a half-length, life-size portrait of a man in the costume of the latter part of the last century ... . The features were irregular and small, with intensely red lips and a crimson flush beneath the transparent bronzed skin ... . The face was not beautiful; it had something at once sullen and effeminate, something odd and not entirely agreeable; yet it attracted and riveted your attention with its dark warm colour, rendered all the more striking for the light, pearly powdered locks, and the general lightness and haziness of touch (1927, 159–60).

Inexplicably haunted by the portrait, Winthrop returns the next day and views it once more. Upon close examination of the painting he discovers that Rinaldi 'was apparently singing, or rather about to sing, for the red, well-cut lips were parted; and in his hand he held an open roll of notes', the score which he later hears in such disturbing circumstances (1927, 163). Returning again the following year Winthrop sees the portrait for the last time and tells his listeners:

> I pushed open the door and entered; a long ray of the declining sunlight, reflected from the neighbouring red church tower, fell across the face of the portrait, playing in the light, powdered hair and on the downy, well-cut lips, and ending in a tremulous crimson stain on the boarded floor (1927, 178).

Lee never refers explicitly to Rinaldi as a castrato, yet Fa Diesis, the owner of the portrait, calls Rinaldi 'a very great singer' and dates his death as 1780, locating Rinaldi's fame at the height of the castrati's popularity (1927, 166). More subtle, but no less significant are Rinaldi's perceived effeminacy and the intensely red lips that displace, and yet reflect, the crimson stain that can only 'borrow' its colour from the phallic church tower, in a metaphoric relationship that marks the source of the singer's power.[11] Spurred by his curiosity, Winthrop searches for the villa in which Rinaldi died and, on a rainy night amidst the revels of St John's Eve, he finally finds the 'gaunt, grey villa, with broken obelisks on its triangular front' (1927, 181).[12] He spends the night in its vast ruined halls where the rain pours in through unglazed windows. Through the 'dull falling rain' and the 'water splashing from the roof', Winthrop hears other sounds, the 'notes of some instrument' that 'proceeded from the interior of the house' (1927, 195–196).

Working his way through dark, damp, and empty rooms, Winthrop arrives at the foot of a spiral staircase. Here the sounds are 'quite distinct, the light, sharp silvery sounds of a harpsichord or spinet' that 'fell clear and vibrating into the silence of the crypt-like house' (1927, 196). As he climbs the stairs he hears a chord and observes that 'delicately, insensibly there glided into the modulations of the instrument the notes of a strange, exquisite voice' (1927, 196). Instrument and voice become one, eliciting a response that is both pleasurable and perturbing: 'It was of a wondrous sweet, thick, downy quality, neither limpid nor penetrating, but with a vague, drowsy charm, that seemed to steep the soul in enervating bliss; but, together with this charm, a terrible cold seemed to sink into my heart' (1927, 196–197). In the dimness of the room at which he arrives, Winthrop sees a figure in eighteenth-century dress wearing the clothes in which Rinaldi is pictured in his portrait. The passage that follows is worth quoting in full as it traces the voice's metamorphosis from musical instrument to primordial cry:

> He was singing intently, and accompanying himself on the harpsichord ... . The wonderful sweet, downy voice glided lightly and dexterously through the complicated mazes of the song; it rounded off ornament after ornament, it swelled imperceptibly into glorious, hazy magnitude, and diminished, dying gently away from a high note to a lower one, like a weird, mysterious sigh; then it leaped into a high, clear triumphant note, and burst out into a rapid, luminous shake ... . At that moment a shadow was interposed between me and the lights, and instantly, by whom or how I know not, they were extinguished, and the room left in complete darkness; at the same instant the modulation was broken off unfinished; the last notes of the piece changed into a long, shrill, quivering cry (1927, 197–198).

This transmutation of the voice is signalled earlier in the text. Like the maternal voice, Rinaldi's 'voice' is experienced in a figurative womb. His voice when actually heard emerges from the 'interior' of the 'crypt-like house'; a house of vast, dark, empty halls which drip with damp and harbour death, a uterine 'bath of sounds' that is simultaneously comforting and threatening, awash with a voice that, like Poizat's operatic cry, leads to a terrifying immobilization. Mesmerized, Winthrop's blood is frozen, and his limbs are 'paralysed' and 'almost insensible' (1927, 198). The emasculating power of this voice is clearly indicated and, more importantly perhaps, this 'castration' manifests itself in Winthrop's waning creativity.

As his hostess begins to sing he is in the process of sketching, his book littered with a strange combination of designs: sirens' tails that suggest his fear of the feminine voice, satyrs that seem to signify a triumph of Dionysian chaos over Apollonian order, and 'manikins', diminutions that are symptomatic of his artistic impotence. These images coalesce, reflecting both the hybridity of the castrato voice, and the dissolution that marks his own ambiguous response to that voice. At the point at which the music enters his consciousness, Winthrop suddenly stops drawing. As in his first encounter with this song, which ends in a fruitless journey to Venice where he is laid low by a debilitating fever, Winthrop's creativity is here suspended once more, paralyzed this time, by the sound of Rinaldi's aria from the throat of his female host. Winthrop's tale ends with the artist's confession that Rinaldi's air had become something of an obsession, that he had vainly attempted to trace its source until his failure to do so made him doubt 'whether it had not been all a delusion, a nightmare phantasm, due to over-excitement and fever, due to the morbid, vague desire for something strange and supernatural', prompting him to ask whether his experience was grounded in reality or fiction: his audience is unable to give an adequate reply, and Winthrop is left in limbo, knowing only that they 'wouldn't believe a word of it' (1927, 204–205).

'A Wicked Voice'

Winthrop's tale appeared in a more intricate and intriguing form as 'A Wicked Voice' in *Hauntings: Fantastic Stories* (1890).[13] Perhaps taking her cue from Winthrop's own removal to Venice, Lee shifts the location to the Venetian lagoon where the castrato voice once more claims a victim who succumbs, like Winthrop, to a disabling fever. The protagonist here is Magnus, a nineteenth-century Norwegian composer who declares himself, 'a follower of Wagner' (2006, 155). Having arrived in Venice to compose his opera *Ogier the Dane*, which is Wagnerian in style and content, Magnus finds his inspiration flagging, his mind and body thrown into confusion by the stagnant Venetian waters that exhale 'like some great lily, mysterious influences, which make the brain swim and the heart faint' (2006, 156). During his stay at a Venetian boarding-house he is shown an engraving of a famous singer, Balthasar Cesari, known as 'Zaffirino'.[14] A fellow border, Count Alvise, recounts how his great-aunt, the Procuratessa Vendramin, had succumbed to the singer's bewitching power, killed by the mere beauty of his mesmerizing voice. Haunted by the singer's portrait and Count Alvise's story, Magnus himself begins to hear the singer's voice both in his dreams and in his waking hours, increasingly possessed by its beauty to the detriment of his own composition. Becoming progressively feverish and unstable, Magnus leaves Venice to stay at the Count's home at Mistrà where the Procuratessa had died. Here, in the very room where Zaffirino exerted his fatal magnetism, Magnus re-experiences the scene of death which has already contaminated his dreams, and is subsequently not only unable to complete his work, but is forever compelled to reproduce the eighteenth-century music that made Zaffirino's voice famous, whilst denied the sound of the singer's voice.

As in 'Winthrop's Adventure', the word 'castrato' is never used but it is evident from Magnus's description that Zaffirino shares Rinaldi's effeminacy whilst bearing a mark of cruel beauty which is lacking in the latter: 'That effeminate, fat face of his is almost beautiful, with an odd smile, brazen and cruel. I have seen faces like this, if not in real life, at least in my boyish romantic dreams, when I read Swinburne and Baudelaire, the faces of wicked, vindictive women' (2006, 162). Zaffirino's voice is infected similarly with the decadent qualities of these dangerous *femmes fatales*: it has 'the same sort of beauty and the same expression of wickedness' (2006, 162). Later, it becomes clear that Zaffirino is indeed a castrato: he has 'a man's voice which had much of a woman's, but more even of a chorister's, but a chorister's voice without its limpidity and innocence' (2006, 170).

Magnus first hears the singer's voice in his dreams where, reliving the scene of the Procuratessa's death, he finds himself in 'a real ballroom, almost circular in its octagon shape' (2006, 164). Gradually he begins to perceive sounds which draw his attention:

> little, sharp, metallic, detached notes, like those of a mandoline; and there was united to them a voice, very low and sweet, almost a whisper, which grew and grew and grew, until the whole place was filled with that exquisite vibrating note, of a strange, exotic, unique quality. The note went on, swelling and swelling. Suddenly there was a horrible piercing shriek, and the thud of a body on the floor, and all manner of smothered exclamations (2006, 164–165).[15]

As in 'Winthrop's Adventure', voice and instrument are here 'united'. Moreover, although our knowledge of the Procuratessa's story tells us that the shriek belongs to her, the passage does not make this clear and once again the song merges with the cry and its fatal consequences. At night, in search of inspiration, Magnus seeks the solitude of the Venetian lagoon. Here, gently swaying 'to and fro on the water' whilst his gondola 'rocked stationary', he hears Zaffirino's voice once more: 'there came across the lagoon, cleaving, chequering, and fretting the silence with a lacework of sound even as the moon was fretting and cleaving the water, a ripple of music, a voice breaking itself in a shower of little scales and cadences and trills' (2006, 166). The sounds teasingly abate momentarily but begin again: the 'murmur of a voice arose from the midst of the waters, a thread of sound slender as a moonbeam ... full, passionate, but veiled, as it were, in a subtle, downy wrapper' (2006, 167). Emanating from incalculable points in threads forming a 'lacework of sound', Zaffirino's voice connotes Chion's maternal voice, forming an 'umbilical net' that surrounds Magnus as he sways in the amniotic fluidity of the Venetian waters (2006, 166; quoted in Silverman 1988, 74). Yet the voice's femininity, wrapped in its 'downy wrapper' masks an hermaphroditic phallicism: its note grows stronger and stronger until at last 'it burst through that strange and charming veil, and emerged beaming, to break itself in the luminous facets of a wonderful shake, long, superb, triumphant' (2006, 167).

In its final manifestation at Mistrà where the Procuratessa's death is replayed once again for Magnus's conscious eyes, the composer is lured into a dark room where a brilliant light blinds him. He finds himself in a symbolically vaginal location, a 'sort of dark hole with a high balustrade, half-hidden by an up-drawn curtain' (2006, 178). Once again the voice becomes phallic:

> I heard the voice swelling, swelling, rending asunder that downy veil which wrapped it, leaping forth clear, resplendent, like the sharp and glittering blade of a knife that seemed to enter deep into my breast. Then, once more, a wail, a death-groan, and that dreadful noise, that hideous gurgle of breath strangled by a rush of blood. And then a long shake, acute, brilliant, triumphant (2006, 180).

Penetrated by Zaffirino's voice which, like Donna Elvira's cry in Mozart's *Don Giovanni*, 'pierces the nerves like a blade', Magnus is metaphorically emasculated and castrated for as Caballero points out, Magnus, 'will never again recover his "voice" as a composer' (1992, 391). Not only is his creativity figuratively 'castrated', but his response to the voice is clearly marked by a form of feminine dissolution. Earlier in the tale, succumbing to the voice in the acoustic splendour of an empty church, Magnus states: 'my hair was clammy, my knees sank beneath me, an enervating heat spread through my body; I tried to breathe more largely, to suck in the sounds with the incense-laden air. I was supremely happy, and yet as if I were dying' (2006, 174). Later, at Mistrà, this '*petit mort*' becomes even more explicit. Hearing the voice as it 'wound and unwound itself in long, languishing phrases, in rich, voluptuous *rifiorituras*', Magnus feels his body melting 'even as wax in the sunshine' and it seems as though he, too, is 'turning fluid and vaporous, in order to mingle with these sounds as the moonbeams mingled with the dew' (2006, 179). Magnus is doubly feminized: his desire for the 'male' singer cannot but be tinged with homoeroticism, and the fluidity of his orgasmic sensations seemingly define him as feminine.

Yet perhaps the voice's most threatening quality is its androgyny, for it is this hybridity which links its power to the threatening female voices of the past. Emerging from, and aligned with the undulating waters of the Venetian Lagoon, Zaffirino becomes synonymous with Venice herself, whose sobriquet, 'La Serenissima' is pregnant with meaning, for the word 'serene' from which 'serenissima' is constructed, (as well as meaning 'calm'), is also an obsolete form of 'siren' (*O.E.D.*). Like Zaffirino, the siren, too, is a hybrid being, 'half bird, half woman' who enchants, and raises 'the voices of the dead, to bring the past to life in the present' (*O.E.D.*). Moreover, a 'siren' was also once known as 'an imaginary species of serpent', a mythological beast that has obvious connotations with Medusa: an association which is heightened by the maternal fluidity of Zaffirino's voice and echoed in the serpentine waters of Venice that paradoxically immobilize Magnus in a state of fluid suspension between bliss and paranoia (*O.E.D.*). Significantly, the 'siren' was also an acoustical instrument invented by Cagniard de la Tour in 1819, that produced musical tones and was used in numbering the vibrations in any note (*O.E.D.*). It seems that here, in 'A Wicked Voice', the Apollonian instrument of Lee's ideal reverts significantly to a 'violin of flesh and blood' that recalls not only the bloody monstrousness of Medusa's maternity, but also the disturbing quality of the gorgonian cry (2006, 181). Aligned with the threatening femininity of the past, and the phallic and disturbing contemporary *femmes fatales* from the pages of Swinburne and Baudelaire, Zaffirino symbolizes a menacing femininity that remains sexually ambiguous.

'Sarrasine'

As Carlo Caballero has observed, 'Winthrop's Adventure' and 'A Wicked Voice' form an interesting relationship with Balzac's 'Sarrasine' (1832), that is now perhaps best known as the novella which Roland Barthes analyses in his seminal work, *S/Z*. Balzac's tale, like Lee's, is fraught with sexual ambiguity and transgressive desire. Like Winthrop and Magnus, Sarrasine is an artist – a sculptor. Arriving in Rome 'filled with a desire to make his name', Sarrasine is one night drawn to the opera. Here, his senses are 'lubricated', and the voices plunge him 'into a delicious ecstasy' which renders him 'speechless, motionless' (1992, 237). As the singer Zambinella takes centre stage Sarrasine's excitement is heightened and he cries out with pleasure. In Zambinella the sculptor's gaze finds his ideal beauty for she 'displayed to him, united, living, and delicate, those exquisite female forms he so ardently desired' (1992, 238). Her physical perfection is matched by the beauty of her song that elicits a kind of rapture:

> When La Zambinella sang, the effect was delirium. The artist felt cold; then he felt a heat which suddenly began to prickle in the innermost depth of his being, in what we call the heart, for lack of any other word! ... he experienced an impulse of madness, a kind of frenzy ... . Fame, knowledge, future, existence, laurels, everything collapsed (1992, 238).

The singer's voice, 'fresh and silvery in timbre, supple as a thread shaped by the slightest breath of air, rolling and unrolling, cascading and scattering', assaults his body with an orgy of sensations that overwhelms him and provokes 'involuntary cries torn from him by convulsive feelings of pleasure' (1992, 239). Exhausted, Sarrasine is obliged to leave the theatre feeling 'limp, weak' with a sense that he had 'experienced such pleasure, or perhaps he had suffered so keenly, that his life had drained away like water from a broken vase', feeling 'a prostration similar to the debilitation that overcomes those convalescing from serious illness' (1992, 239). Love-stricken, Sarrasine returns night after night to his box at the opera, and eventually his diligence and faithfulness are rewarded when he is invited to attend a supper with Zambinella. On arrival he is disappointed to find that he is not the only guest. However, during the course of the evening, drunk with wine and with lust, Sarrasine sweeps Zambinella off her feet, carrying her into a private boudoir. Here, Zambinella draws a dagger, ostensibly to protect her virtue, secretly to prevent Sarrasine's discovery of the truth behind her voice. Zambinella escapes, briefly, but after several days of coquettish evasion, Sarrasine's ardour is at its peak and he resolves to kidnap the singer. His plans are thwarted, however, when he attends a private concert. Here, he finds Zambinella, this time dressed like a man and at last is told the truth, that the singer is a castrato.

Like Lee, Balzac shies away from the word itself. Instead the nobleman who illuminates Sarrasine asks 'Has there ever been a woman on the Roman stage? And don't you know about the creatures who sing female roles in the Papal States?', leaving Sarrasine and the reader to draw their own conclusions (1992, 250). This, together with the excellence of Zambinella's voice and the other clues that litter Balzac's text, can leave no doubt about the singer's problematic gender. Sarrasine, however, is more difficult to convince. Unable to accept the evidence of his eyes and his ears, he proceeds with the kidnapping plot and has Zambinella brought to his studio where he has been working on a sculpture in her image. When the truth is finally revealed, the impact of Zambinella's deception on Sarrasine's talent are made explicit. Looking at the statue Sarrasine exclaims in despair:

> I shall forever think of this imaginary woman when I see a real woman ... . I shall always have the memory of a celestial harpy who thrust its talons into all my manly feelings, and who will stamp all other women with a seal of imperfection! Monster! You who can give life to nothing. For me, you have wiped women from the earth (1992, 252).

At this point he raises his sword to kill Zambinella, but her protectors come to the rescue and Sarrasine is himself murdered 'stabbed by three stiletto thrusts' (1992, 252).

The pattern is by now familiar: a male artist is enthralled by a feminine voice, a voice that evokes both pleasure and pain, an obsession which terminates in an artist's metaphorical castration and, in Sarrasine's case, in death. For Barthes, this voice is essentially phallic, its 'lubrication' of the hearer's faculties is linked to its 'seminal fluid' which 'floods with pleasure' as it diffuses through the pores of Sarrasine's body (1992, 110). However, as Frank argues, 'there is nothing necessarily masculine about the qualities of "lubrication" and "diffusion" which could apply equally well to sexual qualities that are specifically feminine' (1995,

105). For Frank, the interest that lies behind Zambinella's voice is its duality, its hermaphroditism. Yet, this duality is eschewed in both Barthes's and Balzac's texts; in the former, as we have seen, it is phallicized and in the latter it is negated entirely for, although Zambinella can 'give birth' to a voice, Sarrasine states that she 'can give life to nothing' (Balzac 1992, 252). Written in 1832, during a period which was fraught, as Margaret Reynolds has pointed out, with sexual anxieties which contributed to the devaluation of the castrato, Balzac's tale nevertheless resonates with the voice's androgyny. Its 'femininity' is encased in a woman's form, Zambinella, and its affective quality is linked to both the female operatic voice that immobilizes the hearer, and to the maternal voice – for Sarrasine's responses of orgasmic bliss and undefined depression as he listens to the silvery web-like threads of the singer's voice, are results of an experience that takes place in a darkened auditorium reminiscent of the womb. Moreover, Zambinella is described as a celestial 'harpy', a figure that bears a horrific female face and the body of a vulture, connoting the half-woman, half-bird physiology of her equally dangerous mythical sister, the siren. Yet Zambinella is also a 'phallic woman' and her fatal beauty foreshadows the decadent women Magnus will later find hidden in the cruelty of Zaffirino's face and voice. Stabbed by stilettos, Sarrasine's death is perhaps fitting: a 'castration' of life that is effected by the 'little knife', the colloquial expression for the castrative operation, and by its symbolic counterpart the 'little phallus' that marked the castrato's often stunted genitalia. Despite their similarities the significant difference that separates Balzac's tale from those of Lee's is the castrato's body. Balzac chooses to mask the castrato's body in the female form. More specifically this form is an ideal – Pygmalion's Galatea – an artistic perfection that is a fetishized idealisation of femininity, a form that contains and controls the contaminating and dangerous fluidity of the female body including the voice. In 'Sarrasine' it is only when the castrato's body is exposed that it becomes truly dangerous, for the threats it embodies no longer remain implicit.

Ariadne in Mantua

Lee's own cross-dressed and star-crossed lover appears in her play *Ariadne in Mantua* as a woman who adopts male attire in order to be close to her love, Ferdinand, the Duke of Mantua.[16] Taking her inspiration once again from Farinelli, whose sojourn in the Spanish court had given rise to a legend that his voice had cured the King of Spain's melancholy madness, Lee transposes this castrato voice onto the page Diego, a 'most expert singer' who has been summoned to the Mantuan court to cure the young duke of his melancholia so that he may marry his cousin Hippolyta (1903, I, 15). Diego is actually Magdalen, a Venetian courtesan and the duke's former lover who facilitated his escape from captivity at the hands of the Infidels. A love triangle ensues in which Hippolyta is attracted to Diego, Diego is in love with the duke, and the duke develops a homoerotically-charged affection for his page whilst lamenting his lost love, Magdalen. In the last scene Magdalen as Diego plays the part of Ariadne on a floating stage amidst the waters of the lake that surround the duke's palace. Having sung her final song, Magdalen drowns herself in the lake, and the duke and Hippolyta finally learn the secret of her 'true' gender.

The action takes place 'during the reign of Prospero I of Milan, and shortly before the Venetian expedition to Cyprus under Othello', highlighting the play's Shakespearian associations, which are acknowledged by Lee in the epigraph from *Twelfth Night* that precedes the first act, thus locating the play's use of cross-dressing and sexual ambiguity firmly within the tradition of Elizabethan theatre (1903, 12). Whilst indubitably playing with the erotic tensions of Elizabethan drama, one must not forget that *Ariadne in Mantua* evolved from Lee's attraction to the castrato figure and, significantly, the drama is propelled by the power and effect of Diego's voice. Moreover, the importance of this sexually-ambiguous singing voice, and the cross-dressed body from which it emerges forces obvious connections with eighteenth-century opera and the transsexual figure of the castrato who plays both male and female parts and sings in a voice that eerily encompasses the tones of man, woman, and boy. Described as 'a Spaniard of Moorish descent', Diego's assumed nationality also indicates that his voice is supposedly the product of castration, for as one of his admirers, the Bishop of Cremona, remarks in the final act: 'A wondrous singer, your Signor Diego. They say the Spaniards have subtle exercises for keeping the voice thus youthful. His Holiness has several such who sing divinely under Pierluigi's guidance' (1903, V, 57). If one considers that the castrati first appeared in Europe in the Moorish courts of southern Spain, and were later employed in the papal chapel, the connotations are clear.

The indeterminate nature of Diego's gender and sexuality is complicated even further, for Diego is not only a cross-dressed woman, but that woman is Magdalen, one of the many Venetian courtesans who were well known for their propensity to wear breeches beneath their skirts and who presented themselves as enticing hybrids of boy and woman (Astern 1994, 92). Furthermore, in the context of the Elizabethan stage this female figure would have been played by a boy whose hybridity was perceived as dangerous, particularly so when it emerged in song for it was 'the combination of boy actresses' erotic, costumed beauty with the seductive love-songs that their roles often required which made theatrical music so dangerous to the listener, their songs the deadly songs of Sirens' (Astern 1994, 89). The boy actor here becomes inevitably linked with the eighteenth-century castrato, as it is the sexual ambiguity of the voice that presents a threat to its audience. Moreover, the siren-like quality of this voice is heightened in *Ariadne in Mantua* for, like Zaffirino, the Venetian courtesan bewitches her listeners with the power of her vocal and musical dexterity. In a passage from *Coryats Crudities* (1611), the famous Jacobean traveller, Thomas Coryat, analyses her skill and warns of her charms:

> Shee will endeavour to enchant thee partly with her melodious notes that shee warbles out upon her lute, which shee fingers with as laudable a stroake as many men that are excellent professors in the noble science of Musicke: and partly with the heart-tempting harmony of her voice (quoted in Astern 1994, 93).

Transgressing the boundaries of masculine artistry, the courtesan is scarcely differentiated from her lute; the threatening femininity of her voice is encased, melding imperceptibly with the Apollonian instrument which accompanies her. Alternatively, as in *Ariadne in Mantua*, the courtesan's voice is submerged in and contained by her body so that she herself becomes an art object. Speaking to Diego of Magdalen, the duke tells him:

> She was like music – the whole art: new modes, new melodies, new rhythms, with every day and hour, passionate or sad, or gay, or very quiet; more wondrous notes than in thy voice; and more strangely sweet, even when they grated, than the tone of those newfangled fiddles, which wound the ear and pour balm in, they make now at Cremona (Lee 1903, III, 39).

Like those strange, sweet voices once heard by Lee at St Peter's in Rome, Magdalen's voice cuts the soul, 'only to pour into the wound some mysterious, narcotic balm' (quoted in Gunn 1964, 38). Yet the threatening quality of that cut requires that her voice, like Zambinella's, be bound by art, confined by the aestheticized female body. Lee's text suggests that Diego's voice, too, must be contained. Having discovered Diego's secret and perhaps fearing the emasculating effects of his hybridity, the duke's cardinal bids him be 'merely a singer: a sexless creature' (1903, I, 18). Unlike the synthetically formed voice of the castrato, Diego's is interpreted as a miracle of Heaven. Yet, like the former, it is merely an instrument in which 'sounds, subtly linked, take wondrous powers from the soul of him who frames their patterns' and the singer is 'merely ... the reed through which he blows' (1903, II, 22). Magdalen's siren song is ostensibly made 'safe', sanitized and contained within the Apollonian mechanism of Diego's body, that recalls the Athenian flute. At the same time, the disturbing ambiguity of this human 'flute' is acknowledged. Diego is simultaneously comforting and disconcerting; 'having seen passion but never felt it' he is 'yet capable ... of rousing and soothing it in others' with his voice (1903, I, 18).

In Act IV, the disruptive nature of Diego's voice is revealed during a duet that he sings with Hippolyta. The Princess begins singing in a 'full-toned voice clear and high', and Diego follows, 'singing in a whisper' in a voice that is 'a little husky, and here and there broken, but ineffably delicious and penetrating, and, as he sings, becomes, without quitting the whisper, dominating and disquieting' (1903, IV, 54). Disturbed and distracted, the Princess 'plays a wrong chord, and breaks off suddenly' (1903, IV, 54). Diego asks the cause of her distress and Hippolyta answers disjointedly: 'I know not. I have lost my place – I – I feel bewildered. When your voice rose up against mine, DIEGO, I lost my head. And – I do not know how to express it – when our voices met in that held dissonance, it seemed as if you hurt me – horribly' (1903, IV, 54).

Like Zaffirino's voice, Diego's is both phallically penetrant and femininely disruptive. Hippolyta, whose body it 'penetrates' and whose art it disrupts, has masculine attributes. She has the 'strength and grace, and the candour, rather of a beautiful boy than of a woman', her brows 'are wide and straight, like a man's', her voice is 'more like a boy's' than a maiden's and she has been brought up by her father 'in such a wise as scarcely to lack a son, with manly disciplines of mind and body' (1903, IV, 43–55). Hippolyta's 'masculinity' is threatened by Diego's voice. Like the male artists we have already met, her art, too, is cut short, metaphorically castrated, by the elusive ambiguity of Diego's song that combines the phallic power of the 'mannish woman', the dangerous hybridity of the Siren's vocality, and the simultaneously soothing and disturbing attributes of the maternal voice. Yet Hippolyta is herself a 'mannish woman', who is named after the queen of the Amazons, a race of virginal women, 'unlike their vain and weakly sex' (1903, IV, 44).[17] Why then is Diego able to exert his power over her voice? The answer may lie in Hippolyta' s female body whose Amazonian virginity remains intact despite being symbolically penetrated by Diego – an expert 'player on the virginal' – with his hermaphroditic voice (1903, I, 15). The scene suggests a fantasy of lesbian desire, that ends in 'dissonance', or disharmony, and is played out within an ostensibly heterosexual coupling – Hippolyta's voice is 'like a boy's' and Diego's 'like a woman's' – while still retaining a thread of erotic ambiguity in its sexual reversals.

In the final act of the drama, Diego plays the mythological figure, Ariadne, in a masque that is performed to celebrate the marriage of the duke to Hippolyta. In Greek myth, Ariadne, having helped Theseus to evade the Minotaur by means of a thread that leads him out of the Cretan labyrinth, is then abandoned on the island of Naxos, whilst her lover proceeds to marry the young duchess's namesake, Hippolyta. It is here, on Naxos, that Ariadne is wooed by Bacchus whom she rejects, pleading to be allowed time to lament her lost love. The figure of Ariadne functions as an allusion to the duke's personal device, a labyrinth, which is carved in gold on the deep blue ground of the music room ceiling and inscribed with the words *Rectas Peto*, meaning 'I seek straight ways' (1903, III, 33). Earlier in the play, the duke explains its meaning:

> The maze, Diego, carved and gilded on that ceiling is but a symbol of my former life. ... When I entered it, I was a raw youth, although in years a man; full of easy theory, and thinking all practice simple; unconscious of passion; ready to govern the world with a few learned notions; moreover never having known either happiness or grief, never loved and wondered at a creature different from myself ... . The maze, and all the maze implied, made me a man (1903, III, 33).

But the maze, as Diego observes, is symbolic also of the reality of the duke's former imprisonment at the hands of the Infidels, from which he escapes with Magdalen's assistance: Magdalen, like Ariadne, having provided a clue, or 'thread' by which he might achieve his freedom. The music room, whose ceiling bears the labyrinthine carving has windows on both sides 'admitting a view of the lake, so that the hall looks like a galley surrounded by water', a room which paradoxically seems to function as a locus of release and entrapment (1903, IV, 43). Here, the duke has engraved his symbol of freedom and emergence into manhood, and it is also the place in which Magdalen, as Diego, liberates him once more from the labyrinth of his melancholy. For Hippolyta, however, it is a site of confinement for it is here that her song is stifled and her voice silenced: contradictory effects, recalling those created by Chion's maternal vocality, this time produced by Diego's voice in the music room surrounded by the uterine fluidity of the Mantuan lake.

Amidst a stage peopled by Bacchanalian figures, Satyrs and Nymphs, Ariadne appears, dressed in 'a floating robe and vest of orange and violet ... with particoloured scarves hanging, and a particoloured scarf wound like a turban round the head, the locks of dark hair escaping from beneath' (1903, V, 60). Ariadne speaks accompanied by viols and harpsichord. As her speech becomes more dramatic, her declamation is echoed by 'a rapid and passionate tremolo of violins and viols' (1903, V, 62). The accompaniment becomes more and more agitated until at last she sings, and as her song ends she flings herself into the waters of the lake as a 'hautboy suddenly enters with a long wailing phrase' (1903, V, 64). In this scene of Dionysian excess Ariadne sings in garments that symbolize the disruptive quality of her voice, her particoloured dress suggests her hybridity, her Medusan locks escape threateningly from the serpentine scarves that drape her hair. Yet her singing voice is effectively 'silenced', allowed only to speak whilst the flute, the viol, or the harpsichord echo her emotions, culminating in the hautboy's mournful wail that displaces the gorgonian cry of mourning. The threatening nature of her voice manifests itself only at the point of death, as she drowns herself in the lake that, in its sunset colours, mirrors the deep blue and gold of the labyrinthine pattern that adorns the duke's music room. Ariadne, led by the thread of her own song, dies engulfed by the maternal liquidity of the Mantuan waters.

Inverted Images and Acoustic Mirrors

At the heart of Lee's supernatural tales, 'Winthrop's Adventure' and 'A Wicked Voice', as in Balzac's 'Sarrasine', lies the theme of the thwarted artist. Winthrop is unable to complete any sketch he begins, Magnus can no longer write what he chooses, and Sarrasine's sculpture of Zambinella is nothing but a cruel illusion, a mockery of his artistic vision. As we have seen, in all three tales the cause of this disruption is the castrato. In Balzac's story, the castrato's dangerous voice and physical deformity are safely hidden in the feminine curves of Zambinella's body. When the castrato body is finally exposed, the artist's inspiration becomes void, both literally and figuratively, for Zambinella lacks what a woman's body should have, and hides a 'void', the castration wound, which is mirrored in the artist's castrated creativity. Zambinella and Sarrasine are, arguably, mirror images: as Barthes observes, 'S and Z are in a relation of graphological inversion: the same letter seen from the other side of the mirror' (1992, 107). Although Barthes contends that it is Zambinella's voice with which Sarrasine falls in love, Balzac's text suggests otherwise, for it is Zambinella's physical attributes that first attract him:

> Her mouth was expressive, her eyes loving, her complexion dazzlingly white. And along with these details, which would have enraptured a painter, were all the wonders of those images of Venus revered and rendered by the chisels of the Greeks ... . This was more than a woman, this was a masterpiece! (1992, 238).

Zambinella is 'Pygmalion's statue, come down from its pedestal', locating her in a tradition of woman as object, of woman as a reassuring mirror to the male gaze (Balzac 1992, 238). While it is certainly true that Sarrasine responds sexually to Zambinella's voice, that voice is nevertheless already contained by the exquisite aesthetic form of her physical body. This effectively 'silences' Zambinella's voice and displaces the threat implicit in the castrato's voice onto the body that is later exposed with such fatal effects. In contrast Lee's tales centre on the voice: Rinaldi's portrait depicts him with open lips in the process of singing and the engraving of

Zaffirino prompts the young ladies at Magnus's boarding-house to ask the young composer to sing one of Zaffirino's favourite songs, so that Magnus momentarily 'becomes' Zaffirino. It is open to question whether the ghostly manifestations of these voices are heard by anyone other than the artists themselves. During one of Magnus's nocturnal excursions a mystery voice is apparently heard not just by himself but by others. Yet the voice emerges seemingly from the waters of the Grand Canal where a music-boat is providing entertainment for the people who grace the balconies of the neighbouring hotels, and it is never clear whether the voice heard by Magnus is that which is also heard by others. As in 'Winthrop's Adventure', it is therefore debatable whether the source of the voice is internal or external.

The spatial indeterminacy of this voice has interesting implications. Winthrop and Magnus, like Sarrasine, respond erotically to the castrato voice, but in Lee's tales the castrato body is aurally, and not physically, explicit: its sexuality is disembodied by its ghostliness, displaced and made to 'lodge in the throat' (Barthes 1992, 109). If Sarrasine falls in love with Zambinella's body before he falls in love with her voice, Winthrop and Magnus have no such option. The locus of their desire is the voice itself. In his essay 'On Love' (composed 1818), Shelley suggests that the self 'thirsts after its likeness' (1977, 473). If this is the case then one might argue that the voice which haunts the artists in Lee's tales is, in fact, a facet of their own, an auditory image which functions as an 'acoustic mirror' that is potentially disruptive to their subjectivity. As Guy Rosolato observes:

> The voice [has the property] of being at the same time emitted and heard, sent and received, and by the subject himself, as if, in comparison with the look, an 'acoustic' mirror were always in effect. Thus the images of entry and departure relative to the body are narrowly articulated. They can come to be confounded, inverted, to prevail one over the other (quoted in Silverman 1988, 79).

Kaja Silverman notes that this 'notion of an "acoustic mirror" can be applied with remarkable precision to the function which the female voice is called upon to perform for the male subject' (1988, 80). She points out that within 'the traditional familial paradigm, the maternal voice introduces the child to its mirror reflection': not only does the child learn to speak by imitating the mother's sounds, but even before its entry into language the maternal voice plays a major part in the development of the child's subjectivity, generally being 'the first object not only to be isolated, but to be introjected' (1988, 80). In this early period of a child's development:

> the object has as yet no externality, since it is no sooner identified than it is assimilated by the child. Nor, since the subject lacks boundaries, does it as yet have anything approximating an interiority ... . Since the child's economy is organized around incorporation, and since what is incorporated is the auditory field articulated by the maternal voice, the child could be said to hear itself initially through that voice – to first 'recognize' itself in the vocal 'mirror' supplied by the mother (Silverman, 1988, 80).

She goes on to argue that 'the male subject later hears the maternal voice through himself – that it comes to resonate for him with all that he transcends through language ... projecting onto the mother's voice all that is unassimilable to the paternal position' (1988, 81).

So how do Winthrop and Magnus function within this scenario? As I have illustrated, the castrato voice appears to embody both the comforting and disturbing qualities of the maternal voice, whilst simultaneously aestheticizing and projecting the emasculating threat represented by the powerful speaking woman and her Medusan cry. Vernon Lee, like many of her female contemporaries, and writers like George Eliot before her, was aware of the need to reject the feminine voice in order be taken seriously by the male literary establishment. While regretting that most female novelists had embraced the idea of 'imitating men's cuffs and collars and documents' instead of exploring the world from the female consciousness, Lee was often guilty of this herself (quoted in Gunn 1964, 9). Like Eliot, Lee retained her male pseudonym throughout her literary career and is listed amongst the small number of female contributors writing non-fiction prose for the leading periodicals which served as the principal venue for what has come to be known as 'sage writing' (Christ 1990, 22). This genre was dominated by writers such as Carlyle, whose lecture, 'The Hero as Man of Letters', forms what Carol T. Christ calls 'the paradigmatic Victorian text which establishes the ideal of the writer as prophet, priest, or sage' and 'defines that role as exclusively male' (1990, 20).[18] It was in these periodicals that many of Lee's articles on musical aesthetics were published and it is perhaps therefore unsurprising that her work in this field should be characterized, as we have seen, by a rejection of the feminine and a penchant for Apollonian form and order. But like Athena, that 'figure for the incorporation of the otherness of female creative energy into the polis', who bears the head of Medusa on her dress, Lee's theoretical work carries within it traces of Medusa's threatening femininity which emerge in the contradictions of her factitious aesthetic system and are then refracted through her fiction (Segal 1994, 31).

The increasing feminization of the voice in that fiction, which can be traced in a clear trajectory from Rinaldi, through Zaffirino, and finally to Magdalen-Diego in *Ariadne in Mantua*, might suggest that in Magdalen, who must appear a man even when she plays Ariadne, Lee expresses her frustration with the male persona she maintains in order to achieve success in the critical world. As Caballero observes, what Lee refuses in her aesthetic system, 'what would otherwise remain unwritten ... became a rich fund for her imaginative writing' (1992, 403). Winthrop and Magnus then are arguably facets of Vernon Lee's public persona: aspects of her artistic 'masculinity' that project onto the maternal voice 'all that is unassimilable to the paternal position' she adopts (Silverman 1988, 81). Yet the castrato is also the artist's mirror image, a figure of formidable vocal power that emasculates and disempowers the masculine for, like George Eliot's diva, Armgart, who functions as 'a metaphor for female empowerment in a culture that traditionally places women on the side of silence', the castrato might also declare, 'I carry revenges in my throat' (Pope 1994, 140; quoted in Pope 1994, 146). It is worth noting that in Lee's tales the artist's nemesis is the 'cry', a sound which Lee, in her aesthetic system, associates with the declamatory voices of Wagnerian opera. The disturbing nature of these voices is illustrated in Lee's essay 'The Religious and Moral Status of Wagner':

Attentive or inattentive, able to follow or not able to follow, your mind is imprisoned in that Wagner performance as in the dark auditorium, and allowed to divagate from the music only to the stage; not the literal stage ... but the inviolable stage of your own emotions, secretly haunted by the vague ghosts of your own past ... by the vaguer fatamorgana figures of your own scarce conscious hopes and desires (1911, 879).

Interestingly, these voices are heard in the womb-like darkness of the auditorium amid a maelstrom of unruly and disordered sensations. In Lee's fictions these disruptive and disconcerting voices are displaced onto eighteenth-century singers, vessels that feature in her aesthetic system as symbols of Apollonian form and order: a contradiction indicative of those that Caballero locates in her work and a ghostly reminder of the feminine power that haunts not only Lee's fiction but appears as an unacknowledged presence in her theoretical writing.

But why should this figure appear as a ghost? The answer lies perhaps in the homoerotic tensions that underlie these tales. In her book *The Apparitional Lesbian: Female Homosexuality and Modern Culture*, Terry Castle illustrates the ways in which the lesbian is 'apparitionalized' in the Western imagination, and argues that the 'literary history of lesbianism ... is first of all a history of derealization' (1993, 34). Using texts as disparate as Daniel Defoe's 'The Apparition of Mrs Veal' (1706) and Djuna Barnes's *Nightwood* (1936), Castle traces the spectral metaphors that have accompanied expressions of lesbian sexuality since the eighteenth century. In Baudelaire's 'Femmes Damnées', 'one of the numerous lesbian obsessed poems in *Les Fleurs du Mal* (1857)', Castle notes that Delphine and Hippolyte, 'the tortured lovers, are presented as damned spirits, enslaved by a sterile passion and doomed to wander ceaselessly in a hell of their own creation' (1993, 36). In Swinburne's 'Faustine' (1862), the Roman empress Faustine in whom 'stray breaths of Sapphic song that blew/ Through Mitylene' once 'shook the fierce quivering blood' by night, is 'surrounded in death by the phantoms of the women she has debauched in life' and acquainted with that 'shameless nameless love' (Castle 1993, 37–38). Given Zaffirino's affinity with these ghostly Baudelairian and Swinburnian figures of transgressive sexuality, we can conceivably discover erotic tensions that reputedly remained unacknowledged in Lee's private life. In an unsympathetic description of Lee, Bertrand Russell comments on Lee's relationships with young women. He writes:

She was a woman of almost unbelievable ugliness and probably never aroused desire in any man. She had a whole series of young girls to whom she was a vampire, and when one of them had been used up, she would throw her away and get another. She sapped their life and their energy. She was a very masterful, dominant person – a bloodsucker! And that endless stream of talk. She sucked the blood of all of them (quoted in Gardner, 1987, 85, 60).

Here, significantly, Lee's 'lesbian vampirism' is equated with her vocal prowess, her voice saps one's energy, drains one's life, immobilizes. Supposedly denying her sexuality even to herself, it is unlikely that Lee would consciously have chosen the phantom castrato as a figure of lesbian empowerment. Yet it is worth noting that the hermaphroditic qualities that mark the castrato were often associated with lesbian sexuality during the chronological periods in which Lee sets her fictional singers. At this time the label 'hermaphrodite' encompassed both 'feminine men' and 'masculine women', but the tag was most frequently applied to those who exhibited lesbian desire:

> In texts circulating in Britain in the seventeenth and eighteenth centuries, women who had sex with women were often denounced, mocked, and exiled from womanhood; one of the most common strategies was to call them hermaphrodites. There was constant slippage between concepts of sexual deviance at this time, but two ideas in particular – lesbian desire and hermaphroditical anatomy – became tightly bound into the figure of the tribade, a woman whose phallic 'member'... was thought to enable her to have penetrative intercourse with women (Donoghue 1993, 199).

Emma Donoghue points out that the medical, or pseudo-medical, literature on the subject expressed a veiled hostility: 'Rather than attacking lesbianism directly as a sin, they explained it away as an anomaly. By cutting lesbians off from their sex, from their own femaleness, these writers ... could reduce them to exceptional, and therefore harmless, freaks of nature' (1993, 201). The phallic 'member' was often a prolapsed vagina or an enlarged clitoris, which was commonly termed 'a miniature version of the penis' (Donoghue 1993, 204). In his treatise, *Onanism* (1766), the Swiss doctor Samuel Tissot argued that these 'imperfect' women with a 'semi-resemblance' to men 'glorying, perhaps, in this kind of resemblance, seized upon the functions of virility' (Donoghue 1993, 206). Donoghue observes that:

> It was one of the ironies of eighteenth-century sexuality that Tissot could present these women's abnormal imperfection as something to 'glory' in, since even a 'semi-resemblance' to men was an honour. Though as freaks they were less than whole women, Tissot could not help admitting that in some sense they were more than women too (1993, 206–207).

The concept of the 'hermaphroditic' lesbian resonates interestingly with Sarrasine's ideal, Zambinella, for she, too, is described by the artist as 'more than a woman' (Balzac 1992. 238). The similarity between Balzac's castrato and Tissot's lesbian does not perhaps end there. What is perceived to be the lesbian's 'miniature penis' recalls the castrato's stunted member, and whilst the latter is the result *of* castration, the former was often subjected *to* castration. Quoting from various eighteenth-century texts, Donoghue highlights the fate of the offending anomaly, noting that the concensus of opinion was generally that 'hermaphrodites both deserved and needed castration' (1993, 209). One might suggest, then, that the figure of the castrato is an inverted incarnation of the lesbian 'hermaphrodite'. As a fictional representation in Lee's texts, however, the castrato functions possibly as an 'inscription of the unintended' creating 'the quality of resonance, that rich wake of meaning which rocks our conscious life and disturbs us in our dreams': expressing, perhaps, an alternative subjectivity that is played out in the 'potential space' of Lee's fictions and explored within the 'safe' holding environment provided by the 'maternal' voice of the castrato, which is simultaneously an 'acoustic mirror' of her own (Sprengnether 1993, 95).

Arguably this musical 'maternal' voice provides the framework for Lee's play, *Ariadne in Mantua*, which she sees as an allegorical dramatization of the 'contending forces of history and life', the struggle between 'Impulse and Discipline' (1903, x). The play is inspired not only by her own fascination with the 'palace of Mantua and the lakes it steeps in', that she had written of earlier in *Genius Loci* (1899), but also more specifically by a piece of music. In her preface to the play Lee writes:

> looking into my mind one day, I found that a certain song of the early seventeenth century – (not Monteverde's 'Lamento d'Arianna' but an air, 'Amarilli', by Caccini, printed alongside in Parisotti's collection) – had entered that palace of Mantua, and was, in some manner not easy to define, the musical shape of what must have happened there. And that, translated back into human personages, was the story I have set forth in the following little Drama (1903, viii).

Lee's acknowledged indebtedness to Shakespeare associates the play with the male literary canon, and her adopted 'masculine' intellectualism. However the play is fraught with sexual ambiguities that, whilst consistent with its Elizabethan antecedents, destabilize its apparent simplicity. I have suggested that, in Lee's fiction, these sexual reversals can be read as indicative of the insecurities that haunt the 'male' subjectivity she displays in her theoretical work. The music she sees as 'orderly' in her aesthetic system becomes disruptive, the powerful and threatening qualities of the female voice, which she ostensibly aestheticizes and reforms, return in her fiction, and the desire for the feminine which she seemingly negates is expressed in the homoerotic tensions that characterize 'Winthrop's Adventure' and 'A Wicked Voice'.

So what is one to make of the gender instabilities in *Ariadne in Mantua*? It is important to remember that the latter is a 'play'. Here, in a drama that is inspired by the singing voice, set in a palace surrounded by the waters of the Mantuan lake, Lee plays with a variety of sexual roles. Neither the duke, nor Magdalen/Diego, nor Hippolyta 'represent the male and the female exclusively' (Gunn 1964, 178). The duke, whose 'strange moodiness is marked by an abhorrence of all womankind', is attracted to his page Diego in whom he sees traces of Magdalen: he sees 'glances of her' in Diego's eyes, hears her voice in his, and tells him that not music 'but love, love's delusion, was what worked my cure' (Lee 1903, I, 16; III, 40). It remains unclear whether 'love's delusion' is that he sees Magdalen in Diego, or that in Diego he responds to the same androgynous quality that Magdalen, as a Venetian courtesan, is reputed to possess.[19] A similar ambiguity hampers one's interpretation of the scene in which Diego sings with Hippolyta. Is it the man or the woman in Diego to whom Hippolyta responds? Having been raised as a substitute boy by her father, Hippolyta is herself sexually ambiguous, an ambiguity that is heightened by her mythological counterpart, the Amazon, who cut off her right breast in order to use the bow more easily in warfare, thus mutilating her body and creating a physical hybridity.[20] But it is Diego's sexuality that most frequently transgresses the borders of socially demarcated gender. Throughout the play he embodies the hybridity of the Venetian courtesan, the 'asexuality' of the castrato, and a fluid homosexuality that eludes definition. This fluidity is heightened by the play's affinity with Elizabethan drama and one's own awareness that, in that setting, the role of Diego would have been played by a boy. However, if one steps outside one's own imagination and onto the nineteenth-century stage, the figure of Diego takes on an added significance.

Here, the role would have been played by a woman, a woman who plays the part of a castrato, a figure that is empowered by its voice. Yet when that voice returns to the female body in Ariadne, it is 'silenced', initially by the instruments that displace her voice, and drowned both literally and figuratively in the Mantuan waters.

In a letter to Maurice Baring, Lee writes of *Ariadne in Mantua* that the 'whole piece was written in a more inevitable, unconscious way than anything else I have ever done, and I respect its integrity just because it made itself without any act of writing or judgment' (quoted in Gunn 1964, 178). As an expression of Lee's 'unconscious', *Ariadne in Mantua* sheds light on the contradictions between her theoretical writing and her supernatural fiction. In the latter the castrato emerges as a figure of feminine empowerment who simultaneously bears the phallus and the castration wound: a version of the phallic woman that haunts the *fin-de-siècle* imagination. In *Ariadne in Mantua*, the castrato figure is untenable on the nineteenth-century stage. Here, the castrato must be played by a woman and the part of Diego is transformed from that of a womanish man, into that of a mannish woman who dies unable to exist in the heterosexual order that is reimposed as the play ends. In a play that is in itself a form of 'song', set in the womb-like waters of the palace lake, Lee 'plays' and attempts to develop her artistic subjectivity, and to find her voice, exemplifying perhaps Winnicott's observation that, 'In a search for the self the person concerned may have produced something valuable in terms of art, but a successful artist may be universally acclaimed and yet have failed to find the self that he or she is looking for' (Winnicott, *Playing and Reality*, 1971, 54). If the 'maternal' voice of the castrato is the 'holding environment' in which this subjectivity is being explored, it is significant that this voice, as it appears in Lee's fiction, symbolizes both release and entrapment. The castrato figure whose voice embodies the tones of both man and woman and cannot be confined by its gender is a potent symbol of empowerment for the lesbian writer who must masquerade as male, and negate her sexuality. Yet the demise of the 'castrato' in *Ariadne in Mantua* acknowledges the impossibility of this position. The castrato remains a ghostly figure embedded in the rejected 'enchanted garret' of Lee's imagination, returning only in her fiction and hiding its implications in musical fantasy for if 'you speak a secret you lose it; ... But if you sing the secret, you magically manage to keep it private, for singing is a barricade of codes' (Koestenbaum 1994, 157). In Lee's tales, however, such ghostly personae are not concealed in song alone, but emerge reconfigured, and sometimes, disfigured, in the art forms that are the subject of the chapters to follow.

Notes

[1] 'Contralto', Gautier 1903, 71, ll. 29–32.

[2] Carlo Broschi, known as 'il Farinelli' (1705–1782) was one of the most famous castrati of the eighteenth century. Farinelli retired at the height of his fame to sing exclusively for Philip V of Spain, who suffered from depression, and continued in the service of the Spanish Court for more than two decades.

[3] For Winnicott, the process of individuation via which an individual develops his/her distinct personality, takes place within children's creative play, thus bridging their internal and external worlds prior to the acceptance of an independent subjectivity.

[4]   Max Beerbohm (1872–1956), parodist and caricaturist. In *Gospels of Anarchy*, Lee devotes essays to Emerson, Tolstoi, William James, Rosny, Ruskin and H.G. Wells.

[5]   For further references to the reception of Lee's 'talk' among her contemporaries, see Gardner, 1987, 53–64.

[6]   Michel Poizat, in his 1991 essay, explains that, for Lacan, 'the voice takes its place alongside other objects of the drives identified by Freud: oval object (the breast), anal object (faeces), [and] genital object (the penis)' (210). Lacan added 'the gaze' to this list of 'partial objects'.

[7]   Interestingly, the castrato and the flute are 'merged' in the 'eunuch-flute', a type of mirliton, an instrument that, according to the *O.E.D.*, is 'not a flute at all, but a tube covered at the small end with a thin membrane. The performer sings, or rather hums, through a hole in the side near the membrane'. My thanks to Carol Barker for bringing this instrument to my attention.

[8]   When I refer to 'castration' in relation to women, I use the term in the Freudian sense.

[9]   Vernon Lee met John Singer Sargent in 1866, and developed a friendship that continued until his death in 1925.

[10]   Giovanni Pierluigi da Palestrina (*c.* 1525–1594), Italian composer of Renaissance music, who had a significant influence on the development of Roman Catholic church music.

[11]   See also Caballero, 1992, 389.

[12]   St John's Eve (23 June), date of pagan celebrations in honour of the goddess Aphrodite.

[13]   'A Wicked Voice' first appeared in French as 'Voix Maudite' in *Les Lettres et Les Arts* (1887).

[14]   Reputedly, 'because of a sapphire engraved with cabalistic signs presented to him one evening by a masked stranger ... that great cultivator of the human voice, the devil' (Lee 2006, 157).

[15]   The instrument is in fact a harpsichord, and not a mandolin. Catherine Maxwell suggests that Lee evokes the mandolin in order to allude to her half-brother, Eugene Lee-Hamilton's poem 'The Mandolin' published in *The New Medusa, and Other Poems* (1882) (2006, 35).

[16]   Lee visited Mantua for the first time in 1896. Struck by the beauty of its lakes, she returned several times and wrote about them in her essay, 'The Lakes of Mantua', published in *Genius Loci: Notes on Places* (1899). For background information on the origin of the play, including historical personages who may have inspired Duke Ferdinand and Diego, see Ermanno F. Comparetti, 1954, and Rita Severi, 1996. The play was performed on two occasions: in May 1916 it was produced at the Gaiety Theatre, London, by the Countess Lytton, with Ben Webster as the Duke and music by Eugene Goossens and Ivor Novello, and later, in Italian, at the Reale Accademia dei Fidenti in Florence in 1934 (Gunn 1964, 180; Colby 2003, 269).

[17]   In Greek myth, the Amazons were a nation of martial women who cultivated manly qualities. They cut off their right breasts so that they might use the javelin more effectively, while keeping their left breasts for feeding their children.

[18]   Phyllis Mannochi has suggested that Vernon Lee's own role in the literary arena was 'based on the original image of the man of letters' (Mannocchi 1986, 130).

[19]   The question of whether the duke was aware of Diego's true identity is one that concerned readers of *Ariadne in Mantua* during Lee's lifetime. In a letter to Maurice Baring, of 12 December 1932, Lee writes that the players in a projected production of the play would ask 'as Ben Webster did in Lady Lytton's rehearsals, whether the Duke did or did not recognize Diego': on that occasion she replied that 'it was for him to tell me, because I didn't know ... what the author intended is neither here nor there ... also I think I like the vagueness better than the realistic possibility' (Smyth 1938, 335). Arguably, her preference for 'vagueness' allows a fictional space for sexual as well as textual ambiguity.

[20]   A similarly androgynous figure, Artemisia del Valore, appears in Lee's novel *Louis Norbert* (1914). Like Hyppolyta, Artemisia is a substitute boy for a father who lacks a son, and is compared to the Amazons (see Pulham 2006).

Chapter 2

A White and Ice-cold World

Where between sleep and life some brief space is,
With love like gold bound round about the head,
Sex to sweet sex with lips and limbs is wed,
Turning the fruitful feud of hers and his,
To the waste wedlock of a sterile kiss.
Algernon Charles Swinburne (1866)[1]

The Magdalen/Diego character in *Ariadne in Mantua* finds its echo, in Lee's aesthetics, in the figure of Orpheus. In her essay 'Orpheus in Rome' in *Althea: a Second Book of Dialogues on Aspirations and Duties* (1894), Lee explores the aesthetic value of music and sculpture via the dialogic exchange between a fictive self, 'Baldwin', and a close circle of friends based loosely on Lee's own, all of whom had appeared some years earlier in her book, *Baldwin: Being Dialogues on Aspirations and Duties* (1886).[2] In this essay, Baldwin first appears at an opera where he is discussing his current jaded responses to those cultural pursuits that had formerly given him pleasure: once moved by the music of Gluck, Baldwin 'doesn't care any longer for old music, any more than he cares – really and actively – for antique sculpture' (Lee 1894, 56). Yet Gluck's music, and more particularly the eighteenth-century castrato Gaetano Guadagni, who first played the title role in *Orfeo ed Euridice* (1762), remain an insistent memory.[3] As Baldwin says, 'It's curious … that one of the few remaining shreds of my old musical lore … one of the few impressions remaining to me from my eighteenth-century days should happen to be that of the original singer of this very opera—the man for whom Gluck composed his *Orpheus*' (Lee 1894, 51).[4]

The forceful nature of this memory is recalled by Baldwin in language that connects the singer to Lee's fictional castrati. He calls Guadagni a 'ghost' and ponders 'by what caprice some particular ghost chooses to manifest himself and haunt' (Lee 1894, 52). However, the Roman Orpheus (to whom the title of Lee's essay refers) is a woman: the notes that attract the company's attention 'belonged to a low soprano voice', that of Helene Hastreiter (Lee 1894, 57).[5] Lee's narrator, Althea, observes that, 'instead of the disturbing fact of a woman dressed up as a man', these notes conveyed to the hearer, 'quite simply, naturally and irrefutably, the existence of a world of poetry and romance, and the presence of a demi-god' (Lee 1894, 57). Although this passage suggests that the importance of the singer's gender is negated by the beauty of her song, it seems significant that at least one of the company, Donna Maria, needs to resolve the question of sexual ambiguity: she prefers to 'think of her as he' and one of the other interlocutors cannot help but return to the figure of the castrato for, when Baldwin asks for the singer's name, Carlo replies 'Did you think … it might be the ghost of Signor Guadagni?' (Lee 1894, 58).

The opera *Orfeo ed Euridice* is one that carries a history of problematic sexuality. The critic Wendy Bashant describes it as 'one of the queerest operas I know' and goes on to point out that:

Orfeo and Euridice do not bend gender. They transform it. How many times have they been conceived? Jacopo Peri, Guilio Caccini, Claudio Monteverdi … Willbald Gluck, … Hector Berlioz … Igor Stravinsky. When the opera was born in 1600 (not by any means its origin – Angelo Poliziano's *pastorali*, *Orfeo*, had been around since 1472), it was unsure of its sex, *L'Euridice*? *L'Orfeo*? All of its composers seem unsure (1995, 217).

This sexual ambiguity is complicated further by the main protagonist of the myth itself. As Bashant observes, 'Orpheus appears to be both asexual and supersexual. He is an artistic figure who creates without a spouse – he invents the world through his song' (1995, 218). Moreover, while the myth suggests the desirability of heterosexual love, it ultimately fails to reestablish heterosexual order. Orpheus loses Eurydice and, in some texts, appears to be homosexual:

Ovid speaks of how 'his life was given to young boys only' … causing the Maenads to tear him into pieces. Others further confuse the tale by describing how his body parts finally find their resting-place on the isle of Lesbos. Orpheus becomes not-man and not-woman, a mythic figure who exaggerates the codes of sexual difference that he himself displays (Bashant 1995, 218).

As Bashant explains, Berlioz's transcription of Gluck's opera for the French stage confuses the gender issue further:

Gluck's title role was originally performed in 1762 by the celebrated castrato contralto, Gaetano Guadagni. When Gluck was called to Paris by Marie Antoinette in 1773, he was forced to transpose the part down a fifth so that a tenor could sing it, since the Paris opera never used castrati. In the nineteenth century the exceptionally talented Pauline Garcia Viardot persuaded Hector Berlioz to restore Orfeo to the contralto line (1995, 219).[6]

Viardot's vocal excellence and striking stage presence recall Lee's castrati. Her biographer, April Fitzlyon, notes that she was a singer with a voice of 'extraordinary range', she could reach notes in the upper soprano register with ease, and also sang comfortably in the contralto register (1964, 39). She had 'a strange, exotic charm' and the power of her performance led Berlioz to write, 'The impression of yesterday still remains. It is a pain, an obsession … I have lost my bearings, like the needle of a compass during a typhoon' (Fitzlyon 1964, 49, 353), language reminiscent of the turmoil experienced by Lee's composer, Magnus, in 'A Wicked Voice', once he has heard the voice of Zaffirino. Viardot's similarity to the castrato figure does not end there. As Felicia Miller points out, Viardot became known as 'aknowledgeable proponent of "antique Italian song" and performed arias by Handel and other eighteenth-century composers' (1997, 81). Like Guadagni, whose gestures would have been 'excellent studies for a statuary', Viardot has a 'statuesque grace', and 'an innate dignity and nobility' that mirror the 'noble simplicity and ... calm grandeur' that J. J. Winckelmann was to assert as the defining quality of the Greek sculptural ideal (Lee 1894, 54; Fitzlyon 1964, 354, 71; Potts, *Flesh and the Ideal*

1994, 1). For Winckelmann, this ideal seems intrinsically related to the androgynous body for, as Simon Richter notes in his book, *Laocoön's Body and the Aesthetics of Pain*, although Winckelmann's conception of 'noble simplicity' and quiet grandeur is initially located in the statue of the Laocoön (fig. 2.1), when he comes to write his history of antique art, this statue 'no longer holds a central place in his aesthetic thinking. It has been supplanted, however discreetly, by the figure of the eunuch' (1992, 48). As Richter goes on to explain, in Winckelmann's *Geschichte der Kunst des Alterthums* (*History of the Art of Antiquity*) (1764), 'every time he looks for the visual instance that best embodies the classical ideal, his eye strays past the Laocoön and the Apollo Belvedere, and fixes on the eighteenth-century Italian castrato' (1992, 50). The sculptural ideal, like the ideal voice, is apparently one that can cross physical and sexual boundaries. Interestingly, these ostensibly male, yet androgynous, bodies immortalized in Greek sculpture are themselves described in musical metaphor.

Fig. 2.1 *Laocoön and His Sons*, c. 1st century B.C.E.

Musical Statues

For example, in *A Problem of Greek Ethics* (1883), John Addington Symonds writes that the Greeks were 'enthusiastic for that corporeal beauty ... which marks male adolescence no less triumphantly than does the male soprano voice upon the point of breaking' and that:

> When distinction of feature and symmetry of form were added to this charm of youthfulness, the Greeks admitted, as true artists are obliged to do, that the male body displays harmonies of proportion and melodies of outline more comprehensive, more indicative of strength expressed in terms of grace, than that of women (1908, 68).

This link between music and the perfection of form had been forged some time earlier by Walter Pater in *Studies in the History of The Renaissance* (1873), in which he observed:

> Art, [is] ... always striving to be independent of the mere intelligence, to become a matter of pure perception, to get rid of its responsibilities to its subject or material ... .
> It is the art of music which most completely realises this artistic ideal, this perfect identification of matter and form ... . Therefore, although each art has its incommunicable element, its untranslatable order of impressions, its unique mode of reaching the 'imaginative reason,' yet the arts may be represented as continually struggling after the law or principle of music, to a condition which music alone completely realises; and one of the chief functions of aesthetic criticism, dealing with the products of art, new or old, is to estimate the degree in which each of those products approaches, in this sense, to musical law (1986, 88–89).

As one of Pater's disciples, it is unsurprising to find that Lee, in her own critical writing, discusses the musical properties of sculpture. In *Belcaro*, in an essay entitled 'Orpheus and Eurydice: the Lesson of a Bas-Relief' she observes that when we look at sculpture we appreciate a work of art at once 'plastic and musical'; she writes that what we enjoy, 'is the work of art itself, the combination of lines, lights and shades and colours in the one case, the combination of modulations and harmonies in the other' (1881, 62). This harmonic fusion of the musical and the sculptural is epitomized in Théophile Gautier's famous poem 'Contralto' (1849).[7] Gautier considers the statue of the *Sleeping Hermaphrodite* in the Louvre (fig. 2.2); 'is it youth or is it maiden sweet?' he asks, and acknowledges the 'fair fascination' of its 'Uncertain sex' that leads him to create a poetic fantasy which equates the statue with the contralto voice:

> O dream of poet passing every bound!
>   My thought hath built a fancy of thy form,
> Till it is molten into silver sound,
>   And boy and girl are one in cadence warm.
>
> O tone divine, O richest tone of earth,
>   The beautiful, bright statue's counterpart!
> Contralto, thou fantastical of birth,
>   The voice's own Hermaphrodite thou art!
> (1903, 71, ll. 29–36).

Fig. 2.2   *Sleeping Hermaphrodite*, Roman copy of Greek original, *c*. 150 B.C.E.

Although thought to have been written for Guilia Grisi, the famous Italian soprano – a contemporary and rival of Pauline Viardot – Miller argues that there is evidence to suggest that the poem refers to Viardot herself. In his review of the latter's debut performance Gautier writes:

> Pauline Viardot's voice was first striking for its expressive intensity … . One was immediately moved, conquered, possessed. And then one noticed the exceptionally extensive resources of her vocal organ. Music critics measure pedantically the extremes … . Three and a half octaves, one says, carried away by enthusiasm … . Let us accept … Berlioz ['s assessment], according to [which] Pauline's voice had as its limits low F and high C, say, two octaves and a fifth … her voice was, as Berlioz says, 'equal in all registers, true, vibrant and agile' (quoted in Miller 1997, 82).

Miller notes that this description of Viardot's voice resonates with that given of Farinelli's voice in Patrick Barbier's book, *Farinelli, Castrat des Lumières*, where it is depicted as 'perfect, efficient, and sonorous in quality and rich in its range from the deepest notes to the highest', thus reinforcing the sexual ambiguity of Viardot's voice (quoted in Miller 1997, 82). It is perhaps fitting, then, that Miller should imply that the link forged between the hermaphrodite statue in the Louvre and the contralto voice refers to Viardot. Moreover, Miller observes that, in the poem, Gautier 'adduces a list of contralto roles, almost all ... from Rossini operas ... roles [that] match those that Gautier imagined for Viardot in his review of her debut' (1997, 82).

That Viardot's contralto voice prompted Gautier to reconsider a sculptural artifact, leads one back to Lee and, more specifically to her alter-ego Baldwin in the essay 'Orpheus in Rome': here, once again, it is the voice that inspires a re-examination of sculpture. After hearing the performance of Gluck's *Orfeo*, Baldwin revisits the Vatican museum and rediscovers his enthusiasm for Greek sculpture, declaring to Donna Maria that 'it is the music which has made me able once more to love the statues – it's the poetry of those divine melodies, of that exquisite expression and gesture, which has made me feel once more the poetry of that silent, motionless people of marble' (Lee 1894, 92). Having spent an unhappy period as a decadent 'modern' who longs for 'some far-fetched allegoric creature, a feeble lived hybrid' from the works of Burne-Jones – 'a creature with a wistful face and dubious anatomy' – Baldwin ostensibly returns to a former, 'classical self' who appreciates the music of the eighteenth century and Greek sculpture, both of which paradoxically find their ideal in the sexual uncertainty that characterizes Burne-Jones's androgynous figures (Lee 1894, 70).

Given the ambiguities traced in the polemic structures of Lee's aesthetics and the identification of the artistic self through the figure of the castrato discussed in the previous chapter, this association between the hermaphroditic voice and the antique statue compels exploration. As we have seen, the androgynous figure of the castrato and the musical perfection of the voice remain consistent motifs in Lee's aesthetic works. Yet the androgynous castrato voice is also implicit in her consideration of sculpture and in her literary fantasies. Like this voice, the sculptural artifact functions as a form of 'transitional object' enabling her to explore an ambiguity of form that she denies in her aesthetics.

Statues and Things: Fantasies of Regression

In an essay on Rodin and Rilke, the art historian Alex Potts notes that the statue can appear to have both a material and a 'dematerialized presence' – recalling the liminal existence of Lee's castrati – and explores the implications of this fantasy, tracing the contradictory responses of plenitude and anxiety that manifest themselves when a kind of animistic power is attributed to the sculptural object ('Dolls and Things' 1994, 355). Although Potts's essay refers primarily to Rodin's art, he tells us that these responses can also be related to the experience of abstract work and traditional sculpture. He argues that, in each case, 'the sculptural object becomes the staging ground for projections of some ideal simplified sense of self', a model which recalls the myth of Pygmalion, which I will return to later ('Dolls and Things' 1994, 335). Potts differentiates between neo-classical aesthetics that sees the statue as 'an ideal autonomous ego' analogous to the fantasy image of the Lacanian mirror phase in the subject's early development, and Rilke's aesthetical response to Rodin's work that is not produced by anthropomorphization, but by sculpture's 'thing-like quality' ('Dolls and Things' 1994, 361–62). According to Rilke, in Rodin's works one no longer sees 'men and women … . And the longer one looks, the more does even this content become simplified, and one sees: "Things"' (1986, 51). Rilke's conception of the sculpture as 'thing' is rendered by acknowledging the sculptor's construction of the sculpture 'not by an image of the whole body, but by a closely felt involvement with modelling' (Potts, 'Dolls and Things' 1994, 362). Rilke writes:

> This work [of modelling] … was the same in everything one made, and had to be carried out so humbly, so obediently, so devotedly, so impartially on face and hand and body that no specified parts remained and the artist worked at the form without knowing what exactly would result, like a worm working its way from point to point in the dark (1986, 52).

For Potts, this focus on sculptural modelling serves a double function: once the spectator's gaze centres on the undulations of the statue's surface, the sculpture may no longer be seen as a human image, but it still retains 'an intangible charge or presence' that is a symptom of its thing-like quality ('Dolls and Things' 1994,

362). The 'dematerialized presence' of the sculptural object is, in Rilke's mind, inextricably linked to early childhood fantasies:

> If possible, out of practice and grown-up as your feelings are, bring them back to any one of your childhood's possessions with which you were familiar … . That something, worthless as it was, prepared the way for your first contact with the world, introduced you to life and to people: and, more than that, its existence, its outward appearance, whatever it was, its final destruction or mysterious withdrawal from the scene caused you to know the whole of human experience, even to death itself (quoted in Potts, 'Dolls and Things' 1994, 367–368).

He argues that in Rilke's essay, Rodin's 'thing' becomes a form of 'transitional object', an object that 'exists when there is as yet no clear distinction between projections of fantasy and what exists beyond the self' and 'when inanimate things and bodily presences blur together as "objects" in the still amorphous landscapes of the infantile psyche' ('Dolls and Things' 1994, 372). According to Potts, the psychodynamic function of the object was to haunt Rilke's writings in which it appeared to summon 'fantasies of unmediated appropriation and nightmares of stark alienation' ('Dolls and Things' 1994, 372). In his essay on dolls, inspired by the wax dolls of Lotte Pritzel, Rilke traces the negative responses triggered in the child who discovers that, far from being attuned to its subjective needs, the doll is in fact an inanimate object, unresponsive and inert. The child finds that the doll is 'soulless' and it is 'unmasked as the horrible foreign body on which we had wasted our purest ardour' (quoted in Potts, 'Dolls and Things' 1994, 372).[8] Interestingly, Potts suggests that the doll and the statue are intimately related:

> Accumulated as inert objects in the alien spaces of a museum, did not Rodin's sculpture threaten to become like the array of dolls that had 'confronted [Rilke] and almost overwhelmed [him] by their waxen nature' and inspired his essay on the hated doll-thing? Would they be able to distinguish themselves from the 'monotonous whiteness of all those great dolls' so disliked by Baudelaire? ('Dolls and Things' 1994, 373).[9]

The sculpture, then, like the doll, engages the spectator simultaneously in a regressive fantasy of interaction and a destructive process of alienation. Lee herself comments on this process. In *Belcaro* she considers the effect of the Vatican museum's statuary through the eyes of a child:

> What … must not this Vatican be for a child: a quite small, ignorant barbarian such as has never before set its feet in a gallery, to whom art and antiquity have been mere names, to whom all this world of tintless stone can give but a confused, huge, overpowering impression of dreariness and vacuity. An impression composed of negative things: of silence and absence of colour, of lifelessness, of not knowing what it all is or all means; a sense of void and of unattractive mystery which chills, numbs the little soul into a sort of emotionless, inactive discomfort (1881, 19).

In Chapter One, I discussed how this initial sense of alienation becomes a fantasy of interaction where the statues 'speak' to the child and stimulate its imagination and its creativity. As Gunn has suggested, the child Lee speaks of is arguably her younger self and it seems significant that this dual experience of alienation and interaction remains in her adult response to sculpture. Later in *Belcaro*, Lee discusses the Niobe group and is concerned that her readers should learn the lesson that 'the only intrinsic perfection of art is the perfection of form' (1881, 48). Yet she acknowledges that the Niobe's 'perfection of line and curve' leads to an emotional paralysis – a response that seems analogous to Rilke's own when confronted by the figure of the doll – writing that:

> by the side of this overwhelming positive sense of beauty there creeps into our consciousness an irritating little sense of negation. For the more intense becomes our perception of the form, the vaguer becomes our recollection of the subject; … our senses cease to shrink with horror, our sympathies cease to vibrate with pity, as we look upon this visible embodiment of the terrible tragedy. We are no longer feeling emotion; we are merely perceiving beauty (1881, 34).

Sculptural beauty, for Lee, apparently induces a form of 'anaesthesia', a paralysis which recalls that induced by the castrato cry. In his own discussion of the Niobe sculpture (fig. 2.3), Potts explains Winckelmann's differentiation between the style of the Niobe and that of the Laocoön. In his book, *Flesh and the Ideal: Winckelmann and the Origins of Art History*, using language that reflects Lee's own response to the Niobe group, Potts writes that 'The "frozen" Niobe achieves its austere intensity through an almost death-like obliteration of signs of feeling, which elevates its expression to the realm of an inhuman beauty' typifying what Winckelmann calls the 'high style' in antique sculpture (1994, 82). In contrast, the Laocoön is 'shown in the midst of an elaborately modulated struggle, its variegated and beautiful forms, exemplary of the subtle and refined naturalism of the beautiful style' (Potts, *Flesh and the Ideal* 1994, 83). For Winckelmann the distinction between these two styles is analogous to that which applies to the differences between Demosthenes' and Cicero's oratory. The former's rhetoric is likened to a thunderbolt, it 'suspends time' and overwhelms its audience; the latter's develops slowly and 'gradually but powerfully ... [takes] it over' (Potts, *Flesh and the Ideal* 1994, 103). Potts suggests that Winckelmann's representation of the two styles of ancient sculpture as two differing rhetorical modes equates them with figures of speech:

> One is the 'high' visual figuration of a sublime figure of speech, the other the 'beautiful' visual figuration of a graceful and a beautiful one. The power of one mode is shown as suddenly overwhelming its audience, suspending or obliterating any capacity to resist, and the other as steadily overcoming it and inexorably carrying it off. To transpose the contrast into the language of semiotics, one figure [Niobe] is the living sign obliterated and stilled by the unmediated presence of an immaterial idea; the other [Laocoön] is the still living sign, refracting or mediating the presence of an immaterial idea in a beautifully and powerfully modulated play of form (*Flesh and the Ideal* 1994, 108).

I will return to the subject of the Laocoön shortly, but before I do so, I wish to reconsider Lee's discussion of the Niobe in the light of Winckelmann's association of sculpture and rhetoric.

Lee's depiction of the Niobe group focuses on the importance of form and she uses the language of music, or more particularly the choral voice, to describe that perfection:

> For, as the various voices of the fugue, some subtly insinuating themselves half whispered, while the others are thundering their loudest or already dying away into silence, meet and weave together various fragments of the same melody, so also do the figures of the group, some standing, some reclining, some kneeling, some rising, some draped, some nude, meet our sight in various ways so as to constitute in their variety, one great pattern; ... the triumphant centre of the rhythm and harmony of lines, is formed by the majestic, magnificent mother between her two eldest, most beautiful daughters (1881, 32–33).

Fig. 2.3 *Niobe*, Roman copy of Greek original, *c.* 2nd century B.C.E.

This perfection, 'as of the single small voice, swelling and diminishing in crisp exquisiteness every little turn and shake', centres on the figure of Niobe whose silent cry of maternal anguish is reminiscent of the operatic cry; a fixed moment of sublimity that wrests the spectator's attention from the 'text' of the Niobe sculpture, just as the operatic cry wrests one's attention from the libretto's written word (Lee 1881, 34). In contrast, as we have seen, the Laocoön apparently produces a gradual effect on the senses which is always controlled by the form. Yet the 'cry' which induces paralysis is also suggested by the figure of the Laocoön. Discussing the role played by the cry in Herder's treatise, 'Abhandlung über den Ursprung der Sprache' ('Essay on the Origin of Language') (1772), Liliane Weissberg notes that, for Herder, the cry is 'pain's music' (1989, 550). The Laocoön, like the Niobe, represents pain: the Trojan priest is depicted in the midst of his struggle against the venomous bites of the snakes sent by the gods to kill him.[10] Interestingly, however, Winckelmann's influential description of the statue's *stille Grösse* or 'calm grandeur' implies a stillness which recalls a death-like paralysis:

> The word *stille* ... [suggests] an absence of signs of life. 'Calm grandeur' projects an image of resonant heroism, the great soul effortlessly in possession of his strength. 'Still grandeur' could be something else – the stillness of an imperturbable calm that might be inanimate or inhuman, perhaps the stillness of death (Potts, *Flesh and the Ideal* 1994, 1).

The 'cry', whether musical or sculptural, induces a paralysis that simultaneously heightens and inhibits the viewer's conception of the sculptural form. Lee's concern with symbolic form is apparently undermined by the semiotic rhythms of the sculpture.[11] Yet this semiotic strand is not restricted to musical metaphor, it pervades Lee's engagement with the Niobe statue itself. She asks the reader to consider 'the powerfully rhythmed attitudes, the beautiful combinations of lines and light and shade produced by the gesture, which now raises, now drops the drapery, opposing to the large folds, heavy and severe, the minute, most supple, and most subtle plaits; and to the strong broken shadows of the drapery, the shining smoothness of the nude' (1881, 33).

This concern with the mouldings and undulations of sculpture appears elsewhere in an essay in *Renaissance Fancies and Studies* (1895). Here, Lee observes that the Greek statue, even if eventually produced in marble, was conceived by sculptors who modelled in clay, and writes:

> The Greek, therefore, was a moulder of clay, a caster of bronze ... . Now clay (and we must remember that bronze is originally clay) means the modelled plane and succession of planes smoothed and rounded by the finger, the imitation of all nature's gently graduated swellings and depressions, the absolute form as it exists to the touch (1895, 144).

In this essay, as in *Belcaro*, Lee's responses to the sculptural form are reminiscent of those of Winckelmann, whose image of the ideal, according to Potts, 'becomes identified with an abstract flow of contour and surface' (*Flesh and the Ideal* 1994, 170). Winckelmann notes that:

The more unity there is in the connection between forms, and in the flowing of the one into the other, the greater is the beauty of the whole ... . A beautiful youthful figure is fashioned from forms like the uniform expanse of the sea, which from a distance appears flat and still, like a mirror, though it is also constantly in motion and rolls in waves (quoted in Potts, *Flesh and the Ideal* 1994, 170).

In Winckelmann's experience, as in Lee's, 'the differentiated and variegated forms of the body have melted away in a continuously flowing curve' (Potts, *Flesh and the Ideal*, 1994, 170). As Potts explains, 'The demand for absolute clarity and definition associated with the highest beauty is realized in a radically contradictory image, an abstract contour that is at one level the figure of geometric precision, but at another a floating, undulating line, dissolving any sense of shape in a free play of form' (*Flesh and the Ideal* 1994, 170). He goes on to point out that, in psychoanalytic terms, this experience can be termed a regression fantasy, arguing that it is an 'archaic, polymorphous, and objectless experience that seems to exist prior to any separation between the self and the world around it, in which there is no sense of things as bounded separate entities' (*Flesh and the Ideal* 1994, 170). Although Potts suggests that, in Winckelmann, this state may be described as auto-erotic, it also recalls Rilke's response to Rodin's sculpture in which the statue becomes a transitional object that exists 'when there is as yet no clear distinction between projections of fantasy and what exists beyond the self' (Potts, 'Dolls and Things' 1994, 368).

In Lee, in particular, the choice of the Niobe, a maternal figure, heightens the fantasy of 'oneness' with the mother that is a feature of the child's perception in the transitional object phase. It seems significant that, as in the child's engagement with the maternal voice, which functions simultaneously as a material and a 'dematerialized presence', this experience can be one of plenitude or one of entrapment that borders precariously on the threshold of alienation (Potts, 'Dolls and Things' 1994, 355). The Niobe sculpture dramatizes this process. There is a fantasy of 'oneness' in its conception; the mother and her children are moulded together. At the same time, however, it represents a moment of suspended separation; the children from their mother through death, and Niobe's consciousness from her body through paralysis. Yet it is not the tangible drama that concerns me here; I suggest that there is an implicit drama that is played out in the semiotic rhythms of the Niobe sculpture.

Madonnas Antique and Modern: Identifications and Desires

Writing of Kristeva's essay, 'Motherhood According to Giovanni Bellini' in which she argues that Bellini's Madonna paintings play out the child's separation from the mother, Mary Bittner Wiseman claims that the maternal body 'comes to be seen through its painted representations and, finally, through the lines and colors that paintings are, no matter their subject' (1993, 97). She argues that, insofar as the paintings exemplify what Kristeva calls 'the intersection of sign and rhythm, of representation and light, of the symbolic and the semiotic', they are a record made by the unconscious of 'those clashes that occur between the biological and social program of the species' (1980, 242). Informed by Kristeva's analysis, Wiseman suggests that, in Bellini's paintings, the separation of the child from the mother is depicted in terms of the mother's psychic absence: 'Bellini portrays the absence of the mother by the split in the maternal body, between hands that hold the child as close as ever womb held its guest and dreaming, inward-looking face. Her body is there, she is not' (1993, 98). This resonates interestingly with Lee's Niobe whose hands clutch her children in a desperate gesture, whilst her body is 'frozen' and her mind paralyzed and therefore 'absent'.

Wiseman's essay is prompted by a reconsideration of Freud's 'Dora' (1905), whose eponymous subject remains '*two hours* in front of the Sistine Madonna, rapt in silent admiration' (Freud 1977, 135–136). She observes that Freud's interpretation of Dora's fascination with the Madonna is explained as a form of identification, because 'the notion of the "Madonna" is a favourite counter-idea in the mind of girls who feel themselves oppressed by imputations of sexual guilt' (Freud 1977, 145, n. 1). Yet, as Wiseman argues, there are other ways in which Dora might have responded to the Sistine Madonna: 'She could have wanted to have the Madonna rather than to be her, loving a woman as Freud later discovered she did. She could have wanted to be the child in the Madonna's arms, loving her mother and wanting to be loved by her as she once was' (1993, 93). She attributes Freud's reluctance to acknowledge either of these possibilities to the problem that, through the process of psychoanalytic transference, in which 'some earlier person is replaced by the person of the physician', Dora's transference, in this instance, would make a woman of him (1993, 96). In a later work, however, 'The Psychogenesis of a case of Homosexuality in a Woman' (1920), Freud was to acknowledge the role of the mother as 'love-object' in female homosexuality. Discussing the case of a young girl who displays lesbian tendencies after the birth of a younger child in the family, Freud writes:

> The analysis revealed beyond all shadow of doubt that the lady-love was a substitute for – her mother. It is true that the lady herself was not a mother, but then she was not the girl's first love. The first objects of her affection after the birth of her youngest brother were really mothers, women between thirty and thirty-five whom she had met with their children during summer holidays or in the family circle of acquaintances in town (1979, 382).

Yet why should Dora's homosexuality or her regressive fantasy be expressed via her response to a work of art? Wiseman's argument stems from Kristeva's theory of interpretation which suggests that the idea of transference is implicit in the multiplicity of ways in which a painter or spectator responds to a painting. Here, as Wiseman explains, it is asserted that 'in the encounter with art, any earlier object or drive or desire aroused and made conscious during the encounter may be replaced by any element of the artwork. Moreover, by a natural extension of the theory, the artist or spectator may replace herself by some other' (1993, 96).

What, then, of Lee's engagement with the Niobe? Lee's choice of sculpture is perhaps significant in itself. Rejecting the sculptural perfection of the male body so favoured by the aesthetics of Winckelmann and, later, of Symonds, Lee chooses instead the maternal body of the Niobe on which to focus her gaze. Given Lee's publicly unacknowledged homosexuality it is possible that, for her, as for Dora, this may function as a form of tacit erotic engagement with the body of the mother. At the same time, there is arguably another dimension to Lee's response to the Niobe:

a powerful pull towards regression prompted by what Wiseman calls the 'latent' content of the work of art. Here the content is 'the memory of a time and a place: the time before the mother became an object and the place (in the womb or at the breast) where what would eventually construct an identity (build up an ego) was neither something nor nothing' (Wiseman 1993, 99). In this context, Lee's engagement with the sculptural figure re-enacts on a psychic level, a moment of infantile plenitude.

Yet, as we have seen, it is not only through this particular regressive fantasy that the self is negotiated. The sculpture also functions as an 'ideal autonomous ego' recalling the Lacanian mirror stage which augurs entry into language and the symbolic (Potts, 'Dolls and Things' 1994, 361–362). In her discussion of the Enlightenment, Catherine Glyn Davies observes that 'Eighteenth-century theorists were increasingly aware of the self as a three-dimensional physical being, occupying external space' and that, consequently, the animated statue became 'one of their most popular and striking analogues of the self' (1990, 143). Inevitably, the model of the animated statue leads to the Ovidian myth of Pygmalion. Davies notes the use of this myth by eighteenth-century writers such as A. F. Boureau Deslandes and Jean Jacques Rousseau. For Deslandes, the statue's animation is only the beginning. In his fable, *Pigmalion ou la statue animée* (*Pygmalion or the Animated Statue*) published anonymously in 1741, he hopes for the entity's progression in understanding and sophistication; Pygmalion 'expects to see his statue changing and becoming more perfect, progressing towards a condition where she will be able to think' (Davies 1990, 143). According to Deslandes, prior to attaining self-consciousness, she is like a child: 'c'est ainsi qu'un enfant au berceau ressemble à quelque chose de brut, et de plus brut encore, de plus informe que du marbre' (quoted in Davies 1990, 144).[12] However, in Rousseau's drama, *Pygmalion*, written in 1763 and performed in 1770, Galatea functions as an epipsychic projection of Pygmalion himself. Describing the moment of animation, Potts explains:

> What so compels him [Pygmalion] about the idea of the sculpture coming alive is not, as is usually supposed, that he will be faced by some adored other, but that he will discover in it an emanation of his own self ... . It is this narcissistic phantasy that is quite literally enacted in his climactic orgasmic delirium as the statue actually comes to life. Galatea steps off her pedestal, the boundary between herself and the sculptor is abolished and she becomes quite literally one with him. Touching herself she says: 'This is me'; touching a block of marble, the alien matter that remains indifferent to the sculptor's self-projection, she utters: 'This is not me.' Then, as she holds her hand to Pygmalion's palpitating heart, she declares: 'Ah! myself again' (1992, 38).

If we return to Lee's *Althea*, these animated projections of the self share interesting properties with her eponymous protagonist. As noted earlier, this book of essays is linked to an earlier collection entitled *Baldwin*. In her introduction to *Althea*, Lee writes:

> A volume of dialogues similar to these, which I collected some eight years ago, was prefaced by an elaborate account of a personage called Baldwin ... about whose real existence and identity I once seemed so certain, [who] has ceased to exist ... . Baldwin has died because, like certain insects, he was organized to live only a few days. He belonged, like many of

our dead selves, of the youthful predecessors of our identity, to a genius of ephemera which require a universe without rain, wind, or frost, in fact, made on purpose for them; for the lack of which they suffer horribly, and after brief draggling and fluttering, speedily decease; die to resuscitate most often, alas (the reverse in this of butterflies), as some humbler kind of creature, less devoted to sunshine, more agreeable to mud (1894, ix–xi).

The passage seems worth quoting in full because, in using the insect metaphor to explore the process of death and rebirth in our own development, it recalls not only the first womb, that sheltered environment in which our physical selves are held, but also holding environments outside the womb from which we emerge as other selves. According to Lee, the 'new' Baldwin is Althea who is:

the pupil of Baldwin; for being all she is by the mere grace of God, she is, at first inarticulate, unreasoning, ignorant of all why and wherefore, and requires to be taught many things which others know. But, once having learned the names, so to speak, of her instincts, the premises of her unconscious arguments, she becomes as necessarily the precursor of many of Baldwin's best thoughts, the perfecter of most of them (1894, xvii–xviii).[13]

In view of the Enlightenment models of the self discussed above, the stress which Lee places on the process of Althea's development and perfectibility recalls Deslandes's Pygmalion and one might suggest that his 'Galatea' is both phonetically and metaphorically implicit in her mythical descendant, Baldwin's 'pupil' and Lee's creation, 'Althea'. That Althea also functions, like Rousseau's Galatea, as a projection of the self and a love object is made clear in Gunn's biography of Lee in which he writes, 'Althea herself is based partly on Kit [Clementina] Anstruther-Thomson; "she is naturally the pupil of Baldwin" … And in real life Kit Anstruther-Thomson did stand in this relation to Vernon Lee' (1964, 112).[14] Anstruther-Thomson was Lee's close friend and companion, and reputedly an object of her erotic desire. Yet as Lee's introduction to *Althea* acknowledges, this fictional creation is a development of Baldwin, and it is perhaps important to note Gunn's observation that 'Vernon Lee always projected into others the virtues she wished to find there' (1964, 165). It is therefore clear that, although inspired by Kit, Althea remains very much a projection of Lee herself and, although ostensibly feminine, Althea, is a hybrid creature of indeterminate and fluid sexuality.

It seems that, despite Lee's concern with sculptural form, her own ideals, as they emerge in her aesthetics, are undermined by the processes of metamorphosis inherent in the models she chooses to represent or voice her aesthetics. Orpheus and Niobe and, by implication, Galatea, are all mythological figures in Ovid's *Metamorphoses*; like Althea, they are subjects in the process of change. They demonstrate, in varying ways, a concern with the complexities of the self, through regression, identification, and projection. In doing so, they arguably function as 'transitional objects', objects that are separate from, and at the same time perceived as part of, the self. It is these complexities that I aim to explore as they emerge in three of Lee's tales, 'Marsyas in Flanders' (1927), 'St Eudaemon and His Orange Tree' (1904), and 'The Featureless Wisdom' (1904).

'Marsyas in Flanders'

Lee's tale, 'Marsyas in Flanders', was inspired, like 'A Wicked Voice', by a childhood recollection. Addressing Maurice Baring (to whom the collection of tales is dedicated), Lee writes:[15]

> The Story called Marsyas though evidently embodying the legend of the Holy Face of Lucca ... has its true origin in a book wherein you and I, dear Maurice, at a due distance of years, learned the graces and horrors of the French language: *Cours de Dictées* par MM. Noel et Chapsal ... . There, in the *Cours de Dictées* ... was 'Tadolini'. This was the ghostly adventure (by no ascertainable author) of an unidentifiable sculptor of the Middle Ages. It was the story of my marble crucifix cast up on the Northern Coast of France and behaving with miraculous unruliness every time you, that is the sculptor Tadolini, tried to fit it with a missing pair of arms, until ... well! I forget what (1927, xiii–xv).

The specifics of the 'Tadolini' tale may have eluded Lee, but the story itself, like its predecessor, concerns the adventures of a marble crucifix which is cast ashore at Dunes in Northern France in 1195, and which has held pride of place in the little church there ever since. Arriving at the church during the vigil of the Feast of the Crucifix, the narrator notices that the crucifix on display is not the Byzantine image he had expected from a sculpture reputed to be the work of St Luke. The Antiquary to whom he expresses his reservations, tells him that he is right, and that a substitution was made some time ago. He then relates the bizarre events that led to this exchange, telling how the original statue was washed ashore without its cross, and (like Tadolini's sculpture) without its arms, for these were made from separate blocks. Skilled stonemasons were employed to make a new cross and the effigy was finally erected in the little church of Dunes. However, in the days and years that followed, the effigy was often found in contorted positions that signalled its desire to free itself from the cross until one day, some ten years after its arrival, 'the burghers of Dunes discovered the Effigy hanging in its original outstretched, symmetrical attitude, but ... with the cross, broken in three pieces, lying on the steps of its chapel' (1927, 78). The Prior of the church, attributing this to some impurity in the cross itself, ordered another cross which was erected and consecrated some years later. At the same time the Prior had a warder's chamber built in the church where this precious relic, whose popularity had resulted in the increasing wealth and development of the village of Dunes, could be guarded day and night. Hopes were that, once the new cross was in place, there would be no further incidents.

These hopes turned out to be in vain: in 1293, rumours that the figure was 'writhing' on its cross continued to spread and on Christmas Eve of the same year, the cross was once again found dashed in pieces, and the warder on duty found almost dead. A third new cross was made and consecrated, but lasted only a short time: in 1299, the church was struck by lightning, the new warder 'found dead in the middle of the nave, the cross broken in two'; and the effigy missing, later discovered 'behind the high altar, in an attitude of frightful convulsion' and supposedly 'blackened by lightning' (1927, 82). After this disturbing occurrence, the church had been shut for nearly a year and, when it reopened, a new chapel was built and the crucifix once more displayed, 'dressed in more splendid brocade and gems than usual', its head nearly hidden 'by a gorgeous crown' (1927, 82). The people of Dunes were told that a further miracle had occurred, and that the original cross, on which the figure had hung, had been cast ashore on exactly the same spot where the statue had been found some hundred years before. The Prior assured the people that, now that the effigy had been reunited with its original cross, it 'would rest in peace and its miraculous powers would be engaged only in granting the prayers of the faithful' (1927, 83). The Antiquary tells the narrator that part of this prophecy came true, the effigy remained still and the cross intact, but the reason for this lies in the archives of the Archepiscopal palace of Arras, where a stonemason's receipt is found for a life-size figure sculpted in the year 1299, the year when all supernatural events surrounding the crucifix ceased to occur. The original figure, he explains, lies buried deep beneath a vaulted passage, an 'iron stake [run] through his middle like a vampire, to prevent his rising' (1927, 91). The narrator describes the disturbing sight:

> The Effigy was erect against the dark wall, surrounded by brushwood. It was more than life-size, nude, the arms broken off at the shoulders, the head, with stubbly beard and clotted hair, drawn up with an effort, the face contracted with agony; the muscles dragged as of one hanging crucified, the feet bound together with a rope. The figure was familiar to me in various galleries. I came forward to examine the ear: it was leaf-shaped ... 'this supposed statue of Christ is an antique satyr, a Marsyas awaiting his punishment' (1927, 92).

Lee's choice of Marsyas as the satyr responsible for these supernatural events seems particularly interesting if we consider the story of Marsyas in Greek myth. According to Robert Graves, the satyr, a follower of the goddess Cybele and cursed by Athena, is challenged by the god Apollo to a contest in which he pits his talent on the lyre against Marsyas's skill with the flute. The winner of the competition may impose any punishment he chooses on the loser. They are evenly matched until Apollo challenges Marsyas to play his flute in any way that the god can play his lyre. Apollo asks that Marsyas should turn his flute upside down, and play and sing at the same time. Unable to do this, Marsyas loses the contest and the god inflicts his punishment: Marsyas is flayed alive and his skin is nailed to a tree (Graves 1992, 77).

If one considers that, in Chapter One, the flute figures as a transmutation of the gorgonian cry, which is then further aestheticized by the 'flute-like' voice of the castrato, it appears significant that Marsyas, who is equally adept at producing exquisite sounds, should be a follower of the goddess Cybele whose 'male devotees tried to achieve ecstatic unity with her by emasculating themselves [performing self-castration] and dressing like women' (Graves, 1992, p. 117). Moreover, the Dionysian ambiguity that is, as we have seen, inherent both in the flute and in the castrato, can also be traced in the figure of Marsyas. The writhings and contortions that disfigure the Effigy of Dunes occur on stormy nights on which 'howls, groans, and the music of rustic dancing' can be heard (1927, 81). Witnesses affirm that there was also often 'a noise of flutes and pipes ... so sweet that the King of France could not have sweeter at his court' and on one of these occasions a 'Great Wild Man' is seen to break the Cross in two, before playing the pipes on the high altar (1927, 86, 89).

The Dionysian nature of these events is evident, but Marsyas and Dionysus are more explicitly linked by the flute in Walter Pater's, *Greek Studies* (1895):

There is one element in the conception of Dionysus, which his connexion with the satyrs, Marsyas being one of them, and with Pan, from whom the flute passed to all the shepherds of Theocritus, alike illustrates, his interest, namely, in one of the great species of music. One form of that wilder vegetation, of which the Satyr race is the soul made visible, is the reed, which the creature plucks and trims into musical pipes (1928, 9).

Marsyas, then, like the castrato, is the embodiment, the 'soul made visible' of the reed, and, by implication, of the flute. This association between Marsyas and Dionysus can also be traced in Pater's, 'Denys L'Auxerrois' (1887), a story which, like Lee's, explores the effect of a pagan influence on a Christian community. The narrator in Pater's tale first encounters the figure of Denys in a fragment of stained glass and in a series of tapestries both of which carry the same theme displaying musical instruments, 'pipes, cymbals' and 'long reed-like trumpets' (1910, 53). Among the stories traced in the tapestries is one that shows the building of an organ. Those listeners shaped in the threads of the tapestries, 'appear as if transported, some of them shouting rapturously to the organ music' and a 'sort of mad vehemence prevails ... throughout the delicate bewilderments of the whole series': these show 'giddy dances, wild animals leaping' and 'one oft-repeated figure ... that of the organ-builder himself' (1910, 53–54).

Intrigued by this figure, Pater's narrator traces the history of Denys L'Auxerrois whom the archives show played his part in creating the works that adorned the cathedral of St Etienne. A carnivalesque figure, whose presence inspires desire in the women and girls of Auxerre and an unnatural, almost Bacchanalian gaiety in any gathering he attends, Denys finds that, eventually, his unconventionality is deemed dangerous. His fondness for odd children and wild animals is seen as a sign of his witchcraft and the people of Auxerre turn against him. Following a period of dark indulgence, Denys seeks refuge, and joins the monks of Saint Germain where his own experiences seem to influence their work; the transitions of his life etched in the arts they produce:

> In three successive phases or fashions might be traced, especially in the carved work, the humours he had determined. There was first wild gaiety, exuberant in a wreathing of life-like imageries, from which nothing really present in nature was excluded. That, as the soul of Denys darkened, had passed into obscure regions of the satiric, the grotesque and coarse. But from this time there was manifest ... a well-assured seriousness ... . It was as if the gay old pagan world had been blessed in some way (1910, 70–71).

Furthermore, it is Denys who creates the church organ. 'Like the Wine-god of old', Denys is 'a lover and patron especially of the music of the pipe, in all its varieties' that can be traced in its 'three fashions or "modes"': – first, the simple and pastoral, ... then, the wild, savage din, that had cost so much to quiet people, and driven excitable people mad' and finally a new combination that Denys would compose 'to sweeter purposes': phases that mirror once again the three stages of his nature (1910, 71–72). The organ was to be 'the triumph of all the various modes of the power of the pipe, tamed, ruled, united' and only 'on the painted shutters of the organ-case Apollo with his lyre in his hand, as lord of the strings, seemed to look askance on the music of the reed, in all the jealousy with which he put Marsyas to death so cruelly' (1910, 72). Here, the Dionysian quality of the 'power of the pipe' is 'tamed' and 'ruled', recalling the aestheticization of the Medusan voice and its chthonian disorder in the 'man-made' body of the castrato.[16] Yet, the organ, like the castrato, retains a certain ambiguity – it remains fundamentally linked to 'the music of the reed' and to unruliness and disorder via its association with Apollo's formidable opponent, the satyr, Marsyas. Denys's demise proves as violent as that of Marsyas. Taking the leading part in a pageant during a local festival in which 'the person of Winter' is 'hunted blindfold through the streets', Denys becomes the victim of the townspeople who hunt him down in earnest, and his body, when they catch him, is 'tossed hither and thither, torn at last limb from limb' (1910, 75–76).

In her article, 'From Dionysus to "Dionea":Vernon Lee's Portraits', Catherine Maxwell retraces Lee's own visit to Auxerre which is recaptured in her memorial essay for Walter Pater entitled 'Dionysus in the Euganean Hills' (1921). Here Denys's Dionysian character is confirmed as Lee 'recognizes in the carved niches of the cathedral the images that inspired Pater's "Denys L'Auxerrois"' (1997, 259). This prompts 'a long reverie on the Gods in Exile, of Dionysus, of the symbolism of the vine, of Friedrich Nietzsche's contrasting of the Apolline and the Dionysiac characters of art, and it concludes with Lee's own experience of Dionysus' (Maxwell, 1997, 259).[17] Gods in exile, Lee argues, partake 'of the nature of ghosts even more than all gods do': they are '*revenants* ... tragic beings' who are 'likely as not, malevolent towards living men' (1921, 348). This exile, 'implying an in-and-out existence of alternate mysterious appearance and disappearance', is therefore, according to Lee, 'a kind of haunting' (1921, 348). Dionysus, she suggests, is perhaps the most curious of all the gods in exile for, she asks, 'Was he not the mystery, in human or divine shape, of the unaccountable dreams and transformations, the sublimations and degradations due to the supreme mysteriousness, one might say, the supreme elemental mystery, of fermentation and its effects?' (1921, 348–349). Moreover, he is 'the symbol of moods which seek deliverance from reality in horror as well as excessive rapture, what Nietzsche taught us to distinguish as the Dionysiac, as opposed to the Apolline side of art' (Lee 1921, 348).

The liminality that characterizes the figure of Dionysus extends to his sexuality. As Lee observes, although a seducer, Dionysus is 'little more than a woman himself': his effeminacy is 'like that of those beautiful languid Arabs ... who strike one as women in disguise, the beard against their jasmin [*sic*] cheeks seeming some kind of ritual half-mask' (1921, 349–350). Inhabiting an inbetween location in time, in nature, and in sexuality, Lee's Dionysus is reminiscent of the ghostly castrati that haunt her tales. Neither man, nor woman, Dionysus is a god of transformation, embodying the elemental powers of nature in an occult space that simultaneously allows, yet sublimates 'the hopes and fancies, the ecstasies and barbarities which humdrum existence has said No to' (Lee 1921, 351). According to the cultural critic, Camille Paglia, his attributes are 'variability', 'playfulness, wantonness, and frenzy': he is 'Lusios, "The Liberator" – the god who by very simple means, or by other means not so simple, enables you for a short time to *stop being yourself*, and thereby set you free' and the 'aim of his cult was *ecstasis* – which could mean anything from "taking you out of yourself" to a profound alteration of personality' (1992, 97).

The presence of Dionysus, then, provides a carnivalesque space that encourages the expression of those repressed desires, those alternative subjectivities that remain hidden in everyday life. But the Dionysian revel, as we have seen, can be fraught with violence. In Pater's tale, the Dionysian figure is torn limb from limb, a fate which is also that of Orpheus who, in one version of the Orphic myth, suffers this brutal death at the hands of the Maenads who commit the atrocity at Dionysus's instigation (Graves 1992, 112). In other myths the figures of Dionysus and Orpheus are similarly conflated: Orpheus does not 'come into conflict with the cult of Dionysus', he *is* Dionysus, and he plays 'the rude alder-pipe, not the civilized lyre' (Graves 1992, 114). In addition, Proclus, in his commentary on Plato's *Politics*, tells us that 'Orpheus, because he was the principal in the Dionysian rites, is said to have suffered the same fate as the god', and elsewhere, Apollodorus credits him with having invented the Mysteries of Dionysus: the 'violent principle' of which is '*sparagmos*, which in Greek means "a rending, tearing, mangling" and secondly "a convulsion, spasm"' (Graves 1992, 114; Paglia 1992, 95).

The relationship that can be traced between Marsyas, Dionysus and Orpheus in Greek myth prompts an examination of the significance of these figures in Lee's writings. Their mythical deaths seem particularly suggestive: Dionysus and Orpheus are dismembered, Marsyas is skinned alive and, in Lee's tale, is also figured as dismembered, for the effigy's arms are missing from its body. Moreover, it seems important that the violence of Orpheus's death emerges, not in the aesthetic context of Lee's essay, 'Orpheus in Rome', but in intricate associations traced via the occult tale, 'Marsyas in Flanders'. In this supernatural space, Marsyas's violent rejections of the cross, and apparent 'convulsions' figure as a form of resistance to the restrictions of a fixed identity: a resistance that resonates with the sexual fluidity of Orpheus in Lee's 'Orpheus in Rome'. Although, in Lee's tale, the effigy is still in full possession of its 'skin', the fact that it is the satyr Marsyas means that one cannot help but think of his ultimate fate at the hands of Apollo. Skinned alive, Marsyas body becomes a kind of disturbing double for the body in its embryonic state, in which the blood and veins of the foetus are visible through the translucence of the skin. It is perhaps unsurprising, then, that Marsyas should be found 'buried deep beneath a vaulted passage' a space reminiscent of the maternal womb, a literal space of infantile regression that is echoed in the elemental 'space' provided by the effigy's associations with the chthonian deity, Dionysus, in which Marsyas 'plays' and resists his Christian misrecognition.

However, these three figures from Greek myth are also linked by their indeterminate gender and sexuality: in archaic vases Dionysus is shown 'in a woman's tunic, saffron veil, and hairnet ... . He is called Pseudanor, the Fake Man'; Orpheus, although best known for his tragic love for Eurydice, is configured, by Ovid, as homosexual; and Marsyas, a follower of Cybele, is arguably castrated (Paglia 1992, 89). Yet it is not only the mythical Marsyas that is associated with castration: Richter posits the sculpted figure of Marsyas, as one of 'Laocoön's others' and accords it an intermediate position:

> Certainly one of these counter-images is that of the satyr, Marsyas, whose statue stands in the Uffizi in Florence, a copy of the same in the Capitoline Museum in Rome [fig. 2.4]. While the eighteenth century enthusiastically discussed the Laocoön and statues of Niobe and her daughters, it generally avoided Marsyas, even though these three groups are the primary instances of antique representations of pathetic subjects (1992, 34).

Marsyas, then, is a liminal figure in aesthetics: something 'not-man' and 'not-woman' that exists in the silent space between the Laocoön and the Niobe. For Winckelmann, as noted earlier in this chapter, the figure of the Laocoön is 'supplanted ... by the figure of the eunuch': he finds his classical ideal in the body of the eighteenth-century castrato (Richter 1992, 48). Richter links the statue of Marsyas (and by implication his mythical counterpart) to the castrato by the medium of pain. 'Beauty', Richter observes, 'wields a knife' that mutilates and castrates: a knife that may be the sculptor's scalpel, Apollo's blade, or the surgeon's 'little knife' (1992, 192). Moreover, Richter's Marsyas, like Lee's, is confused with Christ, but in Richter's text this confusion occurs via the castrato's body. Discussing Winckelmann's problematic engagement with the conflation of beauty and pain in aesthetics, he explains how, for Winckelmann, the castrato body becomes the site of negotiation for this seemingly irreconcilable difficulty:

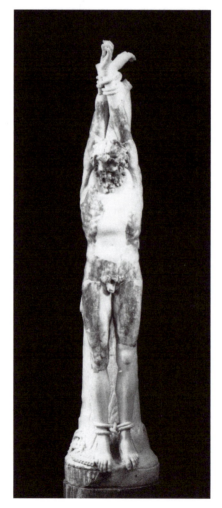

Fig. 2.4   Statue of Marsyas, Roman copy of Greek original, 4th century B.C.E.

The castrato better exemplified classical beauty, and resolved the conflict of aesthetic and semiotic demands in its *Unbezeichnung* or 'Undesignation' as Winckelmann termed his new concept. Pain seemed no longer to be a force of representation, though when Winckelmann described the castrato's body, his gaze finally came to rest on the eunuch's buttocks, the expanse of flesh over the 'heiliges Bein,' his German translation for *os sacrum* or, more commonly, *Kreuz* (cross). *Unbezeichnung* turned out to be a euphemism for castration understood as a type of crucifixion (1992, 190).

The crucified Christ, then, or more particularly those 'medieval or baroque images of a gruesomely tormented or dead Christ', becomes a similarly androgynous figure. In his essay, 'The Image of the Androgyne in the Nineteenth Century', A. J. L. Busst observes that, in Oskar Pfister's Freudian analysis of work by the German pietist, Ludwig von Zinzendorf, 'the androgyny of Christ, apparent in his depiction of the wound in Christ's side as an equivalent of the female genitalia', is attributed to Zinzendorf's childhood speculations on 'the nature of the vulva' for, according to Freudian analysis, 'the external female organs are often considered in childhood as a wound' (1967, 7). This wound, the wound of the castrated female, is also identified with Christ's wound through parturition; the wound at his side echoing that formed by the birth of Eve from Adam's rib (Busst 1967, 7). Furthermore, as Busst goes on to point out:

> Throughout the ages, the mystical tradition has considered Christ as an androgyne, from gnosticism through Jacob Boehme to Mme. Blavatsky. As for the comparison of the wound in Christ's side with the external organ of birth, the image of Christ producing his bride, the holy Mother Church, through the wound in his side in the same way as the first Adam produced Eve, is to be found in the most orthodox Christian theology and liturgy, and in St. Augustine himself (1967, 7).

Added to the images of embryonic regression and childhood fragmentation, Lee's Marsyas, is associated not only with Dionysus and Orpheus, but also with Christ via the androgynous body. The statue of Marsyas in Lee's tale appears to embody that fluid sexuality that characterizes a child's amorphous existence prior to the formation of a 'fixed' subjectivity.

In the supernatural space of Lee's tales, the figure of Marsyas, whose unruliness is normally contained by the lines of sculptural form, is employed to express alternative sexualities and identities. If one returns for a moment to Marsyas in Greek myth, it seems important that Marsyas is in conflict with Apollo. Lee's aesthetic concern with Apollonian form and line in her analysis of sculpture is undermined by the physical contortions of the effigy in her tale, and by the latent regression to infantile androgyny which find their expression in the echoes and associations that emerge via the figure of Marsyas, the satyr.

'St. Eudaemon and his Orange Tree'

'St. Eudaemon and His Orange Tree,' like 'Marsyas in Flanders', takes for its subject the discovery of a pagan artifact that disrupts the equanimity of a Christian community. Eudaemon, of whose history we learn little, other than he once had a bride who died on the eve of their wedding day, whose wedding ring he still wears, makes his home amidst the remnants of pagan society on the Caelian slopes of Rome. As his land is being prepared for planting, a statue of Venus is uncovered that the peasants believe to be an 'embalmed Pagan' or 'a sleeping female devil' (1904, 181). Eudaemon's neighbours offer to destroy the figure, fearing its evil powers, but Eudaemon mends one of its arms and sets the statue up 'on a carved tombstone of the ancients, at the end of the grass walk through the orchard, and close to the beehives' where it can be seen, 'shining white among the criss-cross reeds and the big fig-trees of Eudaemon's vineyard' (1904, 181–182). All proceeds peacefully until 'the vigil of the Birth of John the Baptist', a night on which Eudaemon provides a feast at which the peasants are allowed to 'make merry' and play games; a generous act that engenders disapproval as these revels are deemed an undesirable form of celebration as they coincide with the pagan feast of Venus (1904, 183–84).

Joining in the games, Eudaemon notices that his wedding finger is beginning to swell from the exertion and removes his ring which he places on the finger of the marble Venus. Returning later to reclaim the ring he finds that 'The marble she-devil had bent her finger and closed her hand. She had accepted the ring ... and refused to relinquish it' (1904, 185). Seemingly unperturbed, Eudaemon continues his tasks whilst the last rays of the sun fall 'upon the marble statue ... making the ring glimmer on her finger ... reddening and gilding her nakedness into a semblance of life' (1904, 186). Eventually, Eudaemon addresses the Venus directly, reminding her of the hospitality he has shown her, and asking her to return his ring, but the statue does not move and merely stands 'naked and comely, whiter and whiter as the daylight faded and the moon rose up in the east' (1904, 188). Addressing her once more, Eudaemon asks her to prove that she is not the 'she-devil' people suppose by restoring his ring. Still the statue does not move and only grows 'whiter, like silver, in the moonbeams' (1904, 188). Seeing that his pleas have not worked, Eudaemon assumes a commanding tone and orders the statue, 'as one of God's creatures', to restore his ring to him: in response, 'A little breeze stirred the air. The white hand of the statue shifted from her white bosom, the finger slowly uncrooked and extended itself' (1904, 189). Thanking her for her acquiescence, Eudaemon begs her to forget, 'the malice which foolish mankind have taught you to find in yourself' and asks her to accept 'a loving punishment', begging her 'in the name of Christ' to 'be a statue no longer, but a fair white tree with sweet-smelling blossoms and golden fruit' (1904, 189–190). At Eudaemon's sign of the cross there is 'a faint sigh, as of the breeze, and a faint but gathering rustle' and 'beneath the shining white moon', the statue of Venus changes its outline, and transforms into 'a fair orange-tree, with leaves and flowers shining silvery in the moonlight' (1904, 190).

Like the story of Marsyas, 'St Eudaemon and His Orange Tree' has its literary predecessors. In his book, *Disenchanted Images: a Literary Iconology*, Theodore Ziolkowski traces the multiple variations of the legend of 'Venus and the Ring' on which the story of Eudaemon, among many others, appears to be based. The earliest known version of this legend seems to have been told by William of Malmesbury in his twelfth-century text, *Chronicles of the Kings of England* (c. 1125), in which a young man unthinkingly removes his wedding ring while playing a game, and places it on the finger of a statue of Venus, only to find that, later, the statue imposes itself between himself and his wife in their marital bed (1977, 18).[18]

Venus's 'she-devilry' in this story is linked, as Ziolkowski observes, to Christianity's general demonization of the pagan. However, Ziolkowski points out that of all the Pagan deities 'Venus managed to sustain herself most vividly in the medieval imagination, for she represented the seductive passion to which an ascetic Christianity was austerely opposed' (1977, 27). In French versions of this tale, (*c.*1200), the young man places his ring on the finger of a statue of the Virgin Mary. When, on the wedding night, he attempts to embrace his bride, the Virgin's statue lies between them, and she reminds him that he is 'wedded' to her. The youth gives up his human bride, and dedicates his life to the service of the Virgin Mary. Here, as in Lee's tale, where Venus metamorphoses into an orange-tree, whose white blossoms are associated with the chastity of Our Lady, the demon Venus is assimilated and transformed into an image of Christian virtue – the Virgin herself.[19] But perhaps the most famous version of this story is Prosper Mérimée's 'The Venus of Ille' (1837), in which the statue of a bronze Venus is discovered in the ground. As in its antecedents, there is a bridegroom who gives Venus his ring and is subsequently unable to retrieve it. Mérimée's tale, however, departs from tradition. On the morning after the wedding night, the bridegroom is found dead: his 'clenched teeth and blackened features', signs of his struggle, 'a livid imprint' on his ribs and back suggesting that he has been 'squeezed in an iron hoop' (1989, 157). The story of the Venus's wickedness in the marital bed is told by his widow-bride, whose madness lends the tale a sense of ambiguity that foreshadows the 'psychological' supernatural that is later employed in the works of Vernon Lee and Henry James. The bridegroom's distraught mother, however, takes no chances. She insists that the bronze Venus be melted down and recast as a church bell: the pagan is once more transformed into the Christian.

In his discussion of the various transmutations of the tale, Ziolkowski notes other well-known texts that are linked thematically to the legend of Venus and the Ring. Among these he lists the stories of Pygmalion and Don Juan. Pygmalion's tale or, more particularly, Rousseau's *Pygmalion* (referred to above), appears to have initiated a new theatrical fashion – the 'attitudes', popular among European intellectuals, where famous statues would be imitated by living beings, thus blurring the border between animate and inanimate.[20] For Ziolkowski:

> This bizarre conceit of representing 'living statues' is simply another example of the late eighteenth-century obsession with statues ... . During the 1780's, for instance, it was a vogue in Italy to visit the galleries at night in order to view the statues by torchlight, which produced the illusion that the statues were alive and moving (1977, 34–35).

He attributes this eighteenth-century interest in statues to 'a remarkable resurgence of interest in the art of sculpture' due to the 'new awareness of Greek classicism' prompted by Winckelmann's *Thoughts on the Imitation of the Greek Works of Painting and Sculpture* (1755); Lessing's *Laokoon* (1766); Herder's *On Plastic Art* (1778); and Goethe's *Italian Journey* (1768–88) (1977, 33). But, as Prosper Mérimée's 'The Venus of Ille' illustrates, this interest continued into the nineteenth century, generating, as Ziolkowski observes, E.T.A. Hoffmann's 'The Sandman'

(1816); Heinrich Heine's essays 'Elemental Spirits' (1837) and later 'Gods in Exile' (1853); Sacher-Masoch's *Venus in Furs* (1870); and Henry James's 'The Last of the Valerii' (1874). To these one might also add Thomas Hardy's, 'Barbara of the House of Grebe' (1891), in which a statue, once again, comes between man and wife.[21] Ziolkowski suggests that this second flowering may be due to the discovery of the *Venus de Milo*, which arrived in Paris in 1820. He writes that 'The widely celebrated occasion touched off a veritable cult of Venus that lasted for several decades' (1977, 44).

Whatever the reasons behind these stories of animated sculptures, however, what seems particularly significant for the purpose of my discussion is that each statue seems to act as a trigger for transgressive or 'unnatural' desires. Winckelmann's own engagement with the plastic form is, as we have seen, informed by his desire for the eighteenth-century castrato and, according to Ziolkowski, Heine's is likewise propelled by lustful longings:

> Almost to the point of predictability he [Heine] compares lovely women, in their radiance and inviolability, to statues ... . Not only does Heine attribute to women statuesque characteristics; he treats statues as though they were women. The narrator of *Florentine Nights* (1836) recalls a beautiful statue lying in the grass in the park of his mother's estate. Smitten by its beauty, he creeps out one night to embrace the stone deity: '... finally I kissed the lovely goddess with a passion, a tenderness, a desperation, as I have never again kissed in all my life' (1977, 45–46).

Similarly, Hoffmann's text is driven by Nathaniel's desire for the animated doll, Olympia; James's Italian count in 'The Last of the Valerii' falls in love with a statue of Juno; and Hardy's Barbara of the House of Grebe worships the pristine statue of her former husband. It is intriguing, then, to find that desire is apparently absent in the exchange between Eudaemon and his statue. This is perhaps due to Eudaemon's position as a celibate priest. Regardless of this seemingly non-erotic exchange, we cannot but be aware that the statue chosen for the story is the statue of Venus, a goddess who is inextricably linked to the processes of desire. Moreover, the focus of our gaze on the statue and its 'whiteness' has interesting implications. In her book, *H.D. and the Victorian Fin de Siècle*, Cassandra Laity points out the significance of the statue in the Hellenist imagination, and outlines Hilda Doolittle's 'encodings of female desire through the Victorian Hellenist's principal icon for Platonic and Dorian male-male love – the nude male bodies of Greek statuary that poets such as Swinburne, Pater, and Wilde summoned frequently as objects of the male homoerotic "gaze"' (1996, 65). This gaze, Laity suggests, expresses itself in a variety of 'trace images' that represent the object of its desire: 'whiteness, crystal, marble statuary, the burning "hard gemlike flame," or the transparently veined white body', which H.D. appropriates to 'write the elusive body of mother-daughter eroticism, love between equal men and women, and homoerotic love' (1996, 65). The most explicit example of this appropriation of what Laity calls, 'statue-love', occurs in H.D.'s novel, *Paint It Today* (1921). In an allusion to Oscar Wilde's poem, 'Charmides' (1881), which takes as its source a tale by Boccaccio (evidently based on the legend of Venus and the Ring), H.D.'s narrator, Midget, imaginatively becomes a 'sister of Charmides' when she expresses her lesbian desire as she gazes at the *Venus de Milo*. In a visual parallel to Pater's Winckelmann who sensuously 'fingers' the pagan marbles, Midget, looks 'with eyes that [long] to trace like fingers, "the curve of the white belly and short space before the breasts brought the curve to a sudden shadow"': a desire that manifests itself in the 'whitest passion' (quoted in Laity 1996, 69).

In his fascinating, but ultimately reductive analysis of Lee's 'lesbian imagination', Burdett Gardner suggests that figures such as St Eudaemon's Venus, and Magnus's Zaffirino, that appear in Lee's works, are examples of what he calls the 'semivir idol' whose 'characteristic colour ... is a deadly white' (1987, 326).[22] For Gardner, this idol represents:

> the feminine counterpart of [Lee's] ... own idealized image. The exalted 'Vernon,' ... required an opposite number – a person 'fit' for 'Vernon' to love. As a derivative of Miss Paget's own mask, the idol shares all of the qualities which she, in her more confident moments, took pride in, and, like the 'Vernon image,' embodies the opposites of all of her weaknesses ... . The idol is static and dead. It is a pure, abstract essence – the essence of female superiority – and can be more satisfactorily superimposed upon an inanimate substratum than a living one (1987, 316).

That the 'semivir idol' functions as a form of epipsychic other for Lee, is not in dispute. Zaffirino, for example, certainly appears to perform the role of both self, and maternal other – that primary object of desire. Similarly, the Pygmalion-like relationship between Lee's creations, Baldwin and Althea, discussed earlier bears out Lee's tendency to create fictional selves, and to project onto objects of desire attributes that mirror those selves. However, I suggest that the role of the 'semivir idol' in 'St Eudaemon and His Orange Tree' is far more complex than Gardner's thesis implies. After the statue's direct engagement with Eudaemon, symbolized by the taking of his ring, it is seen, in an image reminiscent of the fashionable torchlit statues of the eighteenth century, in the fading light of day: its body reddened and gilded 'into a semblance of life' (1904, 186). Here, the idol seems neither 'static' nor 'dead'. Its 'life' may be artificially imposed by the warming tints of the setting sun, but, like the waxed 'flesh' that stains John Gibson's *Tinted Venus* (fig. 2.5), this 'lascivious warmth of hue ... demoralizes the chastity of the marble' and arguably imbues it with desirability (Hawthorne 1990, 475).[23] As the moon rises it becomes whiter; its golden colour bleached by the rays, as a wave of light sweeps across its shadowed body and, in the smoke of the incense, it appears to grow whiter still, 'like silver' (1904, 188). Its 'whiteness' then, is never the stark white of death – it is first dappled by the *chiaroscuro* formed by the shades of dusk and the rising moon, and becomes almost mercurial, a volatile silver shimmer glimpsed through an incense-laden mist. Its form seems to disappear, its objecthood dissolved in the varying light and dark of day and night.

Lee's Venus, then, seems to have much in common with those properties that Laity associates with the Greek statuary of Pater, Wilde and Swinburne, displaying the 'whiteness,' and 'light' that 'write a vanishing body' (1996, 70). One might also argue that another of these 'trace images' of homosexual love – the transparently veined white body – can be found in the body of Lee's Marsyas, for his flayed body is suggested beneath the cold white of his naked marble effigy. Laity writes that this

Fig. 2.5   John Gibson, *The Tinted Venus* (*c.* 1851–1856).

body of female desire' the 'differently sexed/gendered male body ... must evade the object status of conventional inscriptions' (1996, 70). In same-sex relationships this process is possibly inherent in their very nature, for the 'blurring' between lover and beloved undermines the subject/object dichotomy of conventional desire. As Laity observes, the 'traditional I-you subject/object position therefore unravels in the transition to the homoerotic' (Laity 1996, 70). Moreover, 'used by Plato in the *Symposium* to indicate homosexual love' and belonging 'specifically to the homoerotic vocabulary or code of late-Victorian Aestheticism' the Greek term *poikilos* also seems particularly appropriate when applied to Lee's Venus, for the word can be used to describe 'the play of light or texture', and, as Robert Crawford points out, 'has a range of meanings including "pied," "dappled," "flashing," "intricate," [and] "ambiguous"' (Laity 1996, 73; quoted in Dowling 1989, 1).

If one returns to Wiseman's discussion of Bellini's Madonna paintings, what seems particularly suggestive is her argument that Bellini's re-enactment of the drama of the separation of child from mother sees the mother transformed into 'dazzles of light'; an expression of Kristeva's 'homosexual-maternal' semiotic that manifests itself in 'a complete absence of meaning and seeing', in 'feeling, displacement, rhythm, sounds [and] flashes' (1980, 239–240). I would suggest that Lee, a close friend of Walter Pater, may well have been aware of the implications of the play of light on her Venus. Consciously, or unconsciously, however, Lee's Venus appears to represent simultaneously a fantasy of lesbian desire and a fantasy of infantile regression. If her Venus is an example of what Gardner calls, the 'semivir idol', a projection of both the self and desired other, the 'flashes' and 'dazzles' of light that characterize this figure function as a return to the maternal semiotic: a regression to the pre-Oedipal stage in which the mother is experienced as part of the self and is, at the same time, sanctioned as the object of desire. Furthermore, the association of Lee's Venus with the Virgin Mary, both through the legend of Venus and the Ring, and through the statue's own metamorphosis into the orange-tree, seems significant.

In her essay 'Identification with the Divided Mother: Kristeva's Ambivalence', Allison Weir shows that Kristeva considers woman's identification with the Virgin Mary a way of dealing with what she describes as 'feminine paranoia', claiming that, in this instance, 'paranoia is a condition produced by the repression of homoerotic desire for the same-sex parent. Thus, feminine paranoia is an effect of the repression of a woman's desire for her mother – and, by extension, for other women' (Weir, 1993, 83). Like Dora's Sistine Madonna, Lee's Venus arguably represents a return to the maternal womb, to the safety of a 'potential space' in which her lesbian identity can be expressed. However, this space, as we have seen, can be both comforting and dangerous, for this fusion with the maternal body brings with it the risk of engulfment. As a projection of the self and simultaneously the object of her transgressive desire for the female body, Lee's Venus suggests a process of duplication which entraps even as it allows the expression of that desire. As Kristeva writes:

> (Re)duplication is a blocked repetition. Whereas repetition extends in time, reduplication is outside of time, a reverberation in space, a game of mirrors with no perspective, no duration. For a while, a double can freeze the instability of the same, ... probing those unsuspected and unplumbable depths. The double is the unconscious depth of the same, that which threatens it, can engulf it (1987, 147).

Reduplication, then, is a process that impedes the development of an independent subjectivity. Lee's desire for other women, expressed through the figure of Venus forms what Kristeva calls 'an echo of the deathly symbiosis with the mother' for 'passion between two women is one of the most intense figures of doubling' (1987, 148). Moreover, the statue's transition from a pagan Venus to a symbol of the Virgin Mary at the end of the tale, suggests that, for Lee, even this covert expression of lesbian identity must be subsumed into an acceptable form – as an expression of maternal and/ or religious love – for, as Weir observes, in 'Stabat Mater', Kristeva argues that 'the medieval cult of the Virgin Mary served to absorb the economy of the maternal – of primary narcissism – into the social order, under the Law of the Father' (1993, 82).

In this context, Lee's Venus is undeniably repressive, but the figure of Venus also allows the expression of an androgynous identity that is famed for its potency. Venus's Greek counterpart, Aphrodite, is a powerful goddess who, in one myth, is born of masculine castration, supposedly rising 'from the foam which gathered about the genitals of Uranus, when Cronus threw them into the sea' (Graves 1992, 49). Often her male followers are emasculated: in her incarnation as Aphrodite Urania, she destroys a king who mates with her upon a mountain top, 'as a queen-bee destroys the drone: by tearing out his sexual organs' and as Cybele, 'the Phrygian Aphrodite of Mount Ida' she is worshipped as a 'queen-bee' – her priests mutilating themselves via acts of 'ecstatic self-castration' (Graves 1992, 71). In the light of these myths, it is suggestive that, in Lee's tale, the statue of Venus is positioned 'close to the beehives' (1904, 181). In certain forms Venus is also depicted as physically androgynous:

> On her native Cyprus, Aphrodite was worshipped as the Venus Barbata, the Bearded Venus ... . Elsewhere, as the Venus Calva or Bald Venus, Aphrodite was shown with a man's bald head, like the priests of Isis. Aristophanes calls her Aphroditos, a Cypriot male name. Aphrodite appeared in battle armour in Sparta ... [and] Venus Armata or Armed Venus became a Renaissance convention (Paglia 1992, 87).

The androgynous nature of Lee's Venus seemingly represents a desire for infantile regression. As Kari Weil explains, in psychoanalytic theory androgyny is often equated 'with a repressed desire to return to the imaginary wholeness and self-sufficiency associated with the pre-Oedipal phase before sexual difference' (1992, 3). In her summary of Aristophanes' myth of the androgyne recounted in Plato's *Symposium* (360 B.C.E.) in order to explain the origins of love, Catriona Macleod explains that human beings were originally divided into three sexes – 'male, female, and male-female':

> The primordial human being was a spherical creature, bountifully equipped with two sets of hands, legs, faces, sexual organs ... . In the second phase of human evolution, following the divine punishment of differentiation, each creature was doomed to seek its lost half, in a quest to achieve completion. Significantly, Aristophanes notes that this urge for plenitude could be fulfilled through either homosexual or heterosexual union (1996, 197).

The search for plenitude that is figured through Venus's androgyny can therefore be seen as expressive of lesbian desire. As shown in Chapter One, those women who display physically androgynous bodies, such as the 'hermaphroditic' tribade, are often figured as lesbian and, as Macleod points out, 'in German, the lesbian was characterized in medical discourse as a "Mannweib," a direct translation of the Greek term "androgyne"' (1996, 96–197). It is therefore unsurprising that, as Laity observes, the hermaphrodite is a seminal figure in Decadent fantasies of homosexuality, and that in *Paint It Today*, H.D. 'joins the tradition of Aesthete poets who used the statue of the Hermaphrodite to fabricate fantasies of bisexuality and androgyny' (1996, 69). Laity points out that 'Even as lines from "Fragoletta" and "Hermaphroditus" run through her mind, H.D.'s heroine Midget – like Swinburne and Gautier before her – is transfixed by the Hermaphrodite, whose "gentle breathing image modeled in strange, soft, honey-colored stone" provokes painful memories of her forsaken bisexuality' (1996, 69).

This link between Lee's Venus and the Louvre *Hermaphrodite* prompts a return to Marsyas and his androgynous counterparts. Like H.D., Lee, employing a complex code of associations, uses the 'hermaphroditic' figures of not only Venus, but also Marsyas, Orpheus, Dionysus and the castrato to express a lesbian identity and transgressive desire. That this desire should manifest itself via the male body of homosexual love is perhaps due, as Susanne Kord suggests, to the lack of a female model that can embody it satisfactorily. It seems that, 'despite Sappho, there was no tradition' for the expression of lesbian desire and that in the rare cases where 'partners clearly stated or alluded to the homoerotic nature of their relationship, their model [was] … male, not female, homosexuality' (1996, 241). Moreover, Laity observes that even though exclusively lesbian writers such as Renée Vivien (who modelled much of her poetry after Swinburne), 'identified themselves as female Aesthetes, claiming Swinburne's Sappho in "Anactoria" as their model of androgyny rather than Fragoletta or Hermaphroditus', this appropriation of the Decadent body can still be considered a form of 'male masking, because, arguably, even Swinburne's Sappho is a "mask" for male homoeroticism' (1996, 79).

The prominence of Greek love in expressions of homosexual desire may be due, in part, to a need to sanitize relationships that would otherwise be deemed unacceptable. In *A Problem of Greek Ethics*, John Addington Symonds notes that, 'Very early ... in Greek history boy-love, as a form of sensual passion, became a national institution' (1908, 4). However, for Symonds, this 'Greek Love' is understood as 'a passionate and enthusiastic attachment subsisting between man and youth, recognised by society and protected by opinion, which, though it was not free from sensuality, did not degenerate into mere licentiousness' (1908, 8).[24] This model of same-sex love is apparently also evident in Greek sculpture:

> The license of Paganism found appropriate expression in female forms, but hardly touched the male ... . Thus the testimony of Greek art might be used to confirm the asservation of Greek literature, that among free men, at least, and gentle, this passion tended even to purify feelings which in their lust for women verged on profligacy (Symonds 1908, 66).

For Symonds, the 'natural desires were symbolised in Aphrodite Praxis, Kallipugos, or Pandemos. The higher sensual enthusiasm assumed celestial form in Aphrodite Ouranios'; 'the wild and native instincts ... received half-human shape in Pan and Silenus, the Satyrs and the Fauns'; and hermaphroditic figures symbolized 'the violent and comprehensive lust of brutal appetite' (1908, 66–67).

Given the unruliness of desires expressed in these female and/or hybrid figures, it is perhaps to be expected that homosexual desire should manifest itself in the coded purity of 'Greek Love'. Yet, despite its sanitary quality, even those texts, such as Plato's *Symposium*, which advocate its morality find themselves infiltrated by the disorder inherent in the androgynous figure of the boy as object of desire. Despite the best efforts of its members to eliminate disruptive influences (such as wine and the flute-girl) that might affect the progression of a serious philosophical discussion whose aim is to distinguish between 'physical, or earthly desire' and the 'form of spiritual or heavenly love that leads to the knowledge of truth', Plato's symposium finds this clear dichotomy undermined from within, by Alcibiades, who tells the story of his love for Socrates (Weil 1992, 22–23). While his eulogy of Socrates reinforces the latter's commitment to a higher love divorced from the physical appetites, the images he uses to describe Socrates are undeniably ambiguous. In Alcibiades's opinion, Socrates is like one of the 'Sileni'. He is like 'Marsyas, the Satyr', the only difference between them being, as he tells Socrates, that 'you don't need any instrument: you produce the same effect with plain words ... when we hear you speaking, ... woman, man or child – we're all overwhelmed and spellbound' (Plato 1994, 61).[25] His voice is likened to the voice of the 'Sirens' and to be smitten by him is to have been 'bitten by a snake' (Plato 1994, 61, 64).

In the context of the symposium's discussion, Alcibiades's speech, as Robin Waterfield suggests, substitutes Socrates for Love. As he points out, in Diotima's speech (ventriloquized by Socrates) which immediately precedes that of Alcibiades, we are told that 'Love is a philosopher' and that 'in the higher mysteries of love the lover becomes a philosopher' (1994, xxxvii–xxxviii). Symbolized by Socrates, Greek Love, then, however pure, contains within it the unruly qualities that are to be found in Marsyas, and in Orpheus, for if Silenus is the chief priest in the Dionysiac mysteries, he must of necessity be linked with Orphic myth, for Orpheus, too, is sometimes accorded this role. Furthermore, the power of Socrates's rhetoric, that overwhelms and enchants, is reminiscent of the castrato voice, or more particularly the 'cry'; a cry that is also implicit in the sirenic quality of his musical voice, and in the serpentine (or Medusan) power of his 'bite'. Interestingly, in Alcibiades's discussion of his relationship with Socrates, the roles of lover and beloved are seemingly interchangeable: he says, 'He [Socrates] takes people in by pretending to be their lover, and then he swaps roles and becomes their beloved instead' (Plato 1994, 70). This interchangeability is in itself disruptive of Socrates's purity for as Weil observes:

> This dislocation of the lover-beloved opposition is figured in Alcibiades' very presence. Drunken, shouting, adorned 'with a massive garland of ivy and violets' claiming to speak the truth, Alcibiades' physical appearance and the story he tells about Socrates make a mockery of the master. The sign of Aphrodite in the violets of his crown, the sign of Dionysus – himself a God of sexual contradictions – in its ivy, he makes a travesty of the Socrates-Diotima duo, as well as of Aristophanes's 'halves.' In Alcibiades, male and female, self and other, body and mind are intertwined into their confused and hermaphroditic paradoxism (Weil 1992, 28).

The latent sexual instability that is, in Plato's text, manifested in mythological terms, mirrors that discovered in the responses of Winckelmann, H.D., Pater, and Vernon Lee to Greek sculpture. If one returns to Lee's statue of Venus, and her effigy of Marsyas, it would seem that the complicated network of associations implicit in these figures serve, like the castrato, to express a Dionysiac liberation of static identity, and a sexual ambiguity that is figured in their metamorphic bodies. Marsyas's effigy may end its days buried and unacknowledged, fixed by a phallic stake, but Venus's final transformation into a tree at the end of the tale has its own implications, for one of Dionysus's titles is 'Dendrites', or 'tree-youth', and the 'Spring Festival', at which 'the trees suddenly burst into leaf ... celebrated his emancipation' (Graves 1992, 107). Eudaemon's tree, though ostensibly a 'Christian' tree bursting into the blossoms associated with the Virgin Mary, carries with it the instability inherent in Dionysus as well as the Dionysiac resonances traced earlier in the figure of the satyr in 'Marsyas in Flanders'.

Objects of Desire: Pagan Spaces and the Metamorphic Body

The sexual fluidity of Lee's sculptural figures is also evident in the statues that appear in the works of two of her contemporaries: Henry James and Thomas Hardy. James's tale, 'The Last of the Valerii', concerns itself with the discovery of an antique Juno in the grounds of a villa owned by Conte Valerio, an Italian count who has recently married the narrator's American god-daughter, Martha. The statue's location is supernaturally announced to Valerio in a dream in which the Juno rises and lays her marble hand on his, and this hand, which is indeed the first fragment found, he keeps 'in a silver box' having made 'a relic' of it (1983, 28). Valerio, a 'pagan' or 'natural man', reminiscent of Hawthorne's Donatello in *The Marble Faun* (1860), who has little interest in contemporary Christianity, becomes increasingly obsessed by the marble statue (1983, 16, 19). He places the statue in the 'casino', a garden-house, built in imitation of an Ionic temple (1983, 25–26). For Valerio, the statue becomes an object of worship. He treats the Juno 'as if she were a sacrosanct image of the Madonna', locks her away and pays her solitary visits (1983, 28). As time goes on, he begins to neglect his wife in favour of the marble statue.

One night, whilst walking in the grounds, the narrator comes across the casino in which the statue is lit by moonlight. Foreshadowing Lee's Venus, the Juno stands 'bathed in the cold radiance, shining with a purity that made her convincingly divine' (1983, 35). The effect, we are told, is 'almost terrible' prompting the thought that 'beauty so expressive could hardly be inanimate' (1983, 35). Lying prostrate at the Juno's feet is Valerio who had come into her presence in obedience to his passion. In the grip of his infatuation, the Count builds an altar and begins to offer pagan sacrifices to his Juno. His wife, Martha, increasingly disturbed, has lost her bloom and become lifeless, and her godfather observes that 'To rival the Juno she is turning to marble herself' (1983, 37). Martha, too, is seemingly aware of the substitution that is occurring between the Juno and herself and says, 'His Juno is the reality; I am the fiction!' (1983, 38). In desperation she decides on a course of action: the Juno is to re-interred. Once the statue is in its grave, Valerio is restored to his wife, although he retains the Juno's marble hand as a memento of his passion.

In Hardy's 'Barbara of the House of Grebe', a statue is similarly the subject of marital discord. Barbara, the daughter of wealthy parents, initially elopes with Edmond Willowes, a handsome young man of no fortune or status, whom she marries in preference to the more suitable, if considerably less beautiful, Lord Uplandtowers. Barbara and Edmond's straitened circumstances force them to seek a reconciliation with Barbara's parents. This is effected on the condition that Edmond spend some time abroad with a tutor so that he can be educated to a standard befitting Barbara's husband. With his good looks no longer in sight, Barbara's passion for Edmond begins to wane, and noticing this, she asks that her husband send her his portrait. Edmond agrees but intends to send a life-size statue of himself, which is currently being sculpted, and asks Barbara to wait. While away, Edmond is dreadfully disfigured by a fire in a Venetian theatre. Upon his return, although wearing a mask made 'of some flexible material like silk, coloured so as to represent flesh', Barbara is perturbed by his appearance, and when he finally removes the mask, she cannot look at him, nor can she hide her repulsion (1979, 226). Edmond leaves and tells her he will return in one year, but dies before he is able to do so.

After some time, Barbara remarries, becoming Lady Uplandtowers and, in due course, having received a letter from Edmond's Italian sculptor, she agrees to take possession of a life-size statue, 'representing Edmond Willowes in all his original beauty ... a specimen of manhood almost perfect in every line and contour', a veritable 'Phoebus Apollo' as Lord Uplandtowers observes (1979, 233–234), evidently recalling the physical perfection of the *Apollo Belvedere* (fig. 2.6). Following its arrival, Barbara falls repeatedly into a trance-like adoration of the statue. Unhappy at his wife's evident attachment to the sculpture, Uplandtowers asks that it be removed from the hall and Barbara places it in a deep recess in her boudoir, where she keeps it under lock and key. Despite the statue's apparent disappearance, 'a sort of silent ecstasy, a reserved beatification' continues to express itself in Barbara's face (1979, 234). Uplandtowers, suspicious, and impatient for their own marriage to be consummated, discovers the location of Edmond's statue and finds Barbara with her arms draped around it, uttering words of love. Under Uplandtowers' direction, the statue is secretly disfigured, and tinted to resemble Edmond's later maimed and mangled features. When Barbara next approaches her 'temple' she can only respond with 'a loud and prolonged shriek' and a loss of consciousness (1979, 238). Although Barbara finally joins Uplandtowers in the marital bed, her refusal to renounce fully her love for Edmond is punished by nightly encounters with the disfigured statue. On the third consecutive night Barbara, progressively unhinged, becomes hysterical and suffers an epileptic fit. From the moment of recovery, Barbara displays a considerable change. Uplandtowers becomes the only object of an obsessive, and oppressive love, one which increases once the statue of Edmond is removed. In time Barbara and Uplandtowers die, and having no male heir, the title passes to the latter's nephew. During the enlargements that take place at his direction, 'the broken fragments of a marble statue were unearthed', a statue which seems to be that of 'a mutilated Roman satyr; or, if not, an allegorical figure of Death' (1979, 242).

What characterizes each of these tales is the relationship between the lover and the object of his/her desire. Count Valerio's desire for the Juno is comparable to that of Pygmalion for his statue. This is particularly evident in the seeming exchange between Martha and the statue. It is Martha's life-force that is being drained to fuel Valerio's desire so that woman and statue are conflated in his imagination. However, his idealisation of the Juno as an object of worship, and his fetishization of the Juno's hand, are also indicative of the anxieties that underlie his desire. Transfigured by the moonlight, 'shining with a purity that made her convincingly divine', James's Juno, like Lee's Venus, displays that 'light', that 'crystal' purity that associates her with decadent images of homosexual desire. Moreover, the Juno's 'terrible' beauty transforms her into a *femme fatale*, or 'phallic woman', a figure that emasculates

Fig. 2.6   *Apollo Belvedere*, Roman copy of Greek original, 4th century B.C.E.

the men that desire her. Finding himself under the Juno's spell, Valerio experiences a disempowerment, a prostration, and perhaps even a 'castration' that is figured in the unidentified blood that stains his pagan altar. The elevation of the Juno to religious status and the fetishization of her hand become, as Laura Mulvey argues, a 'complete disavowal of castration' effected by 'the substitution of a fetish object' or by 'turning the represented figure in itself into a fetish so that it becomes reassuring rather than dangerous', building up 'the physical beauty of the object', so that it is 'transformed into something satisfying in itself' (1975, 13–14). That the figure of the Juno harbours these implications is suggested by the figure's eventual re-interment. For James, the perils of emasculation must be buried, unacknowledged, and obscured under the mask of a woman's jealousy.

Hardy's statue, whilst it remains in pristine condition, functions similarly as a fetish. It is comparable to Phoebus-Apollo, an example of ephebic masculinity.[26] Barbara's desire is based on ideal beauty and, as such, it necessarily recalls Winckelmann's sculptural ideal that is located in the castrato's body. Her love for the statue, and her rejection of Uplandtowers's physical love suggests a refusal of penetration/impregnation that is consistent not only with a woman's desire for the castrated male body, but also with her primordial desire for the maternal female body that also displays a 'castration'. Penetration is symbolically effected when the statue is placed in a figurative womb, a 'deep recess' in Barbara's boudoir, but it remains under Barbara's control – it is she who holds the key that opens the closet door and each time she does so, it is she who enters, arguably enacting a return to the mother's body. The disfigured statue, however, makes its deformity explicit. The mangled flesh, highlights the mutilation implicit in Winckelmann's sculptural ideal and its livid colours make illusion impossible. Faced with its reality, Barbara displays hysterical symptoms that echo the paranoia that Weir suggests is produced by 'the repression of a woman's desire for her mother – and, by extension, for other women' (1993, 83). The unearthed fragments of Edmond's statue, thought to be those of a 'mutilated Roman satyr' (reminiscent of Marsyas), or a figure of 'Death', represent perhaps the perils of pagan ambiguity, or the 'death' implicit in Barbara's transgressive desire, that 'deathly symbiosis with the mother' (Kristeva 1987, 148).

In both James's and Hardy's tales, however, these transgressive desires are externalized. In each tale pagan licence is located not in the statues themselves, but in the human figures that desire them. In Lee's work, desire resides within the statue itself: it is both subject and object of that desire creating that fantasy of oneness that characterizes the child's pre-Oedipal relationship with the mother. Lee's 'marble' images, it seems, can be chiselled away to reveal alternative subjectivities inspired by the nexus of myths that inform their existence. Within the pagan 'potential space' of the supernatural, the antique statues in Lee's tales allow and enable the expression of those transgressive subjectivities that must elsewhere remain concealed.

The Pagan and the Supernatural

That, for Lee, the pagan symbolizes a childhood space that sanctions the revelation of sexual amorphousness and the processes of metamorphosis, is clearly indicated in her essay 'Divinities of Tuscan Summer Fields' in which she writes of the summer antics of Tuscan children:

> A brand-new race appears miraculously from nowhere: tiny boys and girls in that succinct garment, waistcoat and breeches in one, fastened in the back with missing buttons, which reduces sex to a matter of a ribboned top-knot more or less; Gesù Bambinos and San Giovanninos and Santi Innocenti for Donatello and the Della Robbias; cupids, putti, baby fauns for the more pagan Raphaelesques and followers of Correggio, all suddenly

there, like the flowers which appear after a day of showers and sunshine; little moving flowers themselves, flexible, tender, fluffy, rosy, pearly, golden-brown, with indescribable loveliness of brilliant, weather-stained rags, suddenly arising (by that magic rite of diminishing raiment) out of the cobbles of slums and the dust and litter of roadside hamlets (1914, 231–232).

Sophie Goeffroy-Menoux argues that, for Lee, 'marked by the *fin-de-siècle* imagination', pagan antiquity seemingly represents 'a happy time of harmonic fusion with mother earth' (1998, 253).[27] In Lee's essay the young children of Tuscany are transfigured and transformed. What interests me in this description is the children's sexual amorphousness: girls and boys are indistinguishable from one another in their 'unisex' clothes. Moreover, the discernible shift from the Christian to the pagan in this passage suggests that it is the latter that truly symbolizes this image of childhood freedom. For Lee and her contemporaries, the idea of youth and beauty was intrinsically linked to Greek antiquity which was seen as the 'childhood' of western civilization, and the Greeks stood for 'human virtues and normal healthy impulses that had been repressed in an evangelical Christian culture' (Holliday 1989, 95). The pagan, then, functions as a transitional and transformative space in which identity is constantly allowed to shift. This space is perhaps particularly significant in Lee's works for it is a space that is recognizably 'lesbian'. As Martha Vicinus points out:

One of the most characteristic moves of the turn-of-the-century lesbian writers was to rework familiar mythologies, natural imagery, and Decadent metaphors ... a refashioned past, whether Greek or Renaissance – the most popular eras – signaled both learning and an imaginative space where the lesbian imagination might flourish (1994, 101).

For Lee this pagan space, that manifests itself in sculpture, is intimately associated with the supernatural, a mode which, as we have seen, undermines the stress Lee places on the aesthetics of form. In 'Faustus and Helena: Notes on the Supernatural in Art', an essay in *Belcaro*, Lee acknowledges the paradoxical nature of this conflict:

The supernatural, in the shape of religious mythology, had art bound in its service in Antiquity and the Middle Ages; ... . From the gods of the *Iliad* down to the Commander in *Don Giovanni*, from the sylvan divinities of Praxiteles to the fairies of Shakespeare, ... the supernatural and the artistic have constantly appeared linked together. Yet, in reality, the hostility between the supernatural and the artistic is well-nigh as great as the hostility between the supernatural and the logical. Critical reason is a solvent, it reduces the phantoms of the imagination to their most prosaic elements; artistic power, on the other hand, moulds and solidifies them into distinct and palpable forms: the synthetic definiteness of art is as sceptical as the analytical definiteness of logic. For the supernatural is necessarily essentially vague, and art is necessarily essentially distinct: give shape to the vague and it ceases to exist (2006, 295).

The pagan supernatural is particularly problematic as it finds its expression in the sculptural art form. However, Lee finds a solution in what she calls the 'ghostly', the only supernatural form that truly captures the pagan, for it is 'the only thing which can in any respect replace for us the divinities of old, and enable us to understand, if only for a minute, the imaginative power which they possessed, and of which they were despoiled not only by logic, but by art' (2006, 309). However, as Lee points out, this supernatural form is specifically internalized:

> By *ghost* we do not mean the vulgar apparition which is seen or heard in told or written tales; we mean the ghost which slowly rises up in our mind, the haunter not of corridors and staircases, but of our fancies. ... a vague feeling we can scarcely describe, a something pleasing and terrible which invades our whole consciousness, and which, confusedly embodied, we half dread to see behind us, we know not in what shape, if we look round (2006, 310).

She argues that, in the world of the supernatural we seek, 'a renewal of the delightful semi-obscurity of vision and keenness of fancy of our childhood' (2006, 312). Art, according to Lee, provides no substitute: 'no picture, no symphony, no poem, can give us that delight, that delusory, imaginative pleasure which we received as children from a tawdry engraving or a hideous doll; for around that doll there was an atmosphere of glory' (2006, 312). In her supernatural tales, these 'ghosts', these 'dolls' return to provide the childhood 'freedom' she denies herself in her adult dedication to art. Yet these 'dolls', as we have seen, are intimately related to art via sculpture and, in Lee's essay, the focus of our gaze is directed at one particular 'doll' – Helen of Troy – who is for Goethe's Faust, a 'semi-vivified statue', a 'ghostly figure, descended from a pedestal, white and marble-like in her unruffled drapery'; a figure for whom Goethe's Faust feels 'as Goethe himself might have felt, as Winckelmann felt for a lost antique statue, as Schiller felt for the dead Olympus: a passion intensely imaginative and poetic, born of deep appreciation of antiquity, the essentially modern, passionate, nostalgic craving for the past' (2006, 315–316).

Although this 'intensely imaginative' passion, and 'nostalgic craving for the past' is attributed to Goethe, Schiller, and Winckelmann, they are equally evident in Lee's own responses to sculpture in her supernatural tales and, like Marsyas and Venus, Helen's identity is mercurial. Her form is moulded by 'The Mothers', 'blind goddesses' who, like the chthonian Medusa and her sister gorgons, 'occupy an eerie netherworld beyond space and time': a Dionysian dimension of occult transmutation (Paglia 1992, 256). For Paglia, 'The Mothers are Greek Fates combined with Plato's eternal forms'; they are 'Formation, Transformation,/ Eternal Mind's eternal recreation'; their realm is that of 'repressed pagan nature', they represent, 'nature's brute force of metamorphosis' (1992, 256; quoted in Paglia 1992, 256). It is perhaps fitting, then, that the mythical Helen is herself metamorphic in nature for 'Helen[a] and Helle, or Selene' are variations of 'the Moon-goddess', and she is therefore associated with the fluctuating contours of her lunar body. Moreover, Helen is related to the androgynous Aphrodite: like Helen, Aphrodite is a Moon-goddess, and Helen, like Aphrodite, has her masculine incarnations, most particularly in 'Hellen – a masculine form of the Moon-goddess Helle or Helen' worshipped by the Achaeans and the Dorians, and adopted by the Victorian Hellenists (Graves 1992, 161). Helen, an ideal of statuesque beauty, projects that sexual ambiguity that is an essential feature of Winckelmann's sculptural ideal, and that also informs the figures of Marsyas and Venus in Lee's tales.

While in her essay, Lee argues that Goethe's Helen fails as a supernatural entity, it would appear that her metamorphic body and sexual ambiguity are linked to Lee's definition of a 'ghost'. She embodies both the 'pleasing' quality of beauty, and simultaneously, recalls The Mothers' 'terrible' dark womb-like space, in which her form is moulded and reshaped; her indeterminate gender suggesting the amorphousness of the primordial child, in a space that can be both reassuring and dangerous. Furthermore, her lunar changeability implies a 'shapelessness', creating that 'semi-obscurity of vision' in her beholder that Lee sees as an intrinsic part of that internalized childhood experience of the supernatural. Given the fluidity that characterizes Lee's definition of the supernatural, her ideal Helen arguably finds herself depicted in Gustave Moreau's painting, *Helen at the Scaean Gate* (*c*. 1880), where her androgynous figure, wrapped in concealing draperies, displays a 'blank mannequin's face' reminiscent of the 'blank, white glance' of Lee's Vatican statues: like them, she is an 'idol of pagan nature' (Paglia 1992, 500). While Lee does not mention Moreau's painting in her work, it is intriguing that this 'faceless' image appears in similarly androgynous guise in her whimsical short story, 'The Featureless Wisdom'.

The Featureless Wisdom

Here, Lee tells the story of how Diotima, a 'Priestess of Mantineia' comes 'to possess an effigy of Athena, conspicuous by the absence of all features' (1904, 195). We learn that Diotima, an acquaintance of, among others, Socrates and Alcibiades, had decided that 'the only Wisdom to which she could possibly bring worship and service would have to be a Wisdom entirely and exclusively her own' (1904, 195). This being so, she asks the sculptor Pheidias 'to make her an image of Athena of a size to fit into her hat-box, and with a set of features easily distinguishable from those of the idols handed down by the past and still adored by the common herd' (1904, 196).[28] Pheidias obliges and at the end of eight days Diotima calls to collect the sculpture. While admiring its form, she is less happy with its features in which she sees too great a likeness to 'the type of the infernal goddesses' (1904, 196). Pheidias agrees to alter the sculpture but the result is still not to Diotima's taste. This time its head looks 'just a little bit too like that of an Aphrodite' a figure rejected on account of its unsuitable associations (1904, 197). The figure is once again altered, but on her third visit, Diotima is dismayed to discover that one of Pheidias' pupils had fitted onto the image of Athena, 'a very neat and expressive little head of Silenus' (1904, 197). At the end of another fortnight, Diotima returns to Pheidias' workshop to collect the Athena. When it is handed to her, she stares at it in silence for 'the effigy of the goddess ... had indeed a most becoming helmet with three chimaeras tastefully curled round the ostrich feathers; it had even a face, with finely modelled chin and delicate flat ear. But it had no features. No eyes, no nose, no mouth—nothing!' (1904, 198). Believing Pheidias to be playing a joke on her, Diotima is about to leave when Pheidias explains the reasons behind his featureless sculpture:

> You have asked for an impossibility – what your clever friends call a *metaphysical miracle*, I believe; and I have vainly endeavoured to satisfy you by a series of makeshifts which,

I am bound to say, most ladies would not have detected. So there remains nothing for it but to impart to you a remarkable mystery which your ingenious mind ... will doubtless take much pleasure in expounding. To wit: That by a supreme and inscrutable decree, the features of Wisdom must always remain the same as we see them in the great images that are set up ... in public places ... . And any image differing essentially from these must, therefore, be that of some inferior divinity, ill-famed, or ill-favoured, or ill-omened; or else, like this one, a poor little sightless and speechless doll, very suitable as a plaything for persons of refinement (1904, 199–200).

The passage seems worth quoting in full because it highlights the problematic role of the intelligent woman in male society. If one returns to Max Beerbohm's comments on the fly-leaf of his copy of Lee's *Gospels of Anarchy*, quoted in the previous chapter, one finds the image of Vernon Lee as a diminutive woman in constant debate with the writers and philosophers of her time. It is but a short imaginative leap to connect this image of Lee both with the figure of Diotima who appears in debate with Socrates in the *Symposium* and with, significantly, the 'sightless' and 'speechless' doll which seemingly represents woman's powerless position in Victorian society. In Lee's tale, Diotima's wise words are credited to Socrates himself: Pheidias 'had heard his friend Socrates speak of Diotima, and had even suspected that, as may happen between ladies and philosophers, the wise man had attributed some of his own remarks to the Priestess of Mantineia' (1904, 196). It would appear that Diotima's position of power is maintained at the cost of serving as a 'doll' through which the male voice of philosophy can be ventriloquized. It is unsurprising, then, to find that she, arguably like Lee, locates her counterpart in Athena, the goddess of wisdom, that figure which, for Charles Segal, represents the 'incorporation of the otherness of female creative energy into the polis' (Segal 1994, 31).

Yet the figure of Athena is itself complicated by her own ambiguous sexuality. Her 'sexual hybridism' is made evident in Homer, 'who makes her descents a sexual masquerade': in the *Iliad*, she 'appears on earth four times as a male, once as a vulture, and six times in her own form; in the *Odyssey*, she appears eight times as a male, twice as a human girl, six times as herself' (Paglia 1992, 84). The classical scholar, Jane Harrison identified Athena as a patriarchal symbol responsible for turning 'the local Kore of Athens' into 'a sexless thing, neither man nor woman'; she is 'manufactured' and seemingly 'unreal': phrases which connect Athena not only to the Dionysian figures traced in Lee's supernatural tales, but also to the 'unreality' of Lee's ghosts, those vague evanescent figures that inhabit her interiority (quoted in Paglia 1992, 84). It seems significant, then, that in 'The Featureless Wisdom', a fanciful tale that hovers on the uncertain borders of the real and the unreal, Lee rejects the explicitly Dionysian figures represented by the 'infernal goddesses', the 'Aphrodite' and the 'Silenus' sculpted in Pheidias workshop, and settles instead for the doll, a 'transitional object' that features elsewhere in her work, as we shall see, and allows the projection of a similarly fluid and indeterminate, but nevertheless powerful, identity.

Notes

[1] 'Hermaphroditus' (1997, 34, ll. 15–19).

[2] Among these are: Kit [Clementina] Anstruther-Thomson, Carlo Placci, Enrico Nencioni, Elena French-Cini, Maria Pasolini, and Maria Gamba (Gunn 1964, 112).

[3] Gaetano Guadagni (1725–1792), famous castrato who played the role of Orpheus in the first production of Gluck's *Orfeo ed Euridice* in Vienna in 1762.

[4] Being a late nineteenth-century figure, Baldwin's 'eighteenth-century days' here represent his interest in the music of the last century.

[5] Helene Hastreiter (1858–1922), American mezzo-soprano.

[6] Pauline Garcia-Viardot (1821–1910), French mezzo-soprano, renowned for the wide range of dramatic characters she played on stage.

[7] Gautier's poem first published in the *Revue des Deux Mondes* in 1849 and later appeared in Emaux et Camées in 1852.

[8] Rilke saw Lotte Pritzel's dolls at an exhibition in Munich in 1913. Pritzel's dolls, intended as art objects, are figures made of wire and wax adopting poses which suggest dance movements.

[9] Potts here refers to Baudelaire's essay 'Morale du JouJou'. See Baudelaire 1963.

[10] Variations of the Laocoön myth suggest that he merited his punishment either because of his sacrilegious fornication with his wife in front of a sacred image of Apollo, or because he is reputed to have thrown a spear at the Trojan horse, thus threatening the Greeks' invasion of Troy.

[11] The word 'semiotic' is used here in the Kristevan sense outlined in Chapter One.

[12] 'It is thus that the child in its cradle resembles something as yet undeveloped, a primitive being, less complete than the unfinished statue' (my own translation).

[13] This passage presents an apparent paradox. If Althea is Baldwin's 'pupil', how can she be the 'precursor' as well as the 'perfecter' of many of his thoughts? A possible answer lies in Baldwin's and Althea's roles as projections of Lee. In the context of these merged identities, Althea can indeed be the 'precursor' as well as the 'perfecter' of many of Baldwin's thoughts, for they are fundamentally one and the same.

[14] Interestingly, Kit herself had been described to Lee as resembling a statue, the Venus de Milo, and on meeting her Lee evidently agreed with the description as she notes in her introduction to Anstruther's *Art and Man*, 'While as to the Venus of Milo, there was no doubt about the likeness, although she wore the inappropriate coat and skirt and sailor hat of the "eighties"' (1924, 7).

[15] Maurice Baring (1874–1945), was a British diplomat, linguist, author, and member of the banking family of Baring Brothers who became a lifelong friend of Lee's.

[16] Although not pursued in any detail in Greek myth, there appears to be a link between the child Dionysus, as he is described in Euripides' *Bacchae*, and Medusa. In the *Bacchae*, the newly born Dionysus is 'a horned child *crowned with serpents* [my emphasis]' (Graves 1992, 103).

[17] The term 'Gods in Exile' is taken from Heinrich Heine's essay 'The Gods in Exile' first published as *Les Dieux en exil* in the *Revue de deux mondes* (April 1853). Here, Heine explores the idea that the ancient gods continued to live in the Christian world, though in exile, adopting the shape of animals (as in Egypt), or inhabiting their own statues.

[18] Vernon Lee seems aware of the legend's origin and refers to the version told by the 'original mediæval professional storyteller' in her preface to *Hauntings* (2006, 38).

[19] In her tale 'The Virgin of the Seven Daggers' (discussed in the next chapter), Lee appears to employ certain elements of this version of the legend.

[20] Ziolkowski notes that this fashion, 'the "mimoplastic art" of representing works of art by mimic means, especially gestures and draperies' was created by Emma Hart, later Lady Hamilton (1977, 34).

[21] James's and Hardy's tales will be discussed shortly, and Hoffmann's 'The Sandman' will be considered in a later chapter, as will Vernon Lee's 'Dionea' (1890) (to which Ziolkowski also refers) in which the eponymous heroine appears as a form of 'goddess in exile', instilling desires and creating disturbances that are linked to the mythical Venus. While this story may have implicit associations with the legend of Venus and the Ring, 'St Eudaemon and His Orange Tree' that makes explicit use of the story is not mentioned in Ziolkowski's account.

[22] See Gardner, Chapter 7 for a full discussion of the works in which he traces this image.

[23] In the 1850s, John Gibson (1791–1866) produced *The Tinted Venus* and other statues using coloured wax to stain the marble in order to imitate the art practised by the ancient Greeks.

[24] Interestingly, in her introduction to *Art and Man*, Vernon Lee describes Kit Anstruther-Thomson as having 'finely chiselled, rather statuesque features, and a certain ... virginal expression' which 'made one think of a very beautiful and modest boy, like some of the listeners of Plato' (1924, p. 8). Given that Kit's intellectual engagement with Lee has Platonic resonances, her use of this image suggests a similar 'purification' of their relationship.

[25] The plural 'Sileni' is taken from 'Silenus' which was originally the name of a follower, or possibly a teacher of Dionysus, and perhaps the original Satyr. Like Marsyas, Silenus is associated with music and also appears as the chief priest of the Dionysian mysteries (Plato 1994, 103).

[26] The term 'ephebic masculinity' is taken from Abigail Solomon-Godeau, *Male Trouble: A Crisis in Representation* (1997), that discusses representations of ideal masculinity. Godeau notes that 'The feminized masculine' is one of 'a number of available types in the lexicon of ideal bodies, appropriate to ... the representation of ephebic characters.' This 'feminized male body had a venerable pedigree in antiquity: hermaphrodite, androgyne, faun, all of which comprised overlapping categories on a spectrum that fell within the genus ephebe' (1997, 202). In *Flesh and the Ideal*, Alex Potts observes that the statue singled out by Winckelmann as 'the epitome of ideal manhood' is the Apollo Belvedere whose body represents 'an ideal conflation of the austerely sublime and sensuously beautiful' (1994, 118). Potts points out that in the context of Edmund Burke's eighteenth-century aesthetic, the Apollo 'problematizes the relation between images of masculinity' and 'the category of the beautiful,' which for Burke is intrinsically feminine (Potts, *Flesh and the Ideal* 1994, 118).

[27] All translations are my own.

[28] Pheidias (also Phidias) (*c.* 490–430 B.C.), ancient Greek sculptor involved in the construction of The Parthenon, and famous for the colossal statues of the goddess Athena he built on this former site of worship.

Chapter 3

Painted Dolls and Virgin Mothers

An old-fashioned doll, that is not like nature,
Can never pass for a human creature;
It is in a doll that moves her eyes
That the danger of these misfortunes lies!
William Brighty Rands (1899)[1]

The 'sightless and speechless doll' that appears in 'The Featureless Wisdom' manifested itself earlier in a different context in Lee's article, the 'Economic Dependence of Women' in the *North American* in 1902. Here the doll figures as an analogue for the powerless Victorian woman, subject to male power and control. Living in a patriarchal society where she is handed from father to husband, the woman functions, according to Lee, as a commodity 'amalgamated with the man's property', a possession, 'a piece of property herself, body and soul' (1908, 270).[2] She observes that, by this process, 'the man and the woman ... do not stand opposite one another ... but in a quite asymmetrical relation: a big man, as in certain archaic statues, holding in his hand a little woman; a god ... protecting a human creature; or ... a human being playing with a doll' (1908, 270).

This is a position that Lee sees as unacceptable and undesirable, and is one which is questioned implicitly by this doll's sculptural counterpart, Diotima's 'doll' in 'The Featureless Wisdom', who defies categorization. However, as in her tale, the 'doll-woman' in Lee's article is a masculine construction. She points out that 'women ... have been as much a creation of men as the grafted fruit tree, the milch cow, or the gelding' and that they function as symbols of desirable Victorian femininity, which was required to be 'decorative, passive, and sexually pure' (1908, 294; Hartman 1977, 2). What could be more passive than an 'inanimate' object? And what more sexually pure than 'the seamless body of the doll' in whose 'idealized miniaturisation' the danger of female sexuality and power is lost? (Stewart 1984, 124). Silent and still, woman becomes an object and, 'not simply an object ... [but] in terms of the production of culture ... an art object: she is the ivory carving or mud replica, an icon or doll' (Gubar 1986, 293).

Seamless Dolls and Stainless Statues

The doll's 'seamless' purity resonates interestingly with the pristine, asexual beauty of Greek sculpture, a purity that, according to Walter Pater, is associated with 'white light' from which 'the angry, bloodlike stains of action and passion' have been purged: a 'white light' which the critic Eileen Gregory interprets as that 'of eternal forms, abstracted from finite bodily particulars, such as sexuality' (1986,

137; Gregory 1997, 93). Moreover, this 'white light' is intrinsically linked to the Apollonian ideal that, for Lee, represents the epitome of Greek sculpture: what John Addington Symonds in *Studies of the Greek Poets* (1873) calls the 'clear light of antique beauty' finds its model in the god Apollo who embodies 'the magic of the sun [and whose] soul is light' (1902, 364, 367). Given that for Lee, the 'highest intrinsic quality of form is beauty', this white light and the perfection of form seem intertwined. For Symonds, it is not only Apollo that is represented by light. He writes that a harmonic beauty infiltrates all aspects of Greek culture producing, in religion, 'a race of gods, each perfect in his individuality, distinct and self-contained, but blending, like the colours of the prism, in the white light of Zeus, who was the whole', thus creating an encompassing, and protective halo, containing, and providing form and order (1902, 378). In a footnote to this assertion, Symonds notes that 'The Greek Pantheon, regarded from one point of view, represents an exhaustive psychological analysis. Nothing in human nature is omitted: but each function and each quantity of man is deified. To Zeus as the supreme reason all is subordinated' (1902, 378).

The gods, then, in their various prismatic hues, constitute those psychological aspects of human nature that are controlled under the aegis of reason. The 'white light' that sheds its rays from the perfection of sculptural form would appear to obscure those human frailties and unruly desires which are implicit in the statue and its associations. Yet, as indicated in Chapter Two, the colour white is often appropriated by the homoerotic gaze to express its desire and this transgressive eroticism, present in the very whiteness of the sculptural form, is evident in the works of Winckelmann, Pater, Lee, and H.D. It manifests itself particularly when that whiteness is compromised by a play of light that dapples the sculptural figure, a phenomenon that, captured in the Greek term *poikilos*, serves to encode homoerotic love: the transient movement of shadow and light threatening to expose the 'lurid colour' of those desires. In his analysis of Lee and her works, Gardner argues that '"Whiteness," ... is the common denominator of all her symbols of purity' (1987, 405). In 'Beauty and Sanity', an essay in *Laurus Nobilis: Chapters on Art and Life* (1909), Lee herself refers to 'white' as 'the queen ... of all colours' and goes on to argue that 'Our minds, our very sensations are interwoven so intricately of impressions and associations, that it is no allegory to say that white is good, and that the love of white is akin somehow to the love of virtue' (1909, 133). In contrast, green suggests 'pollution, fertility and sex', and red harbours 'lurid and sinister' connotations linked variously with reality, sacrifice and, on one occasion, with menstruation (Gardner 1987, 349, 405).[3]

In 'The Seeker of Pagan Perfection', Lee's fictional biography of the artist Domenico Neroni, that appears in *Renaissance Fancies and Studies*, Neroni seemingly acts as a mouthpiece for her own sentiments about colour: '"Colour" he writes, "... is the enemy of noble art. It is the enemy of all precise and perfect form, since where colour exists form can be seen only as juxtaposition of colour"' (Lee 1895, 170). That the ancient Romans and Greeks portrayed their gods in 'white marble ... and not gaudy porphyry or jasper', reinforces for Neroni the superiority of colourlessness in the representation of form (Lee 1895, 171). Given Gardner's key to Lee's colour psychology, Neroni's rejection of red and green represented by porphyry and jasper seems important. For Lee, the inclusion of colour apparently suggests an excess that disrupts form and order. Yet, as John Boardman Beazley and

Bernard Ashmole observe, Greek statues were originally painted: stone figures were usually painted in red and blue; while in limestone, male flesh was often coloured a reddish brown; and in marble, colours were applied discreetly, tinting only details such as hair, lips, eyes, and possibly part of the drapery (1966, 15).

Stained and Deadly Dolls

In her book, *The New Sculpture*, Susan Beattie notes that in the latter half of the nineteenth century, certain sculptors had begun to experiment with colour on marble statuary. John Gibson's *The Tinted Venus* (fig. 2.5) was exhibited in 1850, and in 1889 Moreau Vauthier's bust, *Gallia*, appeared at the Paris International Exhibition (1983, 158). Influenced by Vauthier, George Frampton sculpted *Mysteriarch* (1892), and his famous later work, *Lamia* (fig. 3.1), was exhibited at the Royal Academy of Arts 1899–1900 (Beattie 1983, 158, 160). Beattie's descriptions of *Gallia*, *Mysteriarch*, and *Lamia* are suggestive and prompt an exploration of the disturbing quality of coloured statuary.[4] Of *Gallia*, Beattie writes:

Fig. 3.1   Sir George Frampton, R.A. (1860–1928), *Lamia* 1899–1900, ivory, bronze, opals and glass.

It is a conventional, even commonplace image of a female warrior that takes on a startling and almost supernatural quality from the materials and the manner in which it is worked. The fleshy face is of ivory, its smoothness and pallor sharply offset by the richly chased and gilded silverwork of the armour. A Medusa head decorates Gallia's breast and a winged beast surmounts her helmet (1983, 158).

Frampton's *Mysteriarch*, also displaying an 'ivory tint and sheen', set against the 'stiff, metallic quality of the bodice' is indicative of Frampton's regard for Vauthier's work, but it is his *Lamia*, composed of bronze, ivory and opals, that generates, for my purpose, the most compelling effect. Beattie quotes a contemporary viewer's experience of seeing Frampton's sculpture:

I had been in the sculpture gallery some minutes before my eye fell on this strange and fascinating Lamia. Imagine a life-size face of extraordinary beauty ... that in a minute becomes flesh to the eye, the hair and shoulders covered with a close-fitting head-dress and robe. As you gaze, a faint colour comes to the lips – the loveliest, most sensitive of mouths – the eyelids quiver a very little, and her expression changes, but never loses its mystery or its sadness. She makes an absolute silence in the room; whoever turns his head in passing stops and remains as one enchanted (quoted in Beattie 1983, 161).

Lamia's colour, it seems, stimulates an erotic response in the viewer. Here, as in the earlier description of Gallia, ivory becomes flesh and, in a fantasy of sexual animation, the sculpture's lips are stained with a 'faint colour'. Like the 'lascivious warmth' of Gibson's *The Tinted Venus*, that, for Hawthorne, 'demoralizes the chastity of the marble', colour eroticizes the 'purity' of the sculptural form and I will discuss this phenomenon in due course (Hawthorne 1990, 475, note 1). For the moment, however, I wish to explore another effect generated by the coloured statue: that is its ability to fascinate and 'paralyze' the viewer.

Beattie argues that Frampton's *Lamia* shares 'something of the human condition' if only 'by virtue of its existence in three dimensions and its subjection to the same play of light', and that it is this affinity which allows it the power 'to convey an almost oppressive sense of stillness, isolation and silence' (1983, 161). The sculpture's capacity to transmit this sense of immobility and remoteness to its viewer recalls Rilke's essay on the wax dolls of Lotte Pritzel.[5] Faced with their ominous silence, Rilke relives his childhood experience of the doll:

At a time when everyone was concerned to give us prompt and reassuring answers, the doll was the first to make us aware of that silence larger than life which later breathed on us again and again out of space whenever we came at any point to the border of our existence. Sitting opposite the doll as it stared at us, we experienced for the first time ... that hollowness in our feelings, that heart-pause which could spell death (1994, 33).

In her discussion of Rilke's essay on dolls in relation to Freud's 'The "Uncanny"' Eva-Maria Simms observes that, for Rilke, the disturbing quality of the doll lies in her 'lifelessness and her indifference and unresponsiveness to the child's emotions' (1996, 670). Rilke acknowledges a 'hatred, which unconsciously has always been part of our relationship with her' and notes that, looked at from the perspective of adulthood she would be seen, 'finally without disguise: as that gruesome alien body for which we have wasted our purest warmth; as that superficially *painted drowned corpse* [my emphasis], lifted and carried by the floods of our tenderness until it dried out and we forgot it somewhere in the bushes' (quoted in Simms 1996, 670). Later, I will return to this childhood engagement with the doll but, for now, I would like to keep in mind Rilke's image of the doll as 'corpse'.

In 1900 the enraptured admirer of Frampton's *Lamia* wrote of her, 'I cannot recall anything quite like this', but I suggest that her sisters can be found in the wax anatomical models constructed ostensibly for medical purposes (quoted in Beattie 1983, 161).[6] The cultural critic, Ludmilla Jordanova, notes that both male and female bodies were made: male bodies were either 'upright muscle men, with no flesh at all, or severely truncated male torsos' whereas their female counterparts, notably called 'Venuses', lie 'on silk or velvet cushions, in passive, yet sexually inviting poses ... adorned with flowing hair, pearl necklaces, removable parts and small foetuses' (1989, 44–45) (fig. 3.2). Recumbent on soft pillows and bedecked with jewels, these latter-day Galateas are, like *Lamia*, reminiscent of Pygmalion's ivory statue eliciting a fantasy of desire and animation.[7] Jordanova points out that 'the use of wax to imitate flesh produces texture, and colour, which eerily resemble "the real thing"', and 'the naturalistic colouring of all the anatomical parts together with the meticulous details such as eyelashes and eyebrows further reinforce a simultaneous admiration of and unease about the likeness' (1989, 45).[8]

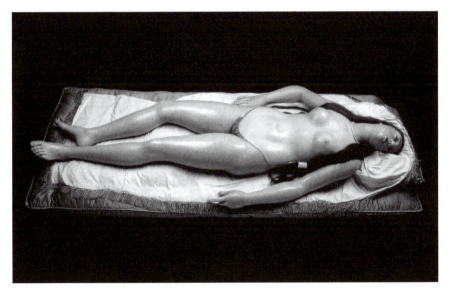

Fig. 3.2   Anatomical Venus.

Sexually inviting, yet corpse-like in their stillness, these anatomical dolls recall both Frampton's *Lamia* and Rilke's childhood doll. Moreover, repeating 'positions and gestures from well-known works of art', and displayed in 'anatomical museums [that] were visited like the great art museums of the eighteenth century', these models are intimately related to statues, '"those great dolls" so disliked by Baudelaire' and the sightless and speechless doll in Lee's 'The Featureless Wisdom' (Jordanova 1989, 45; Bronfen 1992, 99; Potts, 'Dolls and Things' 1994, 373). Yet the difference between them is significant and lies in the use of colour and its role in the creation of an illusory verisimilitude. Writing of responses to the substitution of traditional shop mannequins with stylized and featureless alternatives in the early part of the twentieth century, Tag Gronberg explains that these 'metallic and gleaming figures were often interpreted as a rejection of the *trompe-l'oeil* materials (such as wax or hair) used in mannequins of earlier periods' and argues that these 'modern mannequins assuaged the unease provoked by a too-close resemblance of wax figures to the female body' (1997, 379). A quotation from a 1924 arts magazine in which traditional mannequins are referred to as 'horrific wax cadavers' and 'disturbing counterfeits' substantiates Gronberg's assertion (Gronberg 1997, 379).

The unease caused by the doll, then, apparently lies in its borderline existence between life and death and in its association with the female body. In 'The "Uncanny"', Freud, borrowing from Ernst Jentsch's 'On the Psychology of the Uncanny' (1906), famously locates one experience of uncanniness in our '"doubts whether an apparently animate being is really alive; or conversely, whether a lifeless object might not in fact be animate" ... [an] impression made by waxwork figures, ingeniously constructed dolls and automata' (Freud, 'The "Uncanny"', 1955, XXII, 226). Taking his lead from Jenstch's reference to the works of Hoffmann as examples of uncanny effects in literature, Freud goes on analyse 'The Sandman' (1816), and almost immediately rejects the doll, Olympia – an obvious example of Jentsch's uncanny – in favour of the sandman himself. Freud's reluctance to engage with the subject of the doll's body, and by implication the body of woman, is well documented and discussed by critics such as Ruth Ginsberg, Samuel Weber, and Hélène Cixous. Ginsberg writes, 'Thematically, figuratively and structurally, women and the feminine play a decisive role in Hoffmann's text. They play none in Freud's; at least not in its surface rhetoric', and Cixous points out that, in Freud's essay, the doll is relegated to a footnote which acts as 'a typographical metaphor of repression which is always too near but nevertheless negligible' (1992, 25; 1976, 537). If one agrees with Weber's observation that 'Freud came to the conclusion that it was not "repression ... which produces anxiety," but anxiety which produces repression', one is forced to ask what is it about the doll which makes Freud so anxious that he needs to repress it? (1973, 1110)

For Ginsberg and for Weber this repression is prompted by the doll's affinity with the body of the mother. Ginsberg writes, 'Hoffmann's text offers, quite explicitly, another source of the uncanny – Woman. Woman not as lack or castration ... but as "beginning" – origin and as heterogeneous plenitude' (1992, 26). In Weber's assessment, Freud's understanding of anxiety as a symptom of repression is linked to fears of castration. As he points out, in Freud's 1926 paper, 'Hemmung, Symptom und Angst' ('Inhibition, Symptom and Anxiety'), 'the particular anxiety which now became paradigmatic for the structure of anxiety itself was castration-anxiety' under which the notions of separation from the maternal body and object-loss are also subsumed (Weber 1973, 1111). For Cixous, however, the uncanniness of Hoffmann's doll lies in its liminal existence: 'Olympia is not inanimate. The strange power of death moves in the realm of life as the *Unheimliche* in the *Heimliche*, as the void fills up the lack' (Cixous 1976, 543). This 'dead' body has its own affinity with the body of woman. If one revisits the anatomical Venuses, the association between them becomes clear. As Elisabeth Bronfen notes in her book *Over Her Dead Body: Death, Femininity and the Aesthetic*:

> These wax models were initially created to give medical students access to the human body without having to be present in the anatomical theatre, so repellent because of its horrible putrefaction and its ghastly forms of dismemberment. The wax specimens were modelled directly from cadavers in a technique also used to recreate relics of saints and martyrs. Producing a substitute of the corrupt and putrefied dead body that would mask death, these models are endemic to a general cultural effort to eliminate the impure state of mutibility [*sic*] and decay by replacing it with a pure and immutable wax body double (1992, 99).

Bronfen suggests that this artificial 'dead' body 'was meant to afford access to a truth of human existence, in this case the centre and origin of human life as signified by the interior of the feminine body', an access which, Irigaray points out, carries its own risks for 'the openness of the mother ... the opening onto the mother ... appear to be threats of contagion, contamination, engulfment in illness, madness and death' (1992, 99; 1991, 40). However, Bronfen remarks that the particular fascination 'engendered when the wax cast depicts a feminine body has to do with the fact that the two enigmas of western culture, death and female sexuality, are here "contained" [and that] ... their disruptive and indeterminate quality has been put under erasure' (1992, 99). Covering, distancing, and controlling both sexuality and death, these anatomical figures represent 'the mutable, dangerously fluid, destabilized feminine body' in a 'cleansed, purified, [and] immobile form' (Bronfen 1992, 99). But the danger inherent in the fluid and contaminating female body is not so easily erased, and it is evident that it is present even in that apparently innocuous counterpart of the anatomical Venus, the childhood doll that imbues Rilke with a sense of 'hollowness', a word which resonates with that castration anxiety also implicit in Freud's rejection of Hoffmann's doll, Olympia.

Dolls and Mothers

The doll, then, functions symbolically, in cultural terms, as the body of the mother, a role that it also fulfils, in a different context, for object relations theory, in which transitional objects function as 'the first symbols, representations of the mother' that the child employs in the formation of individual identity (Watson 1995, 483). In his paper, 'Transitional Objects and Transitional Phenomena' (1953), Winnicott summarizes the special qualities required of the relationship between the child and the transitional object which is defined as the infant's first possession that 'belong[s] at once to them and to the outside world': the infant 'assumes rights over the object' and the object can be 'affectionately cuddled,' 'excitedly loved' and 'mutilated' according to its whim; it 'must never change, unless changed by the infant' and it 'must survive instinctual loving, and also hating and if it be a feature, pure aggression' (Rudnytsky 1993, xii: Winnicott 1971, 5). Nevertheless, 'it must seem to the infant to give warmth, or to move, or to have texture, or to do something that seems to show it has vitality or reality of its own' (Winnicott 1971, 5). Winnicott suggests that the object functions as 'a symbol of the union of the baby and the mother', and that the use of an object symbolizes the union of two now separate things, baby and mother, '*at the point in time and space of the initiation of their state of separateness*' (1971, 96–97).

Significantly, however, the doll seemingly inhabits both positions and the relationship between child and doll oscillates between the roles of mother and child (the doll representing the child) and those of child and mother (the doll representing the mother). Using the model of the *fort/da* game, Jay Watson argues that, although Freud does not acknowledge fort/da as 'a doll game', the little boy's play, involving the cotton reel's disappearance and re-emergence from a curtained crib, is 'an exercise in identification with the mother that specifically stages the child's own origin' and serves 'the same purpose that Irigaray attributes to the doll games of little girls' allowing 'the child to explore the creative potential of mothering by establishing a relationship to reproduction and playing around with his or her beginning' (1995, 491–492).[9] For Freud, however, doll games are subject to gendered divisions: the boy's fort/da game is seen as an exercise in masculine control; the cotton reel stands for the mother and she is subordinated in 'a ritual of mastery' which 'turns a madonna into a boytoy' (Watson 1995, 469–471). Yet, as Watson points out, 'when Freud observes a little girl playing with dolls, he recognizes exactly what is going on in metapsychological terms. The player identifies with her mother, while the doll symbolizes the child herself', a configuration he 'cannot or will not see in the case of fort/da' (1995, 490). Moreover, because of his own formulation of sexual identity, where 'the experience ... most basic to femininity, [is] the girl's desire to bear her father's child', a desire that entails an already negotiated separation from the mother, Freud finds nothing inherently 'feminine' in the process of playing with dolls, even though girls 'seem particularly drawn to this activity' (Watson 1995, 490). Watson explains that, for Freud, 'doll play only becomes feminine when the doll begins to signify the wished-for father's baby; until then the game functions in a more gender-neutral manner, as a means of identifying with the mother's power to act upon passive objects' (1995, 490–491).

Ironically, 'this active emulation of maternal power' comes to be described 'as phallic activity', phallic because, in Freud's view, such games 'stage identifications with activity per se rather than with maternal activity specifically' (Watson 1995, 491). Freud's understanding of pre-Oedipal doll-games as phallic, and post-Oedipal doll-games as feminine creates a rigidity that is belied by the fluid identification made possible within its experience and I agree with Watson who argues that 'what is at stake ... is a very different mode of identification' – one that Hélène Cixous sees as – 'a kind of pilgrimage, a journey into the strange, sacred territory of another self' (1995, 493; quoted in Watson 1995, 493). It is an identification that permits the transgression of boundaries, 'predicated upon "permeability" of self ... offering access to difference without jeopardising identity, and at the same time enhancing identity without erasing difference' (Watson 1995, 493). The doll, as transitional object, 'performs' in a doll game that creates a transitional space in which identity and power can be explored: boys can become 'mothers' and girls can inhabit the 'phallic' power of the maternal body prior to being subjected to the patriarchal law of the father and the rigidity of a 'fixed' sexual identity, and this sexual fluidity is in evidence in those works by Lee that feature dolls.

In her book, *The Shape of Fear: Horror and the Fin de Siècle Culture of Decadence*, Susan J. Navarette dedicates a chapter to Lee's story 'The Doll' (1927) in which she writes:

> The doll takes pride of place among the effigies, stone idols, marionettes, and puppets littering the lumber room and enchanted garret of Lee's imagination. References to dolls, effigies, puppets abound in her writings and therefore in the studies or commentaries of her work written by her friends and critics. Lee's friend Maurice Baring – the 'Maurice' of *For Maurice* – referred in his memoirs, for example, to the Italian 'effigies, dolls, puppets' between whose world and our own Lee acted as a mediatrix (1998, 157).[10]

Yet it is not only the doll, puppet, or effigy that recurs in Lee's work. As Mario Praz points out, there is also the recurrence 'in her fantastic tales of the figure of a naked woman, always with demoniacal stigmata' and there is an interesting correspondence between these figures in Lee's writings (1966, 313). What Praz fails to add to his observation is that these naked women, bearing demoniacal stigmata, are very often also dead. In 'Prince Alberic and the Snake Lady' (1896), for example, one is left in the final pages with 'the body of a woman, naked, and miserably disfigured with blows and sabre cuts', and in 'A Wedding Chest' (1904), the naked body of Maddalena, wounded and defiled, is returned in death to her lover (Lee 2006, 227). Given the analogies made earlier between the statue, the corpse, and the doll, one might argue that the bodies of these dead women, still, silent, and stained with colour, function as 'dolls' in Lee's work. For Gardner, for whom these dead women are continuations of the motif of the 'semivir idol' discussed in Chapter Two, an idol which manifests itself in 'dolls, images, statues, pictures, puppets and the dead', this is certainly the case: in his view the murdered Maddalena can be added 'to the battered remnant of the Snake Lady in [Lee's] cabinet collection of idols' (1987, 316, 321).

While Gardner notes both the doll-like quality of the dead female body in Lee's work, and independently observes Lee's colour psychology (outlined above), he fails to make any significant connection between the two. He argues that, 'the characteristic colour of the semivir idol ... is a deadly white', a colour that recalls Pater's white sculptural bodies from which those 'angry, bloodlike stains of action and passion' have been removed (1987, 326; Pater 1986, 137). While the statue may maintain its whiteness, dolls, puppets, pictures, and evidently Lee's dead women, are either painted, or marked by colour. Moreover, Praz labels these marks on the female body 'stigmata'; a word which, while retaining religious connotations, is also defined as 'a mark of disgrace or discredit' and 'a visible sign or characteristic of a disease' (*O.E.D.*). These women, in death, bear those very marks that signify a 'disorder'; an excess that the figure of the doll attempts to contain, one that manifests itself in blood and in painted colours on woman and doll alike. In the latter, as in those statues in Catholic legends that 'sweat, bleed, [or] cry' the painted surface seems to merge imperceptibly with the body beneath in a fantasy of animation, its colours functioning as a form of seepage from the 'white' body: the blank 'canvas' of the unpainted doll, or puppet (Ziolkowski 1977, 22). What, then, is the significance of these colours? A clue may lie in their role in eroticizing the white body of sculpture, and in their function as 'stains': impurities that, for Pater, seem associated with animation and desire.

Miss Brown

In spite of being aligned with contemporary notions of decadence, invoking in her supernatural fiction, 'a highly finished, arabesqued, "yellow" style that functioned ... as a projection of and correlative to the fevered states of mind that the Decadents sought to cultivate', elsewhere Lee was to demonstrate a 'touch of something like Puritanism' that made itself felt in her novel, *Miss Brown* (1884), in which she satirizes what she perceives to be the excesses of Pre-Raphaelitism and late-Victorian Aestheticism (Navarette 1998, 144; quoted in Gunn 1964, 111–112). Henry James's criticism of the novel is revealing:

> The imperfection of the book seems to me to reside ... in a certain ferocity ... you take the aesthetic business too seriously, too tragically, and above all with too great an implication of sexual motives ... you have impregnated all those people too much with the sexual, the basely erotic preoccupation: your hand has been violent, the touch of life is lighter ... perhaps you have been too much in a moral passion! (1980, III. 86).

Even more telling, is Lee's own journal entry on New Year's Eve, 1884. Responding to the novel's unhappy reception, Lee writes initially '"I will show fight", I said yesterday or the day before when it came home to me from the letter of Monkhouse, the talk of Benn, etc., that the anonymous reviewer in the *Spectator* was not alone in accusing me of having written what Monkhouse calls a "nasty" book'.[11] Yet as the entry progresses self-doubt creeps in and she asks of her response, 'Is it a mere reaction – one of those almost mechanically explicable phases of feeling whose explicableness and momentariness has given me so strange a sense of unreality? Is it one of those mere reactions which makes me, today, hesitate and pause and say, "I don't know what to answer"?' Reappraising the situation she goes on to write:

> Yet so it is. It strikes me now, perhaps all those people are right, perhaps the British public is right; perhaps I have no right to argue on the matter, because I may be colour blind about the data. Here I am accused of having, in simplicity of heart, written, with a view to moralise the world, an immoral book ... I say to myself, 'What if these people were right, or at least nearer the truth than I?' ... am I not perhaps mistaking that call of the beast for the call of God; may there not, at the bottom of this seemingly scientific, philanthropic, idealising, decidedly noble-looking nature of mine, lie something base, dangerous, disgraceful that is cozening me? Benn says that I am obsessed by the sense of the impurity of the world ... May this be true? May I be indulging a more depraved appetite for the loathesome, while I fancy that I am studying disease and probing wounds for the sake of diminishing both? ... If I could assure myself of having 'nasty' tendencies of mind, I would take my measures, just as I would were I colour blind. I should mistrust the tendency to speculate upon some subjects, entirely put them aside, occupy myself with others; in these submit to the guidance of people about whom no doubt could ever be raised. But how find out? how know? At any rate, the result of all this is not 'show fight', but rather ask my own feelings for their passports (quoted in Gunn 1964, 105–106).[12]

The passage is fascinating both as an exposition of self, and in its use of language. Lee associates her failure to see the eroticism and sexual implications in *Miss Brown* with colour-blindness, and significantly, in the novel, the moral make-up of Anne Brown, 'a lay-figure for Vernon Lee' clothed 'with her own emotional, moral and sociological preoccupations and prejudices' is linked with a refusal to acknowledge or 'see' colour (Gunn 1964, 101–102):

> For all her familiarity with the aesthetic world, in whose apprehension, as Thaddy O'Reilly's Yankee friend had quietly remarked, 'right or wrong don't exist,' – for all her habit of reading poems in which every unmentionable shamefulness was used as so much vermilion or pale-green or mysterious grey in a picturesque and suggestive composition, – Anne had retained a constitutional loathing for touching some subjects, which was like the blind instinctive horror of certain animals for brackish water or mud (Lee 1884, II. 196–97).

Furthermore, Lee's journal entry reveals that this erotic impurity is linked not only with colour, but also with 'disease' and with 'wounds', an association that offers a suggestive illumination of the stigmata that stain her dead and naked women and of their affinity with the painted dolls that inhabit Lee's tales. But before I discuss the tales themselves, I would like to examine the nature of the 'dangerous' eroticism that infiltrates *Miss Brown*.

The plot of the novel revolves around Anne Brown, a young governess living in Italy. Visiting the family she serves, the Pre-Raphaelite poet and artist, Walter Hamlin, is struck by Anne's unusual beauty, and offers to educate her, and to be her guardian, until such time as she is ready to consider whether or not she will marry him. Anne's cousin, Richard Brown, a self-made Scottish businessman who is the antithesis of Hamlin, fails to dissuade her from accepting the latter's offer. When Anne's education is complete, she arrives in England and is set up in a house in Hammersmith where she meets the leading figures of the Aesthetic circle that surrounds Hamlin. Exposed to the literary and artistic excesses of this set, Anne soon makes her disapproval clear: she does not swoon 'over the descriptions of the kisses of cruel, blossom-mouthed women, who sucked out their lovers' hearts, bit their lips, and strewed their apartments with coral-like drops of blood', and argues that 'a woman of her age had no business not to understand the meaning of such things, and understanding them, not to let the poets know that she would not tolerate them' (1884, II. 24–26). Morally disillusioned with Hamlin, Anne begins to take an interest in social issues, encouraged by her cousin Richard who is now an affluent radical reformer and a prospective Member of Parliament. Hamlin, rejected, takes refuge in the attentions of his cousin, the half-Russian Sacha Elaguine, a mysterious and fascinating woman with a past, and travels to Paris with her. Anne sees the relationship between Hamlin and Sacha as a means of escape from her obligations. However, when Hamlin returns from Paris, it is evident that he has indulged in opium, hashish, and drink to drown the knowledge of his immorality. Learning the full nature of Sacha's moral depravity, Anne resolves to marry Hamlin in order to save him from himself and from Sacha. On the evening the announcement of their engagement is made, Sacha reveals to Anne that Hamlin has been her lover. Anne tells her that she knows, and despite her disgust, martyrs herself in marriage to Hamlin.

Miss Brown has been the subject of critical scrutiny in a number of recent works.[13] Kathy Alexis Psomiades writes that Hamlin is 'clearly modeled after Dante Gabriel Rossetti'. One could argue that Hamlin is, in fact, a conflation of Pre-Raphaelite figures and their relationships with their models, but it is not the intimacy between Anne and Hamlin that is Psomiades's primary interest (*Beauty's Body* 1997, 165).[14] In her analysis of *Miss Brown*, it is the subtext of the relationship between Anne and Sacha that provides the most fascinating insight into Lee's seemingly unconscious concerns. According to Gardner, the figure of Anne Brown is yet another version of the 'Semivir Idol'. In descriptions of her one finds echoes of her sculptural counterparts: her complexion is of 'a uniform opaque pallor, more like certain old marble than ivory'; she is 'no living creature, but some sort of strange statue – cheek and chin and forehead of Parian marble' (Lee 1884, I. 24). She exists, like the doll, in a fantasy of erotic animation; she is to be 'a realised ideal ... a creature of [Hamlin's] own making' (1884, I. 174). Hamlin's life is to be 'crowned by gradually endowing with vitality, and then wooing, awakening the love of this beautiful Galatea whose soul he had moulded, even as Pygmalion had moulded the limbs of the image which he had made to live and to love' (1884, I. 121–222).

Anne bears marks of eroticism in the colours that tarnish her whiteness: her lips are 'stained a dull red', her hair is the shade of 'dull wrought-iron', and her eyes are of a 'mysterious greyish-blue' resembling 'slate-tinted onyx' (1884, I. 24). Like the tinted statues of Gibson, Vauthier, and Frampton, her subtle colour eroticizes her purity, and elicits Hamlin's desire. However, it is not Hamlin, but Sacha, who deepens Anne's colour. In her discussion of the sensual engagements between the bodies of the two women, Psomiades notes the presence of physical changes in Anne at these moments. When Sacha flings her arms about Anne's neck crying, 'I want you', and presses her 'hot lips' on her forehead, Anne's response is that of 'a vague undefinable repulsion' (1884, II. 292–293). Later in the novel, Sacha Elaguine's touch is 'like the contact of some clammy thing' and as Psomiades observes, '"some clammy thing" is also Sacha's body and Sacha's sex, the clammy thing makes Anne hot, rather than cold, "her face still burning from this strangling embrace", the clammy thing is [...] most decidedly NOT the old nauseous story of heterosexual marriage' (Lee 1884, III. 198; Psomiades, 'Still Burning' 1997, 26).[15]

Psomiades argues that, 'Anne marries Walter Hamlin not because of what she feels for him but because of what she feels for Sacha Elaguine', and what she feels for Sacha Elaguine is 'a panicky, disavowed, very physical desire' (*Beauty's Body* 1997, 173). Indeed, as she goes on to point out, at the moment when Anne proposes to Hamlin, the latter's limbs and lips metamorphose into those of Sacha Elaguine:

> 'You love me, Anne; you love me!' cried Hamlin, louder; and pressing closer to her, he put out his arms and drew her face to his, and kissed her, twice, thrice, a long kiss on the mouth. It seemed to Anne as if she felt again the throttling arms of Sacha Elaguine about her neck, her convulsive kiss on her face, the cloud of her drowsily scented hair, stifling her. She drew back and loosened his grasp with her strong hands (1884, III. 208).

According to Psomiades, this lesbian desire gives Anne a 'Swinburnian body', the body of 'the perverse desiring subject, the body of Tannhäuser, but also of Anactoria, embraced by Sacha-Sappho, "with such violence that Anne felt her lips almost like leeches and her teeth pressing into her cheek"' ('Still Burning' 1997, 27).[16] Sacha Elaguine's embrace has, it seems, the hypnotic and debilitating quality of a vampire's kiss. Yet, like the vampire's victim, it appears that Anne herself is contaminated by the contact. Implicit in the heat felt on her cheeks is the colour of her blood rising to the surface of her skin, and injecting its redness into her lips.[17] Engulfed in Sacha's embrace, Anne not only has a 'Swinburnian' body but also a 'Swinburnian' face: a face that aligns her with Lee's Zaffirino and those 'wicked, vindictive women' that haunt Magnus's boyhood dreams, as well as with the 'blossom-mouthed women' of Pre-Raphaelite excess (Lee 2006, 162; Lee 1884, II. 24). The penalty one pays for being bitten by a vampire is, as we all know, becoming a vampire oneself. This coalescence of the bodies of Hamlin and Sacha seems to extend to Anne herself and, interestingly, the identities of Anne and Hamlin merge into one another and, more significantly, into that of Vernon Lee in Mabel Robinson's comments on *Miss Brown* in a letter dated December 14th 1885:

> Miss Brown never to my eyes has that Etheopian [*sic*] type you so much admire but in all her sudden impulses and tricks of expression reminds me of a certain animal (not without piquancy and charm) familiarly known as the 'little vermin flea.' Mary tells me that Hamlin is the true portrait of that said flea as seen by itself but if that be so I should advise that lively animal to buy a new mirror and if it be a true one it will see a much more noble looking personage (quoted in Gardner 1987, 366–367).

The amusing nickname, 'little vermin flea' belongs, as Gardner observes, to Vernon Lee, and it is intriguing that, to Mary Robinson, Lee has confessed to identifying herself with Walter Hamlin. In view of the self-searching journal entry quoted earlier, this is perhaps less remarkable than it would otherwise seem. However, this identification has fascinating implications. In aligning herself with Hamlin, Lee indirectly identifies with Sacha and lesbian desire, a desire that is also doubled by identification with Anne Brown. It is telling that Anne is 'Miss Brown' and not 'Miss White' for, implicit in the colour brown are those untouchable subjects, symbolized by that 'brackish water or mud', from which Anne recoils with 'blind instinctive horror' (Lee 1884, II. 196–97).

Colour, implicit in the language of early sexology, underlies far more recent and overt discussions of same-sex friendships and lesbian sexuality. In her book, *The Spinster and Her Enemies: Feminism and Sexuality 1880–1930*, Sheila Jeffreys writes that 'Krafft-Ebing cited a hereditary *taint* [my emphasis]' as the cause of homosexuality, and that the use of this 'defence' in novels such as Radclyffe Hall's *The Well of Loneliness* (1928) 'was the result of the sexologists' work in *stigmatising* [my emphasis] and isolating the lesbian in the first place' (1985, 112–113). Jeffreys frequently refers to this 'stigmatisation' of lesbianism, a word which, stemming from 'stigma', is necessarily associated with both stain and disease. Given these associations, and the rejection of colour and disease implied in Miss Brown, it is particularly interesting that these associations reappear and recur in Lee's fantastic tales. Moreover, these tales, as we have seen, provide a fantasy space in which Lee explores alternative identities, including that of a lesbian subjectivity. Those tales that include dolls or doll-like women seem especially important in this context for, if the doll functions as a transitional object, then it should assist the assertion of an independent subjectivity. However, it would seem that, for Lee, the expression of a lesbian sexual identity creates a complex and circular engagement with the doll. If the doll represents the body of the mother, then the separation from that body is hampered by a need to return to that body as the object of sexual desire. Nevertheless, in the illusory 'potential space' of her fantastic fiction, the figure of the doll facilitates an engagement with the female body, allowing a regression into the fluidity of a pre-Oedipal asexual identity, which simultaneously permits a 'homoerotic' desire for a woman (that is, the mother). But doll games, according to Watson, also stage 'an active emulation of maternal power' (1995, 491), and it is the doll's role in licensing alternative identities and desires that I intend to explore in four of Lee's stories: 'A Wedding Chest' (1904), 'Sister Benvenuta and the Christ Child' (1905), 'The Virgin of the Seven Daggers' (1896), and 'The Image' (1927).

'A Wedding Chest'

As Lee's tale begins, a panel of the wedding chest in question is encountered as item no. 428 in the Catalogue of the Smith Museum, Leeds, in which it is described as:

> A panel (five feet by two feet three inches) formerly the front of a *cassone* or coffer, intended to contain the garments and jewels of a bride. Subject: 'The Triumph of Love.' 'Umbrian School of the Fifteenth Century.' In the right-hand corner is a half-effaced inscription: *Desider ... de Civitate Lac ... me ... ecit.* This valuable painting is unfortunately much damaged by damp and mineral corrosives, owing probably to its having contained at one time buried treasure (Lee 2006, 229).[18]

After this preliminary description of the panel's present location, Lee returns to the past and to the making of the wedding chest and its disturbing story. Readers are told that the chest was commissioned by Messer Troilo Baglioni from Ser Piero Bontempi, the employer and prospective father-in-law of the craftsman Desiderio who was to wed Maddalena, Ser Piero's daughter, on the coming St John's Eve. Working on the front panel of the chest, Desiderio depicts scenes from Petrarch's 'The Triumph of Love', dividing the panel into four sections each 'intended to represent the four phases of the amorous passion' (2006, 230–231). In the middle section, Desiderio had represented Love, as 'a naked youth, with wings of wondrous changing colours, enthroned upon a chariot, the axle and wheels of which were red gold, and covered with a cloth of gold of such subtle device that that whole chariot seemed really to be on fire' (2006, 231). On the youth's back 'hung a bow and a quiver full of dreadful arrows' and round his eyes was bound 'a kerchief fringed with gold, to show that Love strikes blindly' (2006, 231). Around the chariot are pictured those 'famous for their love' among whom are 'Orpheus, seeking for Eurydice with his lute', 'Socrates' and Desiderio himself, as a bridegroom-to-be (2006, 232–233). However, Desiderio refuses to include his beloved, Monna Maddalena, in the procession, arguing that it would be immodest, though the true reason lies in his reluctance to depict Maddalena on a chest to be owned by Troilo (who also desires her) for he had often painted her, albeit in the guise of the Virgin Mary.

Despite Desiderio's precautions, Troilo, 'a most beautiful youth' whose skin is 'astonishingly white and fair like a woman's' is determined to possess Maddalena (2006, 235). On the eve of her wedding to Desiderio, Maddalena is abducted and, although the perpetrators wear Troilo's family colours, rumour decides that Maddalena had fled willingly with a lover (2006, 236). A year after Maddalena's disappearance, she is returned to Desiderio and her father in 'a coffer, wrapped in black baize' - the very same coffer that Desiderio had made at Troilo's request – accompanied by a piece of parchment that declares this to be 'a wedding gift' to Desiderio 'from Troilo Baglioni of Fratta' (2006, 237). What they find inside proves shocking:

> The lid being raised, they came to a piece of red cloth, such as is used for mules; *etiam*, a fold of common linen; and below it, a coverlet of green silk, which, being raised, their eyes were met ... by the body of Monna Maddalena, naked as God had made it, dead with two stabs in the neck, the long golden hair tied with pearls but dabbed in blood; the which Maddalena was cruelly squeezed into that coffer, having on her breast the body of an infant recently born, dead like herself (2006, 237).

Stunned into silence, Desiderio digs a deep grave in Ser Piero's garden 'abounding in flowers and trees' watered by 'stone canals ... fed from a fountain where you might see a mermaid squeezing the water from her breasts' (2006, 237–238). With the help of Ser Piero, Desiderio prepares Maddalena's body for burial, tenderly lifting it out of the wedding chest, washing it 'in odorous waters', dressing it 'in fine linen and bridal garments' before returning her to the coffer and laying her on 'folds of fine damask and brocade' (2006, 238). Her head is laid 'upon a pillow of silver cloth' and 'a wreath of roses, which Desiderio himself plaited', is placed around her hair 'so that she looked like a holy saint or the damsel Julia, daughter of the Emperor Augustus Caesar, who was discovered buried on the Appian Way' (2006, 238).[19]

The chest is filled with herbs and spices and a certain gum believed to prevent the earthly corruption of the body, and Maddalena's corpse is finally laid to rest in the ground. The body of her child, however, is tossed into the *Sardegna*, a place in which dead animals are disposed of, 'because it was the bastard of Ser Troilo, *et infamiae scelerisque partum*' (2006, 239).[20] Seeing the danger of Desiderio's imprecations against Troilo, Ser Piero advises him to leave Perugia in order to escape the wrath of Troilo's family, and Desiderio goes to Rome where his work is a great success. After seven years of self-imposed exile, Desiderio hears of Ser Piero's death and that Troilo is in Perugia raising an army for the Duke of Urbino. Disguised as a Greek, Desiderio returns to Perugia and, having confessed his sins and received the Eucharist, makes a vow 'never to touch food save the Body of Christ till he could taste of the blood of Messer Troilo' (2006, 240). He soon encounters Troilo, 'dressed in grey silk hose, and a doublet of red cloth and gold brocade', his face still young and unbearded, 'a face like Hyacinthus or Ganymede' (2006, 240–241).[21] A fight ensues, and Desiderio stabs Troilo in the chest. As he dies, Desiderio stoops over his chest, and laps up the blood as it flows; his first food 'since taking the Body of Christ, even as he had sworn' (2006, 241). When Troilo's body is found, 'many folk, particularly painters' come to look at him and to admire 'his great beauty' (2006, 242). Having kept his vow, Desiderio unearths the wedding chest and travels to

Arezzo where he preserves with him 'always the body of Monna Maddalena in the wedding chest painted with the Triumph of Love' (2006, 242).

In 'A Wedding Chest' Lee returns to a Renaissance past, one of those imaginative spaces in which, according to Martha Vicinus, 'the lesbian imagination might flourish' (1994, 101). For Vicinus, Lee's imagination finds its outlet, in this tale, in the figure of Troilo, that young, beautiful, beardless, and effeminate boy, who acts as the focus and/or mediator of homosexual desire in *fin-de-siècle* literature. She argues that:

> Even though many male homosexuals were not pederasts and most lesbians did not look like boys, the boy was the defining, free agent who best expressed who they were. We repeatedly are asked to look – and then look again – to see the hidden meaning of the beautiful boy (1994, 92).[22]

Vicinus suggests that, in his role as a subvertor of marriage, Troilo represents Lee revenging herself 'upon husbands and fiancés' that impede her desire and that the other characters in the 'tragic triangle' are also facets of Lee: Desiderio is the lover 'who – like Vernon Lee – desires too strongly' and Maddalena is 'the unfortunate victim who – like Vernon Lee – never speaks' (Vicinus, 1994, 107).[23] While I agree in principle with Vicinus's reading, the interrelationship between the three characters and their significance for Vernon Lee are far more complex than Vicinus's triangle would suggest. Troilo's effeminacy and his affinity with 'Hyacinthus' and 'Ganymede', are suggestive of the castrato, an association that is strengthened when one notes the similarities between descriptions of Troilo and the figure of Love depicted on the wedding chest. The colours of red and gold used to represent Love are repeated in the final image of Troilo who wears 'a doublet of red cloth and gold brocade'; his 'hat of scarlet cloth with many feathers' is a prosaic version of Love's 'wings of wondrous changing colours'; and instead of Love's arrows, Troilo carries a sword (2006, 240–241, 231). As a double of Eros, Troilo, too, is 'double-sexed' and, like his Greek counterpart, his acts of desire are accompanied by a disturbing violence: his 'love', like that of Eros, is charged with the threat of violence and death, a threat which has its own implications, for Vicinus argues that 'Lee frequently used violence and death to represent the destructive nature of same-sex relations' (Graves 1992, 30; Vicinus 1994, 107). Eros's 'blindness' also has interesting connotations for, in Freudian terms, blindness is linked with castration and Troilo is therefore, by implication, linked once more with the 'castrato': a figure which, as we have seen, has special significance in Lee's negotiation of her sexual and artistic identity.[24]

What is even more intriguing, however, is the conflation of the figures of Troilo and Desiderio. Although seemingly antithetical: artisan/noble, man/boy, they are 'unified' in their desire for Maddalena. Moreover, Desiderio's vampire-like lapping of Troilo's blood arguably functions as an act of introjection which, given the 'two stabs' that mark Maddalena's neck, suggests a form of vampiric consummation of his relationship with Maddalena mediated via the androgynous body of Troilo's corpse: an act which 'feminizes' Desiderio in the process, for it involves an homoerotic engagement with Troilo's body.[25] It is perhaps no accident that this 'sexual' consummation should be effected through Troilo, for the word 'troilism' suggested by this act has a particular significance. Not only does it mean 'sexual activity in which three persons take part simultaneously', but it has now come to define 'a psychotic sexual manifestation in which the patient desires the sexual partner of the person for whom he has homosexual yearnings' (*OED*).[26] In the light of this definition, the fusion of Troilo, Maddalena, and Desiderio implicit in the process encodes not only heterosexual, but also homosexual desire. Furthermore, Desiderio's act of introjection seems especially important because it is staged as a religious process, the fulfilment of Desiderio's vow 'never to touch food save the Body of Christ till he could taste of the blood of Messer Troilo' (2006, 240). Involuntarily, we conflate the two actions, and Desiderio becomes an actor in a pagan ritual, reminiscent of a participant in a Dionysiac mystery that allows the transgression of sexual boundaries, and the opportunity to '*stop being yourself*', to access other identities (Paglia 1992, 97).

However, the focus of our gaze, as for Troilo and Desiderio, is the body of Monna Maddalena. Lying dead in her coffer, under red and green cloths, her hair tied with pearls, and her stillborn child at her breast, Maddalena is reminiscent of an anatomical Venus, a doll-like effigy of her former self. Given Lee's dislike of red and green, here symbolizing perhaps penetration and pollution, it is unsurprising that Maddalena's body undergoes a process of purification and 'mummification' that transforms her into 'a holy saint or the damsel Julia' (2006, 238). Yet in referring to Maddalena as another 'Julia', this 'purification' of her body is undermined. Like Julia, Maddalena is now 'at once an artifact and a body': an 'auto-icon', 'signifying a representation that consists of the thing itself' (Pearsall 1992, 57; Bronfen 1992, 96). Unlike the anatomical Venuses and those recreations of the bodies of saints and martyrs, Maddalena's body, though apparently masking the process of putrefaction, still contains the threat of contamination implicit in its internal decay. In addition, despite its purification and the disposal of her illegitimate child, Maddalena's body is the body of a mother and, more importantly perhaps, the body of the Mother – the Virgin Mary – for Maddalena's corpse, which now represents her living body, is doubled in all the still and silent images of 'Our Lady, the Mother of God' that Desiderio painted in her likeness (2006, 233). As 'auto-icon' Maddalena's body also functions as a 'fetish': it is a 'lost object preserved by virtue of the fetish substitute' which represents not only the '"impossible" feminine phallus but an "imagined" maternal body' (Bronfen 1992, 96–97).

In 'preserving with him always the body of Monna Maddalena' (Lee, 2006, 242), Desiderio 'regresses' to a pre-Oedipal space, a space of indeterminate sexuality where he takes the place of Maddalena's dead child, and simultaneously plays a 'doll game' that turns his 'Madonna' into a 'boytoy' (Watson 1995, 469–471). Yet, in order to look at Maddalena, Desiderio must open the coffer and in doing so he enacts a symbolic entry into the maternal body for, in recalling the anatomical Venus, Maddalena's body is like hers, one of those 'wax cases ... whose "lids" are opened up to reveal the insides, the mysterious organs of sexuality and reproduction', an organic counterpart of the wedding chest 'intended to contain the ... jewels of a bride' and containing at one time 'buried treasure' (Showalter 1992, 128; Lee 2006, 229).[27] If in 'doll games' the doll can represent both mother and child, this entry stages an erotic engagement with the body of the mother even as it reconstructs a fantasy of pre-Oedipal symbiosis. The stigmata that stain Maddalena's body and their sexual implications continue to exert their influence despite purification. In 'A Wedding Chest', then, one finds familiar echoes of those processes of regression that enable the assumption of a fluid identity, and sanction a return to the maternal body in Lee's tales. While in this story these elements are veiled in a complex system of identifications, 'Sister Benvenuta and the Christ Child' and 'The Virgin of the Seven Daggers' offer a more direct engagement with the maternal and, more particularly, the Marian body.

'Sister Benvenuta and the Christ Child'

This later tale, by its title alone, evokes an image of the Virgin and child. Yet Sister Benvenuta, born to 'the illustrious Venetian family of Loredan' (Lee 1905, 1), proves an unconventional Madonna. Lee's story begins with an editorial preamble that half-frames Sister Benvenuta's diary entries. Readers are told that after death Benvenuta had become 'the chief object of devotion to young children and their fond mothers in the town of Cividale' and particularly to young girls who would process annually through the town in her honour (1905, 1). Benvenuta's popularity leads to her family's request for her beatification, and it is as a result of this that her diaries are read and are here reproduced by the editor to 'perhaps shed some light both on her real claims to beatification, and on the reason why these claims were not officially admitted' (1905, 2). Her narrative hinges on her love for the doll that represents the Christ Child during the Christmas period and whom she addresses in her journal. Sister Benvenuta's devotion to the Christ doll seems to be linked to her childhood obsession with a portrait of the Madonna and child that she would gaze at for hours in solitary contemplation, and which she describes to the doll in her diary:

> The picture was the most beautiful picture in the world. It was divided by columns, with garlands of fruit about them, and in the middle, on a ground of gold, all divided into rows and all variegated with russet and orange, like the sunset, was the Madonna's throne, with the Madonna on it, a beautiful lady, though not so beautifully dressed as my mother, and with no paint on her face, and not showing her teeth in a smile ... . And on the Virgin's knee who should be lying asleep, fast asleep, but You – You, my dearest Great Little One ... . The whole of Paradise waited for You to awake and smile; and I sat and waited also, perched on the altar, till it was too dark to see anything save the glimmering gold (1905, 13).

The effigy of the Christ Child is not the only doll that appears in Benvenuta's story. At Eastertime, the Abbess decides to hold a puppet show at the convent that is attended by the eminent citizens of the town. For Sister Benvenuta the female puppets are disturbing reproductions of the doll-like women she encountered in the outside world:

> I do not really like the puppets representing ladies, though they have lovely skirts of flowered cloth of silver and *andriennes* making their hips stick out, and bodices full of seed pearl, and patches on their cheeks and red paint, just like the real ladies who used to come and drink chocolate with my mother and my aunts (1905, 5).

Later, the Madonna effigies used for religious ceremonies are conflated with these puppets and the Mother Superior's examination of their 'shoes and stockings and lace pocket handkerchiefs' is labelled 'the continuation of the puppet show in the Mother Abbess' (1905, 9). Amongst these puppets is the figure of the Devil. Unlike the female marionettes, who in their dominoes and hooped skirts recall the women of Venice who inspired fear and unease in the young Benvenuta, this puppet is an object of fun. She writes, 'I know it is wrong, and I have often prayed that I might learn to fear the Evil One, but I never could, and all the pictures of him, and the things they tell ... have always made me laugh' (1905, 5–6). Faced with aborted attempts at making a suitable coat for her beloved Christ doll, Benvenuta enters into a 'Faustian' contract, signing her name in blood and selling her soul for the Devil's assistance when he appears to her in her cell. The postscript to Benvenuta's story is written by a fellow nun who describes the final scene: 'The cell was streaming with light, as of hundreds of tapers; and in the midst of it, and of this fountain of radiance, was seated Sister Benvenuta, and on her knees, erect, stood no other but the Child Christ' (1905, 15). As the light fades, this animated scene quickly converts into a fixed tableau. In a pose reminiscent of the *pietà*, Benvenuta, now 'stone dead and already cold' holds the lifeless 'waxen image of the Little Saviour' in her arms: her mouth and eyes open in rapture (1905, 15–16).

As the 'heavenly advocate' of puppeteers, Benvenuta can evidently be identified with Vernon Lee who, as Maurice Baring observed, acts as 'a mediatrix' between the world of dolls and puppets and our own (Lee 1905, 2; quoted in Navarette 1998, 157). Like Lee, Benvenuta indicates her distaste for painted women and dolls, preferring instead the beautiful Madonna 'with no paint on her face' that presides over the altar in Benvenuta's family chapel (1905, 13).[28] Yet, ironically, this Madonna's face *is* painted, for it is constructed from the colours of an artist's palette and, as such, she is intrinsically related to her doubles, those doll-Madonnas with their embroidered dresses, stockings, and lace pocket handkerchiefs, who are themselves the religious counterparts of the lady puppets, with their 'skirts of flowered cloth of silver ... and bodices full of seed pearl' that remind Benvenuta of the Venetian women of her past (1905, 5). Given the contemporaneity between Freud's 'Dora' (1905) and Lee's story (published in the same year), Benvenuta's hours of contemplation in front of the painting of the Madonna inevitably recall those of Dora, who spent '*two hours* in front of the Sistine Madonna rapt in silent admiration' (Freud 1977, 135–136). Following Wiseman's argument (discussed in Chapter Two) that, instead of identifying with the Madonna – as suggested by Freud – Dora may have either desired the Madonna or wanted to be loved like the Christ Child held in the Virgin's arms, Benvenuta's enchantment with the Madonna painting takes on a deeper meaning. If one accepts that Benvenuta is, at some level, a facet of Vernon Lee, then the former's love for the Virgin and the Christ Child, and her willingness to 'sell her soul' for the pleasure of an eternal fusion in which she 'becomes' the former and unites with the latter, are suggestive.

In her discussions of the maternal erotic, Helene Deutsch cites a lesbian case study in which the relationship between the two women is described as 'a perfectly conscious mother and child situation, in which sometimes the one and sometimes the other played the part of the mother', enacting a process of pre-Oedipal union posited as one of the psychoanalytical models of lesbian desire (quoted in O'Connor and Ryan 1993, 63). That in Lee's tale this image of pre-Oedipal fusion is figured via the image of the Virgin Mary appears significant for, at the turn of the twentieth century, Mariology is often linked with homosexuality. In her book *Sappho and the Virgin Mary: Same-Sex Love and the English Literary Imagination*, Ruth Vanita argues that, 'The figure of the Virgin seems to have had special attractions for same-sex communities, such as the Anglican sisterhoods established under the influence of Edward Pusey, and ... for homoerotically inclined men and women, both individually and as communities' and writes that:

> Mary, flying in the face of biology and heterosexual normativity, is the exemplary figure for the odd lives of male and female saints who choose same-sex community over marriage ... . It does not seem to me accidental that a liturgy to the Virgin is part of every ceremony of same-sex union unearthed by John Boswell; she is called upon to bless these unions along with Christ and other saints but is not invoked in the same way in heterosexual marriage services ... . And, in the nineteenth century, homosexual men were referred to as 'Maryannes' – the combined names of Mary and of the mother who immaculately conceived her (1996, 8–9).

Adding credence to Vanita's hypothesis, in her book *Veronica and Her Cloth: History, Symbolism, and Structure of a 'True' Image*, the painter and art critic, Ewa Kuryluk, tracing a link between the Virgin Mary and St Veronica, observes that both are celebrated in February, a month whose meaning is etymologically linked to purification.[29] The 'most ancient festival in honor of Mary' is celebrated on the second, a feast day that is considered 'the day of homosexuals in Bulgaria' and on the fourth, St. Fiacre, the patron saint of 'hemorrhoids [*sic*], male flux, and gays' is occasionally celebrated 'together with St.Veronica on Mardi Gras' (Kuryluk 1991, 115).

In 'Sister Benvenuta and the Christ Child', a tale framed by its Marian image, it is worth considering the significance of the marionettes that abound in its pages. As Navarette explains:

> the term marionettes, meaning 'little Maries,' refers to the diminutive versions sold by Venetian toy venders [sic] of the 'Marioles' or 'Marie di legno' [wooden Marie] or 'Marione' [big Maries], pious images associated with the annual festival of the Maries, in which mechanical figures eventually came to substitute for the girls who, in the earliest years of the festival, were selected to represent twelve Venetian maidens who had been abducted by Barbary pirates, rescued and then married – the puppets reenacting, that is, the narrative in which the virgin is threatened with dishonor and then reclaimed, her sexuality ceded to the state of marriage (1998, 167).

With its carnivalesque Venetian background, Lee's tale seems to play with the homosexual implications of Marian imagery. For example, Benvenuta's delight in the chapel's Madonna replaces the fear she senses as a child as she looks at the 'coloured prints of nuns of various orders' that hang in her bedroom at the villa by the Brenta in which the nuns, members of same-sex communities, harbour perhaps uncomfortable connotations with that 'autoeroticism or lesbianism' that figures in such works as Diderot's *La Religieuse* (1780) (Lee 1905, 12; Vanita 1996, 30).

Unsurprisingly, then, Benvenuta is 'purified' as she 'becomes' a Madonna in the final moments of the tale. However, this image of Sister Benvenuta as an 'alternative Virgin', does not completely erase those homosexual identifications. As a result of her transformation, worship of her forms a 'regular cultus' and she is celebrated by mothers and children, and, most particularly, by young girls in the town of Cividale, indicating an implicit reference to same-sex desire that is obscured in the image of pre-Oedipal fusion (Lee 1905, 4).[30]

Benvenuta's identification with the Virgin is foreshadowed as the tale progresses and she resolves to make the Christ doll a coat for, in legends and representations, 'a spinning, weaving, and embroidering Virgin' comes to be identified as the seamstress that makes the seamless tunic worn by Jesus during his Passion (Kuryluk 1991, 193). Kuryluk states that this association dates from the late Middle Ages, and that around 1400, 'various allusions to the crucifixion begin to appear in the scenes of nativity and infancy', usually symbolized by Christ's garment (1991, 194). Such allusions appear in a variety of media: on the 'right wing of the Buxtehude altarpiece (ca.1410) Mary is knitting the seamless tunic with four needles on the porch of her house'; a 'Silesian wood carving (ca. 1500)' shows Mary completing 'her child's garment which she has put on a tailor's dummy'; and in a 'fifteenth-century drawing' the Virgin 'contemplates the seamless coat ... in her hands, while a naked infant Jesus, a mini-Narcissus and Amor, gazes at his mirror image in a round washbasin' (Kuryluk 1991, 194–195).[31] Kuryluk argues that the fabric of this 'seamless tunic' 'plays a central role in the passion narratives, and in particular in the Gospel of John which specifies that Jesus wears a "tunic ... without seam, woven from top to bottom" (Jn. 19:23) – a second skin whose removal foreshadows death': a cloth functioning, for example, as 'an empty shell and double' in Gerard David's *Crucifixion* (1480–90), in which Jesus 'is being nailed to the cross which lies on the ground next to his tunic' (1991, 187, 193).

If losing one's skin is associated with death, then gaining one's skin is associated with coming alive, an analogy that Kuryluk traces in biblical stories such as that of Job who, speaking to God, says, '"Thou didst clothe me with skin and flesh, and knit me together with bones and sinews" (Job 10:11)' (quoted in Kuryluk 1991, 185). This analogy has interesting implications for Benvenuta's Christ Child. Although she fantasizes that the Christ doll is animate, believing that he can feel the cold, 'so chilly in that Sacristy cupboard', it is only at the end of the tale, when the garment made by Benvenuta, 'veined' with gold and silver, has slipped to the floor, that the Christ doll momentarily comes alive, before being fixed forever in Benvenuta's arms (1905, 6). One might suggest that it is this magical coat that is instrumental in his animation, and that 'flayed' of his skin, the Christ Child returns to his embryonic body and 'dies' once more. 'Flayed', this body prefigures Christ in his Passion, his naked body stained with stigmata, reminiscent of the naked, and 'marked' dead women in Lee's tales. This body also recalls that of the satyr Marsyas, Jesus's pagan counterpart who, for Kuryluk, as for Simon Richter, represents a 'silently suffering creature, [and is] clearly the prototype of the crucified' Christ (1991, 211). In addition, as suggested in the last chapter, both Christ and Marsyas have a prosaic double in the castrato: a doubling that is figured in this tale in the image of the Christ Child as 'Amor' in the chapel painting, recalling the blind, and therefore 'castrated' figure of Love in 'A Wedding Chest'.[32] Given the association between the castrato figure and Lee's lesbian sexuality, it would seem that the fusion between Sister Benvenuta and the Christ Child is more complex than a superficial reading might imply. It is a fusion that repeats a lesbian engagement with the maternal body both in Benvenuta's appropriation of the Madonna, and in a return to a pre-Oedipal symbiosis of lesbian desire figured through the castrato body implicit in the Christ Child. It appears that, in this tale, Lee manages to create a fantasy that fulfils the desire for the Madonna, and simultaneously shows that love returned. It is perhaps unsurprising, then, that the moment of fusion is represented as a moment of jouissance, figured in a flickering blaze of light reminiscent of *poikilos*: a phenomenon that, arguably, encodes homosexual desire.

Lee's negotiation of a sexual identity via the figure of the Virgin Mary may seem odd to those who are aware of her rejection of conventional religion. In *Baldwin* (1886), two dialogues, 'The Responsibilities of Unbelief' (which appeared in the *Contemporary* in 1883) and 'The Consolations of Belief', set out 'the reasons which led her to reject the Christian conception of God, and to replace the precepts of a theocentric ethics by those of what might be termed an evolutionary humanism' (Gunn 1964, 113). Despite this, however, Lee was to acknowledge the power that the Marian image held for her. In her introduction to *For Maurice: Five Unlikely Stories* (1927), Lee confesses:

> if I have anywhere in my soul a secret shrine, it is to Our Lady. Even I don't like living in places which her benignant effigy does not consecrate to sweet and noble thoughts. For is she not the divine Mother of Gods as well as God, Demeter or Mary, in whom the sad and ugly things of our bodily origin and nourishment are transfigured into the grace of the immortal spirit? (2006, 245).

Significantly, it is Mary's role in 'purifying' conception (therefore, by implication, sexual relations) and the physical engagement with the maternal body that appeals to Vernon Lee. It is only to be expected, then, that her ideal Madonna should be the Madonna who feeds her child from her breast bathed in a halo of immaculate divinity. Explaining to Maurice Baring the origins of her tale, 'The Virgin of the Seven Daggers', Lee expresses her aversion to Spanish Madonnas who do not fit this image:[33]

> And just in proportion to that natural devotion of mine to the Beloved Lady and Mother, Italian or High Dutch, who opens her scanty drapery to suckle a baby divinity, just in proportion did that aversion concentrate on those doll-madonnas in Spanish churches, all pomp and whalebone and sorrow and tears wept into Mechlin lace (2006, 246).

For Lee, these wax doll-madonnas, with their uncanny verisimilitude to the female body, are perhaps too disturbing as objects of adoration and reverence outside the realms of fantasy. Yet, her tale stages a metaphorical journey into this female and, more importantly, maternal body: a journey which once again figures subtle shifts in gender and a negotiation of sexual identity mediated, as in 'A Wedding Chest', via images of heterosexual desire.

'The Virgin of the Seven Daggers'

'The Virgin of the Seven Daggers' centres on Don Juan Gusman del Pulgar, Count of Miramor.[34] Like his legendary counterpart, Miramor is both 'conquering super-rake and super-ruffian', and is known for his sexual exploits and for the ensuing conflicts with husbands, fathers, and brothers that often end in murder (Lee 2006, 246). Don Juan's saving grace is his devotion to 'Our Lady of the Seven Daggers of Grenada [*sic*]', a doll-like effigy attired in tawdry splendour:

> Her skirts bulge out in melon-shaped folds, all damasked with minute heartsease, and brocaded with silver roses; the reddish shimmer of the gold wire, the bluish shimmer of the silver floss, blending into a strange melancholy hue without a definite name. Her body is cased like a knife in its sheath, the mysterious russet and violet of the silk made less definable still by the network of seed pearl, and the veils of delicate lace falling from head to waist. Her face, which surmounts rows upon rows of pearls, is made of wax, white with black glass eyes and a tiny coral mouth ... . Her head is crowned with a great jewelled crown; ... In her bodice, a little clearing is made among the brocade and the seed pearl, and into this are stuck seven gold-hilted knives (2006, 250).[35]

Sated by the pleasures of earthly women, Don Juan eventually seeks fulfilment in other-worldly realms, and asks the Virgin to protect him as he ventures illegally into the Alhambra in search of a sleeping Infanta and her treasures, both of which he aims to take using necromantic means. Employing the occult knowledge of an accomplice (whose assistance is rewarded with death), Don Juan succeeds in raising the spirit whose giant hand 'turned slowly in a secret lock the flag-shaped key engraven on the inside vault of the portal' (2006, 261). The lock and key imagery that precedes Don Juan's penetration of the Alhambra arguably defines this as a 'feminine' space and this image intensifies as Don Juan continues his journey:

> Don Juan Gusman del Pulgar plunged down a narrow corridor, as black as the shaft of a mine, following the little speck of reddish light which seemed to advance before him ... Underfoot, the ground was slippery with innumerable little snakes, who, instead of being crushed, just wriggled under the feet. The corridor was rendered even more gruesome by the fact that it was a strongly inclined plane, and that one seemed to be walking straight into a pit (2006, 261–262).

It is perhaps important that in this threatening female space, with its snakes that can't be crushed, Don Juan hears the plaintive whisperings of the lovers he has spurned and ruined. Like sirens they appear to lure him to the bottom of a shaft in which the reddish speck of light, reminiscent of the blood-red wound of the castrated woman, had meanwhile grown large. As Don Juan approaches the light it turns from red to white, and at the end of the constricting passageway a startled bird tears 'through the veil of vagueness which dimmed the outer light' revealing 'a stream of dazzling light' (2006, 263). For Don Juan it was as if 'a curtain had suddenly been drawn' and he issues, 'blind and dizzy, into the outer world' which he sees through 'singed' eyelids (2006, 263). Unveiled, the wound leads to blindness and, by association, figurative castration. The 'outer world' proves to be an inner courtyard:

> From the court Don Juan entered a series of arched and domed chambers, whose roofs [*sic*] were hung as with icicles of gold and silver, or incrusted with mother of pearl constellations which twinkled in the darkness, while the walls shone with patterns that seemed carved of ivory and pearl and beryl and amethyst where the sunbeams grazed them, or imitated some strange sea caves, filled with flitting colours, where the shadow rose fuller and higher (2006, 264).

The long passage that leads from these chambers to the Infanta is lined with 'a row of sleeping eunuchs' (2006, 264). The Infanta's chamber is 'a vast circular hall, so vast that you could not possibly see where it ended' in which she is attended, again, by 'rows and rows of white-robed eunuchs', and where 'innumerable voices of exquisite sweetness burst forth in strange wistful chants', filling the hall 'with sound, as it was already filled with light' (2006, 265). The Infanta herself is 'an unfinished statue' and doll-like in appearance recalling the Virgin of the Seven Daggers:

> From her head there descended on either side of her person a diaphanous veil of shimmering colours, powdered over with minute glittering spangles. Her breast was covered with rows and rows of the largest pearls, a perfect network reaching from her slender throat to her waist, among which flashed diamonds embroidered in her vest. Her face was oval, with the silver pallor of the young moon; her mouth most subtly carmined, looked like a pomegranate flower among tuberoses, for her cheeks were painted white, and the orbits of her great long-fringed eyes were stained violet (2006, 266–269).

Fuelled by desire, Don Juan begs the Infanta to 'Unveil and arise' that he might fix his affections upon her alone (2006, 267). The Infanta unveils, and raises 'her heavy eyelids, stained violet with henna' fixing upon Don Juan 'a glance long, dark and deep, like that of the wild antelope' and accepts his love only on the condition that he disavow his loyalty to the Virgin of the Seven Daggers (2006, 271). Don Juan refuses to deny his devotion to the latter and as he does so the Infanta and the Virgin merge in his imagination:

> The place seemed to swim about Don Juan. Before his eyes rose the throne, all vacillating in its splendour, and on the throne the Moorish Infanta with the triangular patterns painted on her tuberose cheeks, and the long look in her henna'd eyes; and the image of her was blurred, and imperceptibly it seemed to turn into the effigy, black and white in her stiff puce frock and seed-pearl stomacher, of the Virgin of the Seven Daggers (2006, 271).

Despite his request for the Virgin's protection, Don Juan is beheaded by the Infanta's chief eunuch. But Don Juan's spirit continues to roam the streets of Granada unaware of his death until he is confronted with his own decapitated body. The tale ends with Don Juan's successful plea for the Madonna's mediation. Although he dies unshriven with the full weight of his sins on his now headless shoulders, he appears to rise as if to heaven in full sight of the Madonna's benevolent eyes.

At this moment Don Juan conflates the image presented by the Infanta with the 'purifying' image of the Virgin of the Seven Daggers. Yet this conflation contaminates the latter, and the Infanta's domain with its fountains and strange, jewel-encrusted 'sea-caves' glinting with mother-of pearl, displays features which are themselves associated with Marian images that harbour erotic implications (Lee, 2006, 264).

Referring to Mariological symbols evident in medieval and renaissance texts, Vanita comments on the erotic connotations of images such as 'the garden, the fountain, the sun, and the singing phoenix' and tells us that these are often accompanied by 'those of flowers like the rose, the violet, the lily, of birds, ... and of gems, especially the pearl in the oyster' – the pearl suggesting 'both the child in the womb and the clitoris in the vulva' – in Mariological texts and paintings (1996, 50–51). Moreover, these symbols appear in writings of same-sex desire such as H.D.'s 'The Wise Sappho' in which, Vanita argues, 'rose, violet, lily, star, moon, jewel, shell, purple' are engaged 'to imagine Sappho and her world', and also occur in 'Notes on Thought and Vision', although here the central image is that of 'oyster and pearl' (1996, 255, n. 35).

Living in an underground paradise reminiscent of Villiers de L'Isle Adam's subterranean Eden in *L'Eve future* (*Tomorrow's Eve*) (1886), surrounded by images of 'maternal' caves and passages that are watered by fountains which, for Vanita, function as 'a major image of love between women', Lee's Infanta, for all her apparent youth, becomes a chthonian version of Pater's *La Gioconda*.[36] Her enigmatic beauty echoes that of the *Mona Lisa*, which is 'wrought out from within upon the flesh, the deposit, little cell by cell of strange thoughts and fantastic reveries and exquisite passions'; whose eyelids are also 'a little weary' (Pater 1986, 80). Like Pater's *Mona Lisa*, the Infanta appears to contain mysteries beyond her years, and to have been 'like the vampire ... dead many times' thus learning 'the secrets of the grave' (Pater 1986, 80).[37] The resemblance between Lee's Infanta and Pater's *La Gioconda* adds new significance to the conflation of the Infanta and the Virgin of the Seven Daggers in Lee's text for between them they create a nexus of female images in which mother is indistinguishable from daughter. The animation of the Infanta, 'an unfinished statue', aligns her with Helen of Troy, that 'semi-vivified statue' who, in Lee's *Belcaro*, as we have seen in Chapter Two, is herself associated with the doll (Lee 2006, 316). Yet, in her affinity with Pater's *La Gioconda*, who, for Freud, 'is the transformation of the image of the desired mother', the Infanta is also Leda, Helen's mother, and St Anne, the Virgin's mother (quoted in Gregory 1997, 104; Pater, 1986, 80).

These relationships echo the mother/daughter model of the women in Lee's tale for the Infanta is, literally speaking, an 'infant' and the Virgin is the universal mother: a model which in 'Pater's mythmaking ... is the type of love and desire between women' (Vanita 1996, 68). What is particularly interesting about this relationship is that as their images coalesce, the mother/child roles become indistinct, once again recalling traditional models of lesbian love and pre-Oedipal fusion. Moreover, the homoerotic connotations of the Infanta (the Virgin's subterranean double) are figured not only in the *poikilos* phenomenon – the 'opalescent radiance', the 'glittering spangles' and flashing diamonds, that veil her and echo the 'shimmering colours' worn by the Virgin – but also in the very language that describes her, for the words, 'exquisite', 'strange', 'subtly', 'mysterious', that surround both the Infanta and the Virgin, are akin to those which, in Pater's work, appear to encode homoeroticism (Vanita 1996, 66).

Significantly, the words used by a young Vernon Lee and John Singer Sargent to describe a portrait of the castrato Farinelli in the Accademia Filarmonica in Bologna, quoted in Chapter One, are similar in tone and implication. Farinelli, if we recall, is 'mysterious, uncanny, a wizard, serpent, sphinx; strange, weird, *curious*' and, castration seemingly haunts Lee's tale the 'Virgin of the Seven Daggers' and manifests itself both literally, in the eunuchs that protect the Infanta, and figuratively in Don Juan's decapitation (Lee 1927, xxx). The Infanta's eunuchs are subtly doubled in 'Syphax, His Majesty's own soprano singer' whose voice can be heard in the church of the Virgin of the Seven Daggers both as Don Juan initially begs for the Virgin's protection, and as he rises to meet her after her seemingly successful intercession at the end of the tale (2006, 252). Although not explicitly stated, it is evident that Syphax is a castrato. Lee's tale is set 'two hundred years ago' in the reign of 'Charles the Melancholy', Charles II of Spain (1661–1700), the king who immediately precedes Philip V of Spain who reigned from 1700–1746 and suffered from melancholia assuaged by Farinelli's dulcet tones (2006, 251).[38]

Given the 'exquisite sweetness' of the voices heard in the Infanta's domain it is likely that they emanate from Syphax's counterparts: the white-robed eunuchs who protect her (2006, 265). I suggest that the presence of the castrato in this tale is worth noting and represents castration both physically and psychoanalytically. In Chapter One I established a connection between the castrato and the Medusa via the gorgonian cry, yet there is also a psychic link between them in that, for Freud, Medusa functions as a significant psychoanalytical model of castration predicated, we may recall, on the formulation 'To decapitate: to castrate' (1955, XVIII, 273). The unveiled Infanta, who lives in a threatening maternal space inhabited by snakes and eunuchs, and is the dark double of that Great Mother, the Virgin, reveals a castrative power which is, like Medusa's, centred in her gaze, for it is her glance, 'long, dark, and deep' that causes Don Juan to link her to the Virgin of the Seven Daggers to whom he has pledged his loyalty: an act of faith that results ultimately in his decapitation (2006, 271). At this point in the tale, Don Juan becomes a symbolic 'castrato': Syphax's ghostly counterpart. Although Don Juan's dismemberment occurs towards the end of Lee's tale, his decapitation is prefigured much earlier. When Don Juan springs from his bed (presumably the site of amorous conquests), we learn that that it is 'curtained with dull, blood-coloured damask' (2006, 254). Paintings of his ancestors show them 'with their foot on a Moor's decollated head, much resembling a hairdresser's block' (2006, 256).

As the sun sets over the Sierra, it leaves 'a trail of blood' (foreshadowing the trail Don Juan himself will leave in due course) that turns 'the snows of Mulhacen a livid, bluish blood-red, and [leaves] all along the lower slopes of the Sierra wicked russet stains, as of the rust of blood upon marble' (2006, 257). Given the existing links between the castrato and Christ, one might also argue that the images of 'waxen Christs with bloody wounds and spangled loin-cloths' in the church of the Virgin of the Seven Daggers, serve as doubles of Lee's marked and naked women, like Maddalena and the Snake Lady, thus further blurring the boundaries of gender in her tale and linking the castrato to the wounded and 'castrated' female body (Lee 2006, 250).

Here, as in 'A Wedding Chest', the three main characters in Lee's tale, Don Juan, the Virgin, and the Infanta, function as facets of Vernon Lee's sexual identity that coalesce via unexpected identifications. The Infanta, stained with colour and bearing a Medusa-like stare, represents a dangerous lesbian eroticism.[39] She is the female love-object that is sanctioned in the tale via Don Juan's heterosexual desire. Don Juan, a famous lover of women, is now symbolically castrated, and inhabits an androgynous body that is neither man nor woman. His heterosexual desire for the Infanta is therefore complicated and arguably homoeroticized. In the tale, Don Juan rejects the dangerous engagement with the Infanta's body in favour of an ideal and spiritual love for the Virgin. Yet, as we have seen, the Virgin's purity is compromised when she blurs into the Infanta in Don Juan's perception. As a result, she, too, becomes Medusa-like, a figure that is 'charged with a profound sensuality and physicality that cannot be purged from her matriarchal origins' (Bowers 1990, 219). Moreover, the end of Lee's tale, an ending which seemingly stages Don Juan's ascension to Heaven, is heavy with imagery that suggests a return to the maternal womb: 'The cupola began to rise and expand; the painted clouds to move and blush a deeper pink ... [and] the gold transparency at the top of the dome expanded; its rays grew redder and redder and more golden' (2006, 277). At its centre is the Virgin of the Seven Daggers, her maternal eyes 'fixed mildly upon him' as she accepts him (2006, 277). This description resonates with that of the Infanta's womb-like domain for here, as there, the place is filled 'with [the] sounds of exquisitely played lutes and viols, and voices', among which Don Juan recognizes 'Syphax, His Majesty's chief soprano' (2006, 277). It is Don Juan the 'castrato' who finally enters the desired female body, and it is the now 'asexual' Don Juan who is to remain there in eternal pre-Oedipal fusion with the mother.

Unlike Lee's tales of animated statues in which desire is contained within the statue itself, Lee's 'doll' stories appear to explore fantasies of desire experienced from different sexual viewpoints. In 'A Wedding Chest', Troilo, with his boyish features that, according to Vicinus, link him with lesbian desire, kills Maddalena, which, if we consider the association between the corpse and the doll traced earlier, effectively makes her body doll-like; her dangerous allure controlled but implicit in the bloody marks that stain her skin. Desiderio's love for Maddalena suggests an idealized heterosexual desire, yet for all Lee's attempts to 'sanitize' the object of that desire, Desiderio's introjection of Troilo undermines that purification and reinscribes the homosexual eroticism of the Troilo-Maddalena duo. Moreover, the name 'Desiderio', meaning literally 'a desire', implies that the complex interactions between the three characters in the tale are expressive of same-sex desire mediated via their male and female bodies.[40] In 'Sister Benvenuta and the Christ Child', the desire for the mother, and the desire to be the child loved by her, is negotiated via a fluidity of identity that allows an oscillation between the two relationships, and these shifts of identification are also discernible in 'The Virgin of the Seven Daggers', which, though ostensibly presenting a tale of heterosexual desire and devotion, is implicitly homoerotic. These tales suggest the particularly complicated nature of female same-sex desire in which identities are unavoidably conflated, and in which, traditionally, the roles of mother and child are perceived as interchangeable. In order to highlight the complexity of Lee's negotiation of identity within this framework, I wish to examine the figure of the doll as it occurs in the writings of two male writers, E.T.A. Hoffmann's 'The Sandman' and Villiers de L'Isle Adam's *L'Eve future* (*Tomorrow's Eve*).

'The Sandman' and L'Eve future' (Tomorrow's Eve)

Hoffmann's tale centres on Nathaniel, a university student of nervous disposition whose chance encounter with Giuseppe Copolla, a dealer in barometers and optical instruments, triggers memories of a childhood trauma. For Nathaniel, Coppola is the double of Coppelius, an aged advocate who regularly visited Nathaniel's home and conducted strange and secret experiments in partnership with his father, and who was implicated in the latter's death. In Nathaniel's young mind Coppelius is conflated with the mythical sandman who throws handfuls of sand in children's eyes, 'so that they jump out of their heads all bloody' (Hoffmann, 1982, 86). Nathaniel's fear of Coppola leads to illness and he returns home to his mother and to his fiancée, Clara, to recover. Yet his anxieties persist, manifesting themselves in stories and poems in one of which Coppelius appears and touches Clara's eyes, which spring out 'like blood-red sparks, singeing and burning, on to Nathaniel's breast' (Hoffman 1982, 105). This throws Nathaniel into a circle of fire from which he hears Clara's voice saying, 'Do you not see me? ... I still have my eyes; you have only to look at me!' but when he looks into Clara's eyes, what he sees is death gazing mildly out of them (Hoffmann, 1982, 105).

Eventually, apparently well again, Nathaniel returns to lodgings in the university town, situated opposite the Professor Spalanzani's home, from which he observes Spalanzani's daughter, Olympia, whom he has seen briefly once before, who sits 'for hours on end ... in the same posture' and gazes at him 'with an unmoving stare'; still in love with Clara, Nathaniel resists the beautiful Olympia's charms, only now and then glancing 'fleetingly over his book across to the beautiful statue' (Hoffmann, 1982, 108–109). During this period, Coppola reappears and tries to sell Nathaniel some glasses which he calls 'occe' in his native Piedmontese, but Nathaniel misinterprets the word 'occe' as 'eyes', causing his fears to resurface, and Coppola and Coppelius blur once more in Nathaniel's imagination. In order to placate Coppola, Nathaniel purchases a pocket-telescope which he uses to take a closer look at Olympia. Beholding Olympia's beauty clearly for the first time, Nathaniel is enthralled and from this moment Olympia replaces Clara in his affections. Nathaniel finally meets her officially at a ball where they dance together and, as they do so, the previously motionless Olympia is seemingly animated by Nathaniel's desire:

> Olympia's hand was icy cold; he felt a coldness as of death thrill through him; he looked into Olympia's eyes, which gazed back at him full of love and desire; and at that instant it seemed as though a pulse began to beat in the cold hand and a stream of life blood began to glow (Hoffmann 1982, 113–14).

Despite the fact that fellow students judge Olympia to be 'a wax-faced wooden doll' that is 'rigid and soulless', who plays and sings with the 'regularity of a machine', Nathaniel is totally smitten (1982, 116). He visits her regularly and reads her his creative works to which she listens with apparent rapture and, to Nathaniel, it seems that what Olympia says of his work, 'of his poetic talent in general ... [comes] from the depths of his own being, that her voice was indeed the voice of those very depths themselves' (1982, 118). However, Nathaniel's happiness is shortlived for he soon discovers the awful truth, that Olympia is a doll, an automaton constructed by Spalanzani and Coppola: the latter supplying the clockwork mechanism and, more importantly, her eyes. He witnesses Spalanzani and Coppola physically struggling for possession of Olympia, and Coppola finally leaves Spalanzani's home with the doll trailing lifelessly over his shoulder. Nathaniel catches sight of her now mangled body, and a hideous sight is revealed for 'Olympia's deathly-white face possessed no eyes: where the eyes should have been, there were only pits of blackness' (1982, 119–120). The discovery triggers Nathaniel's insanity and it is only much later, after careful tending by 'his mother, his loved ones and his friends' that he recovers (1982, 122). But, once again, his recovery is only temporary. On a visit into town, Nathaniel and Clara climb the town hall tower where he takes out Coppola's pocket-telescope for a better view, and as he looks through the glass he sees Clara standing before it. The parallel drawn between Clara and Olympia is fatal and he tries to throw Clara from the tower. She is saved, but for Nathaniel there is no relief and he hurls himself to the ground.

Tomorrow's Eve is clearly indebted to Hoffmann's tale, a debt that is tacitly acknowledged early in the text by the epigraph from 'The Sandman' that opens the second chapter in Book One of Villiers's *fin-de-siècle* novel (2001, 8). In addition, as Michelle Bloom observes, Alicia Clary, the woman who serves as the model for the doll in this story, bears a surname that 'recalls that of Hoffmann's Clara' (2000, 301). However, while Nathaniel is an unwitting victim of Spalanzani's and Coppola's machinations, Lord Ewald, for whom Edison creates a simulacrum of his lover Alicia Clary, is a knowing participant in the drama that unfolds. On a visit to the renowned American inventor Edison (a fictional version of Thomas Edison (1847–1931)), Ewald confesses a dilemma that he feels can only be resolved through suicide.[41] He tells Edison that he is a prisoner of his own desire. Alicia's body is sublime: 'Her figure is full, but with the pale glow of lilies; she has … the splendor of a *Venus Victorious*, but humanized' and her voice hypnotic: 'When she speaks, the resonance of Miss Alicia's voice is so penetrating, the notes of her singing voice are so vibrant and so profound' that Ewald trembles with admiration (2001, 30).[42] Yet, what she says continually undermines her beauty: her tastes are bourgeois; her conversation banal and her thoughts cannot, as he wishes, become 'the reflection' of his own (2001, 30). Convinced that it is in his nature 'to love only once', Ewald is compelled to desire a woman whose character he abhors, and asks, 'Who will deliver this soul out of this body for me?' (2001, 48, 44). Edison offers to do just that, giving Ewald the chance to possess Hadaly, a form of sophisticated 'android' whose exterior can be moulded to double Alicia's, and whose voice will be a recorded reproduction of Alicia's own.

After a long, and misogynistic deliberation on the nature of 'real' and 'ideal' woman, that includes a digression on the artificiality of feminine beauty embodied in a fatal woman named Evelyn Habal whose body is stripped of make-up and padding to reveal the horror beneath, Ewald accepts Edison's proposition. Alicia is encouraged, under false pretences, to model for a sculpture and, as Marie Lathers notes, to record the 'unpublished words of [male] nineteenth-century poets, metaphysicians, and novelists' (Lathers 2001, 217). These provide the foundations for Hadaly's body and soul. Once Hadaly is complete, she appears to Ewald as Alicia. For a moment he is convinced that she *is* Alicia transformed, and asks himself: 'was I out of my mind? I was dreaming of a sacrilege, a plaything, a puppet … . A ridiculous, senseless doll' before discovering that the being before him is in fact the very 'doll' he was about to reject (2001, 192). Woman and doll have become indistinguishable. Disturbed, Ewald briefly refuses Hadaly, but is swiftly persuaded by her eloquence and seals his fate when he states 'it's clear to me that set one beside the other, and it's the living girl who is the phantom!' (2001, 204). Hadaly is to be transported to England by ship in 'a long and splendid coffin of black ebony' on which her name is inscribed; its interior lined with 'black satin which exactly modelled a feminine form', but before Ewald can possess her, the steamer on which Ewald, Alicia and Hadaly are travelling sinks and both Alicia and Hadaly are lost at sea (2001, 204).

While Hoffmann's Olympia may be an early prototype of Hadaly, it is clear that the latter's sophisticated construction exceeds that of the simple automaton. Edison makes her superiority apparent. He calls those who produced earlier automata 'Poor fellows' whose 'ridiculous monsters' are 'outrageous caricatures' of humanity that 'deserve to be exhibited in the most hideous of wax museums' (2001, 61). In contrast, Hadaly, as 'Android', is more than 'An Imitation Human Being', she is, as Edison tells Ewald, 'an Apparition whose HUMAN likeness and charm will surpass your wildest hopes, your most intimate dreams!' (2001 63). In Villiers's text, Hadaly (whose name, according to Edison, means 'the IDEAL' in Iranian (2001, 76)) embodies the ambivalence of men towards women. When she first appears to Ewald, emerging from an alcove where she is exhibited on a dais, she presents an unfathomable presence:

> Standing on this dais, a sort of BEING appeared, its form suggestive of nothing so much as the *unknown*. The vision seemed to have features compounded of shadow; a string of pearls across her forehead supported a dark veil which obscured the entire lower part of her head. A coat of armor, shaped as for a woman out of silver plates, glowed with a soft radiance. Closely molded to the figure, with a thousand perfect nuances, it suggested elegant and virginal forms. The trailing ends of the veil twined around the neck over the metal gorget, then, tossed back over the shoulders, were knotted behind her back; thence they fell to the waist of the apparition like a flowing head of long hair, finally dropping to the ground, where they were lost in shadow. A scarf of black batiste was knotted about her waist like a loincloth, and trailed across her legs a line of black fringe into which brilliants had been sewn. Within the folds of this veil was visible the glittering blade of a drawn dagger. The vision rested her right hand on the handle of this poniard, while her left hand, hanging by her side, held a golden flower. On all the fingers of her hands glittered rings set with various stones; they seemed to be fastened to her fine gloves (2001, 57–58).

In this description Hadaly is mysterious and alluring. She shares her 'disquieting beauty' with Vauthier's *Gallia*, and Frampton's *Lamia*, whose images, composed of metal and ivory, elicit a fantasy of erotic animation; with Lee's Virgin and Infanta in 'The Virgin of the Seven Daggers' both of whom are similarly veiled and adorned with jewels; and her spectral presence is reminiscent of Goethe's Helen who simultaneously represents statue, 'doll' and ghost. As a 'Being in Limbo', Hadaly is both like Anne Brown, and Pygmalion's Galatea, and such pristine sculptural bodies served as Enlightenment models for understanding the development of self-consciousness.[43] In *The Treatise of Sensations* (1754), the French philosopher Étienne Bonnot de Condillac uses the awakening statue as a means of exploring self-development and knowledge through the senses, a concept which, at that time, seemed especially feasible. Framed by eighteenth-century theories of sensibility, Condillac's experiment ensured that his statue gained use of the senses one by one, and his argument, as Annette Michelson explains, suggested that 'Sense is sensibility. *To feel is to think*' (1984, 19). In Villiers's novel, Ewald asks Edison whether his creature 'will be capable of self-awareness', to which the latter replies emphatically: 'No doubt about it!' and Michelson observes that the systematic process through which Edison endows his android with human function and 'existence' is reminiscent of Condillac's experiment (Villiers 2001, 67; Michelson 1984, 19). It is worth noting that, as Hadaly 'becomes' Alicia, she is also becoming, like Galatea, a vivified statue, for Alicia is the living image of the *Venus de Milo*. Yet, as noted earlier in this chapter, the statue has much in common with both the doll and the corpse, associations that become particularly evident during Edison's 'dissection' of Hadaly's 'body'. In Chapter One of Book V, Edison shows Ewald how Hadaly is constructed, dividing the android into 'four major parts': 'The living system of the interior'; 'The plastic mediator ... the metallic envelope which isolates the inner spaces from the epidermis and the flesh'; 'The flesh'; and 'The epidermis or human skin' (2001, 129). As Michelson remarks, in this description 'We are reminded of those medical drawings and anatomical models with layered articulations of nervous, digestive, and circulatory systems' (1984, 11). The bejewelled Hadaly whose 'natural' home is a coffin lined with black satin, is reminiscent of the anatomical Venus and therefore of the corpse. Edison's demonstration therefore becomes a form of 'autopsy', signifying a sexual and scientific 'penetration' of Hadaly thus reinscribing masculine power over the female body.

Guys and Dolls

What characterizes these works and separates them from those of Lee's I have discussed so far is that, in each case, the doll is destroyed. In contrast to the dismembered doll-remains that physically litter the stories of Hoffmann and Villiers, Lee's dolls are left intact: Maddalena's doll-like body is preserved, Sister Benvenuta becomes a divine 'doll-statue' in a tableau of religious union, and Don Juan's Virgin doll retains her immaculate perfection. However, the question one must ask is why? In Villiers's story as in Hoffmann's, the anxieties surrounding the doll centre on female autonomy. While Olympia murmurs an appreciative, 'orgasmic', yet empty, 'Ah, Ah, Ah' in response to Nathaniel, she is a 'beam of light from the Promised Land of love', a 'heart' in which his 'whole being is reflected' (Hoffmann 1982, 114). Similarly, it is because Alicia Clary does not adequately reflect Ewald's image of himself that she must be replaced by the android, Hadaly, who will: Ewald, like Nathaniel, seeks an 'objectified projection' of his own soul (Villiers 2001, 66). In other words, as long as these dolls perform the role of the Romantic epipsyche propounded in Shelley's 'On Love', being that 'soul within our soul,' that 'mirror whose surface reflects only the forms of purity and brightness', they can be sure of their suitors' undying loyalty and affection (1977, 474). In Hoffmann's text, contemporaneous with Shelley's 'Alastor' (1816), Olympia arguably represents a prosaic alternative to the veiled maid of Alastor's poetic vision whose 'voice was like the voice of his own soul' (1973, 404, l. 153). Edison promises Ewald a similarly undemanding companion: 'the Being called Hadaly depends on the free will of him who DARE to conceive it. *Suggest it to her from the depths of your self!*' (Villiers 2001, 68).

For each man the doll is an epipsychic figure that Maxwell describes as a 'device that completes [his] ... lack, simultaneously reflecting him back to himself in a reassuring fullness': a function which was once fulfilled for them by the mother for, as Winnicott argues, when a baby looks at its mother's face, 'ordinarily what the baby sees is himself or herself' (1993, 989; 1971, 112). Winnicott goes on to point out, however, that some babies have a long experience of not getting back what they are giving: they look and they do not see themselves' (1971, 112). In denying the reality of Nathaniel's anxieties concerning the sandman, Clara would seem to serve as a 'mirror' in which he cannot see himself reflected for her thoughts are different from his own. Similarly, it is the 'absolute *disparity*' between Alicia Clary's body and soul, a soul that fails to reflect his own, that determines Ewald's fate (Villiers 2001, 31). It is woman, then, or more especially, the mother, who is the cause of anxiety. Without the mother's reassuring look, the child's 'creative capacity begins to atrophy', and it looks around 'for other ways of getting something of [itself] back from the environment' (Winnicott 1971, 112).

Interestingly, in Hoffmann's 'The Sandman' we actually encounter Nathaniel's mother, who also denies the sandman's existence, as Clara does later. In denying Nathaniel's fears, it would seem that she, like Clara, does not function as a suitable 'mirror'. Although in *Tomorrow's Eve* we do not meet Ewald's mother, we can perhaps assume that she is the fundamental source of those anxieties which are later triggered by Alicia, as in stating that it is his character 'to love only once', he is implicitly acknowledging that she must function as a permanent replacement for his original love for his mother (Villiers 2001, 44). In order to reflect reassuringly, the doll must 'see' the man she is to reflect and show signs of animation. When Nathaniel looks into Olympia's eyes, they 'gazed back at him full of love and desire' and 'at that instant it seemed as though a pulse began to beat in the cold hand and stream of life blood began to glow' (Hoffmann 1982, 114). Ewald is initially concerned that Hadaly cannot see, but Edison reassures him that her artificial eyes will provide the illusion that she can. Showing Ewald a box of eyes from which Hadaly's will be selected, Edison exclaims:

> Here now, are some eyes that would put to shame the gazelles of the vale of Nourmahal; they are jewels, gifted with a white so pure, a pupil so deep, that they are really upsetting – don't you find them so? The art of the great oculists has gone far beyond Nature in our time. The solemnity of these eyes gives one, actually, the sense of a soul behind them (Villiers 2001, 159).

The association between the doll and the eye as centres of reflection is perhaps less perverse than it might initially seem for in dialogue with Plato's Alcibiades, Socrates observes that:

the face of the person who looks into another's eye is shown in the optic confronting him, as in a mirror, and we call this the pupil, for in a sort it is an image of the person looking ... . Then an eye viewing another eye, and looking at the most perfect part of it, the thing wherewith it sees, will thus see itself (Plato 1927, 210–211).

Plato's text includes the editors' explanatory footnote for the word 'pupil' which stems from the Greek word kore [κορή] and the Latin word 'pupilla', both of which are defined as 'little girl' or 'doll' (Plato 1927, 210–211, n. 1). It is the eye, then, or more specifically the pupil, that functions as the mirror. Yet eyes, as we have seen, can themselves be a source of anxiety and are particularly so for Nathaniel in 'The Sandman'. From Freud's analysis of 'The Sandman' in his essay 'The "Uncanny"', we learn that eyes, and particularly the fear of losing one's sight, are a source of castration-anxiety linked to the boy's first sight of the mother's 'wounded' genitals. But why should the sight of the mother's genitals be equated with blindness? One possible answer may lie in a desire for blindness that the disturbing vision might remain unseen. Yet blindness itself, especially as it occurs in 'The Sandman' where eyes are torn from their sockets, evokes an image of redundant hollows that echo the 'wound' that marks the 'castrated' Freudian female body. It is also important to remember that the 'pupil' (or 'doll'), in which Nathaniel and Ewald see their self-images, is also literally a hole, one that mirrors the maternal fissure. If this is the case then, as dolls, Olympia and Hadaly cannot be divorced from a connection with lack or castration. Nathaniel's first encounter with Olympia is particularly telling:

> Recently I went upstairs in Professor Spalanzani's house and perceived that a curtain which was always drawn tight across a glass door up there was showing a chink of light ... . A woman, tall, very slim, perfectly proportioned and gorgeously dressed, sat in the room at a little table, with her arms lying upon it and her hands folded ... . She seemed not to notice me, and her eyes had in general something fixed and staring about them, I could almost say she was sightless, as if she was sleeping with her eyes open (Hoffmann 1982, 98–99).

In this moment of unveiling what is revealed is a 'sightless' figure, and what is disclosed to Nathaniel is a figuratively 'castrated' woman, a double to Lee's 'sightless and speechless' doll. The experience makes him 'feel quite uncanny' (Hoffman 1982, 99) suggesting an awareness of his anxiety. In *Tomorrow's Eve*, Hadaly is equally sightless and it is interesting that while every detail of her internal and external body is discussed, her sexual organs are merely intimated. As a fetishized ideal, Hadaly must replace and occlude the dangerous and castrating femininity of women such as Evelyn Habal. Yet, Hadaly herself is potentially equally treacherous. As Edison acknowledges, he cannot be fully sure that his creation is benign: 'Nobody can see the real character of what he creates because every knife blade may become a dagger, and *the use to which an object is put changes both its name and its nature*' (Villiers 2001, 62). The analogy Edison makes between Hadaly and the blade of a knife is apt: she carries a dagger in her belt and, as Edison tells Ewald, 'It's a weapon that no man could possibly parry, and every blow it deals is mortal' (Villiers 2001, 83). In possession of this dagger, Hadaly is, in effect, a phallic woman: both reassuring and dangerous. Moreover, in appropriating Alicia's 'contralto' tones, and projecting them from her artificial body, her 'hauntingly beautiful voice' blends 'a seductive feminine charm with the strange fascination of a transcendently inhuman being', recalling Zaffirino's similarly disturbing castrato voice (Villiers 2001, 173, Frank 1995, 153–154).

In 'The Sandman', woman and doll are conflated. Clara's rejection of Nathaniel's work results in his declaring her a 'lifeless accursed automaton' (Hoffmann 1982, 106), his fragile ego demanding that Clara become the doll and Olympia the real woman, and earlier references to Clara as 'cold' and 'unfeeling' imply that she and Olympia are doubles. In *Tomorrow's Eve*, Hadaly's ability to transform, or be transformed into an endless variety of female 'types' constructs her as 'everywoman', whilst inevitably presenting her as a male fantasy, thus forcing her to occupy an uneasy position between woman and doll. However, around the figures of the doll and the woman lurks the shadow of the mother, and the threat of castration that is present in one is evidently still present in each of the others. Certainly Nathaniel's tale, in which Clara's eyes are gouged by Coppelius, prefigures the episode in which he discovers the eyeless Olympia. In Nathaniel's story Clara tells him, 'I still have my eyes; you have only to look at me!' but when Nathaniel looks into her eyes he sees the same mild look that Don Juan sees in the eyes of the Virgin of the Seven Daggers, a look that in Nathaniel's case prefigures death (Hoffmann 1982, 105). That Nathaniel perceives Clara as a threat is expressed in his fiction and manifests itself in the madness that later overwhelms him when he discovers the corresponding 'pits of blackness' that exist where Olympia's eyes once were: a discovery which recalls not only the anxiety of castration, but also the vaginal fissure of maternal engulfment (Hoffmann 1982, 120). It would seem that, for Nathaniel, as suggested in the work of Luce Irigaray, 'the openness of the mother ... the opening on to the mother' does indeed result in 'engulfment in illness, madness, and death' (1991, 40).

The demise of both Alicia Clary and Hadaly in *Tomorrow's Eve* signals, perhaps, a more prosaic anxiety regarding the ideal construction of femininity. As Jennifer Forrest notes, Villiers's novel forms part of a larger late nineteenth-century debate, one to which, as indicated at the beginning of this chapter, Vernon Lee also contributed:

> *L'Eve future* [*Tomorrow's Eve*] (1886) joins other literary works from the nineteenth century that dramatize the effort to physically reproduce, if not an entire woman, then fragments of women. The proliferation of artificial women in these novels firmly situates the central debate of *L'Eve future* within a particular socio-historical configuration of woman disseminated during the last half of the nineteenth century. In that configuration, an active redefinition of woman's social role often gets entangled with the advent of a middle-class and industrial economy (1996, 18).

Representing an active independence (Alicia) and a potentially draining passive parasitism (Hadaly), neither woman in Villiers's novel can be allowed to live. Similarly, in 'The Sandman' when the active and independent Clara blurs with the passive doll Olympia before his very eyes, Nathaniel seeks her death and attempts to throw her from the tower. It seems that women, in whatever form, are potentially dangerous. Hoffmann and Villiers exhibit an apparently 'traditional' male response to this threat: their dolls, Olympia and Hadaly, are destroyed, enacting a literal destruction of the doll's body that is figuratively repeated in Freud's obliteration of the doll from the surface rhetoric of 'The "Uncanny"'. However, there is one tale by Lee in which the figure of the doll is also destroyed although, as we shall see, for very different reasons from those of Hoffmann, Freud, and Villiers de L'Isle Adam.

'The Image'

The doll in question appears in a short story entitled simply 'The Image', published initially in the *Cornhill Magazine* in 1896 and later renamed and included in the collection, *For Maurice: Five Unlikely Stories,* under the title 'The Doll'.[44] Here, the doll is no longer hidden in the realms of the fantastic tale. Lee claims in the introduction to *For Maurice* that the story was told to her by Pier Desiderio Pasolini, a friend she shared with Maurice Baring, and references to it also appear in *Hortus Vitae: Essays on the Gardening of Life* (1904, 144).[45] The origin of the tale is nevertheless unclear: Lee claims: 'it is not by me at all, nor do I know whether it is by anybody, or, so to speak, a natural product', but what *is* certain is that it was Lee who added 'that little invented *finale* of the burning' (Lee 1927, xlv, 1). Unusually for Lee, the first-person narrator is a woman, and the mention of a telegram situates the tale, like Villiers's novel, in a relatively modern, post mid-nineteenth-century setting rather than in some distant past. The narrator discovers the eponymous doll accidentally while visiting a seventeenth-century palace in Italy, a visit arranged by a curiosity dealer by the name of Orestes, and initially mistakes it for 'a woman in 1820 [*sic*] costume' (1896, 518). Dressed 'to the utmost detail', the doll wears 'open-work silk stockings, with sandal shoes, and long silk embroidered mittens' (1896, 518). On her second visit the narrator observes, 'The clothes which she wore were the real clothes of her poor dead original. And when I found on the table a dusty, unkempt wig, with straight bands in front and an elaborate jug handle of curls behind, I knew at once that it was made of the poor lady's real hair' (1896, 519).[46] We learn that the doll had been modelled on an Italian Count's wife who died only two years after her marriage. Subsequent to her death he had the doll made for him 'from a picture' and spent several hours with it every day (1896, 519).

For the female narrator there is an immediate, if uneasy, bond with the doll:

> I don't know what that Doll had done to me; but I found that I was thinking of her all day long. It was as if I had just made a new acquaintance of a painfully interesting kind, rushed into a sudden friendship with a woman whose secret I had surprised, as sometimes happens, by some mere accident. For I somehow knew everything about her, and the first items of information which I gained from Orestes ... did not enlighten me in the least, but merely confirmed what I was aware of (1896, 520).

She tells us that, married straight from the convent, the young Countess had been kept in isolation by a possessive husband 'so that she had remained a mere shy, proud, inexperienced child' (1896, 520). In Lee's tale, the doll, like the Infanta and the Virgin of the Seven Daggers, is composed of a nexus of female images. Like Hadaly, she is a work of art which is doll, sculpture and portrait all at once bearing a 'Canova goddess or Ingres Madonna face' (1896, 520). She is arguably both 'child' and 'mother' to her husband who, like Hoffmann's Nathaniel, 'knew nothing of the feelings of others and cared only to welter and dissolve in his own' (1896, 520). In all their years of marriage he never attempted to discover 'whether his idol might have a mind or character of her own', and she is condemned to a silence which is merely repeated in death (1896, 520). Her counterpart, the doll, becoming increasingly superfluous during the Count's second marriage, is eventually discarded and forgotten in his old age. For the narrator, however, the doll is not so easily forgotten. 'Couldn't abandon the Doll' she writes, 'I couldn't leave her, with the hole in her poor cardboard head, with the Ingres Madonna features gathering dust in that filthy old woman's ironing-room' (1896, 522). Enlisting Orestes' help, the narrator purchases the doll only to burn her. On her 'funeral' pyre, the doll seems to come alive momentarily: 'Her black fixed eyes stared as in wonder on the yellow vines and reddening peach trees, the sparkling dewy grass of the vineyard, upon the blue morning sunshine, the misty blue amphitheatre of the mountains all round' (1896, 523). Her final gaze on the world is sweet but brief, for her pyre is soon set alight:

> Orestes struck a match and slowly lit a pine cone with it; when the cone was blazing he handed it silently to me. The dry bay and myrtle blazed up crackling, with a fresh resinous odour; the image was veiled in flame and smoke. In a few seconds the flame sank, the smouldering faggots crumbled. The image was gone. Only where she had been, there remained in the embers something small and shiny. Orestes raked it out and handed it to me. It was a wedding ring of old-fashioned shape, which had been hidden under the silk mitten. 'Keep it signora,' said Orestes; 'you have put an end to her sorrows' (1896, 523).

As Mary Patricia Kane observes, this tale 'could be said to rewrite Olympia's story in 'The Sandman' casting 'Nathaniel's analogue, the Count', like Ewald, as an 'active participant' in the creation of an ideal woman adapted to 'the masculine imagination' (2004, 109). The doll's role within the tale appears to have been much like that of Olympia and Hadaly, functioning as a replacement both for the real woman, (the Countess), and for the mother in whose eyes the young Count would originally have seen himself reflected. Having never achieved a level of autonomy, the Countess, like the doll, is non-threatening and is therefore, once dead, reconstructed in full in her counterpart. In negotiating the Count's separation from his wife in death, the doll is arguably what Carol T. Christ refers to as a 'funerary monument – a kind of mourning work – [which] undoes the bodily dissolution that is the work of death' (1995, 392). The doll, wearing the Countess's clothes, and her natural hair, is part auto-icon: an idol constructed of the very thing it represents. It is particularly significant that she wears the Countess's hair for, as Christ observes, 'Hair seems to be the feature of the dead body ... frequently used as a synedoche for the intact corpse; indeed, as such, it often functions as a screen for the decaying body' (1995, 398).

Lee's doll, then, is related to Maddalena, to Julia, the Emperor's daughter, and, with her 'Ingres Madonna face' is undoubtedly linked to both Sister Benvenuta and the Virgin of the Seven Daggers. Yet, as Navarette points out, she is also essentially a 'memento mori, a "reminder" of death', and it is perhaps because of this that she is relegated to limbo as the Count marries his new wife; but on Lee's narrator she has a quite different effect (1998, 158). What is particularly intriguing in her response, is the instinctive understanding she senses between herself and the doll.

Ostensibly, this is because the doll epitomizes the still, silent, and subordinate position that characterized the expected position of women living in a patriarchal society – no distinction being made between the portrait and the original – that the narrator 'knows all about the doll's life ... because she has lived that life' (Navarette 1998, 173). However, it seems to me that this is too simplistic; that the nature of the narrator's identification with the doll is far more complicated. I suggest that this complexity is implied in the language used to describe the narrator's affinity with the doll. After seeing the doll, she thinks of her 'all day long'; their acquaintance is 'of a painfully interesting kind'; the doll harbours a 'secret' which the narrator has instinctively understood, and she 'somehow knew everything about her' (Lee 1896, 520). The narrator's response to the doll is characterized by an intensity that is normally reserved for the love-object of sexual desire. The 'painfully interesting' nature of their friendship that is based on the recognition of a 'secret', and particularly the doubling effect that results from this engagement, suggests the eroticism of same-sex desire for, as Irigaray argues, feminine desire 'may be recovered only in secret, in hiding, with anxiety and guilt', and as Kristeva has said, 'passion between two women is one of the most intense figures of doubling' (Irigaray 1993, 30; quoted in Weir, 1993, 86).

Given that the doll apparently allows the expression of a veiled homoerotic desire, why might Lee have added that 'little invented *finale* of the burning' (1927, 1)? The answer may lie in the figure of the doll itself that, as we have seen, often symbolizes the body of the mother. Whilst the engagement with the doll offers a return to a figurative womb and an asexual identity that sanctions the desire for, and fusion with the maternal body, it also posits the risk of engulfment recalling Kristeva's model of a 'deathly symbiosis with the mother' (quoted in Weir 1993, 86). I would argue that the ritual burning of the doll in Lee's tale allows an alternative means of asserting a fluid sexual identity whilst retaining a symbolic reference to same-sex desire. Navarette notes that the doll's funeral pyre is ignited with 'the flaming pine cone sacred to Dionysus', a detail which implies that the burning of the doll is ritualistic, and therefore, in some way, symbolic (Navarette 1998, 171). Kane explains that this 'ritualistic scene combines symbols of death with symbols that are suggestive of rebirth or regeneration'; the chrysanthemums placed on the doll's body, usually associated in Italy with death, 'are used in Anglo-Saxon countries in bridal bouquets as a floral symbol of truth' (2004, 116). Furthermore, 'the heady scents' of myrtle and bay 'used to fuel the funeral pyre' function 'like the incense of some ancient rite of purification' and 'link the scene to ancient mythology in which myrtle is associated with passion and bay with victory or merit' (Kane 2004, 117). However, it is worth noting that myrtle is also a shrub dedicated to Venus-Aphrodite (Lee 2006, 77, n.2), a goddess who, as indicated in Chapter Two, can embody a fluid sexual identity, and it is also worth remembering that it is to Aphrodite that the Greek poet Sappho, a lover of women, addresses a number of her poems.

In my discussion of 'A Wedding Chest' above, I suggested that the Dionysian rite suggested in Desiderio's introjection of Troilo's blood, allowed him to transgress the boundaries of identity. The burning of the doll functions perhaps in a similar way. It is not only the doll that is liberated by the blaze, but also Lee's narrator. As the doll lies on the funeral pyre she momentarily comes alive. Significantly, the doll, in this final instant, is no longer sightless: she 'sees' and enjoys. In this brief moment of animation the doubling between the two women is at its most intense. Yet the burning of one, appears to allow the release of the other into a separate and individual subjectivity, one that is, however, still imbued with a fluid sexuality for, in accepting the doll's wedding ring, the narrator is both 'husband' and 'wife' to the doll, a bridal scene that is signified by the floral tributes that adorn the doll's 'body'.[47] Yet this scene also highlights the narrator's appropriation of an androgynous identity that sanctions a psychic, if not physical, return to the maternal body.

Phallic Mothers: Pagan and Christian

However, what kind of maternal body is represented by the dolls in Lee's tales? The defining link between these dolls is their affinity with the Virgin Mary. Maddalena's face is used in paintings of Our Lady; Benvenuta, who becomes a doll-like effigy at the end of the tale, is inevitably associated with the Virgin Mary; the image of the Infanta coalesces with that of the Virgin of the Seven Daggers; and the doll-Countess has an Ingres Madonna face. While I would suggest that one of the functions of these associations is the simultaneous authorization and 'purification' of same-sex desire, there appears to be another reason for this recurrent image. A clue lies in Lee's own discussion of the Virgin Mary in her introduction to *For Maurice*. For Lee, the Virgin Mary, as indicated in her preface to 'The Virgin of the Seven Daggers', is intrinsically related to the Greek goddess Demeter and this connection offers interesting implications. In her discussion of Jane Harrison's *Prolegomena to the Study of Greek Religion* (1903), Eileen Gregory notes how Harrison questions the ideality of Olympian religion and asserts 'through an analysis of specific festivals and cults, that Olympian religion is everywhere overlaid upon an older, precedent stratum of worship involving "snakes and ghosts and underworld beings"' (1997, 112). Gregory also notes Harrison's contention that 'patriarchal Olympian religion suppresses an earlier matriarchal religion and that vestiges of this earlier worship can be found in the iconography of extant artifacts' (1997, 114–115). Relying on what Gregory calls 'imaginal association', Harrison 'establishes a network of interrelated and recurring images from artifacts' that suggest 'the survival in memory and tradition of an archaic theology' (1997, 115).

One important example of this method is illustrated by Eileen Gregory as she traces Harrison's argument concerning images of the Kourotrophos, or Great Goddess as child carrier:

> The continual recurrence of a single image in metamorphic form suggests to Harrison increasingly diversified and distant strains of the old unitary and encompassing image. She presents a sequence of these primary images of the goddess from iconographical evidence: the prehellenic image of the Great Mother as the Lady of Wild Things, surrounded by fierce animals; the Kourotrophos; the dyad of Mother and Maid, or Kore; the image of the anodos of the Kore, a head emerging from the earth as from a womb, with attendant gods as midwives; the ubiquitous trinities of Korai in Greek cult, finally crystallizing in the goddesses of the 'Judgment of Paris,' Hera, Athene, and Aphrodite (1997, 115).[48]

According to Gregory, Harrison finds the 'fullest echo of an original goddess in the figure of Aphrodite, who is also, like Persephone and Pandora, figured in terms of the anodos, the rising Kore. She is thus not only the nymphe or bride, but the virgin, and later, in connection with the Orphic cult of Eros, the mother as well' (1997, 115). Gregory's concern is to draw parallels between H.D. and Jane Harrison, tracing in each 'an instinctive affiliation with the mother and with art and thus a rebelliousness toward Olympian rational totality, and at the same time a compulsive affiliation with Apollonian paternal authority' (1997, 110). To H.D. and Jane Harrison we might easily add Vernon Lee in whose work we can see similar tensions. In fact, there may be a closer association to be traced between Harrison and Lee, than between Harrison and H.D. for whereas, 'H.D. never directly refers to Harrison in her writing' (Gregory 1997, 110), Lee had met Harrison in London and was to write on Harrison's work, delivering a lecture entitled 'Sympathy versus Group Emotion, à propos of Miss Jane Harrison's *Alpha and Omega*' to the Cambridge 'Heretics' on 6 June 1915.[49] Harrison is also known to have visited Walter Pater, Lee's friend and mentor, and her intellectual curiosity regarding Dionysian cults would have been of interest to both Pater and Lee.[50]

What is likely, if not certain, is that Lee would have found Harrison's work on matriarchal cults of particular interest for, if we employ Harrison's method of 'imaginal association' to those tales of Lee's I have discussed so far, it is possible to trace the significant presence of the Great Mother in her work. In previous chapters we have encountered Medusa, Athena, and Venus/Aphrodite, and in this chapter, Demeter, Proserpina, the Virgin Mary, and her dark double, the Medusa-like Infanta.[51] These powerful female images are versions of the 'phallic' mother, which Francette Pacteau defines as that 'primitive imago of early childhood located prior to the recognition of sexual difference', the mother 'whom the child perceives as complete and autonomous' (1986, 71). The most obviously 'phallic' mother is the Virgin of the Seven Daggers, whose body is 'cased like a knife in its sheath', and pierced with seven swords, whose image, as we have seen, can be traced in the other dolls that appear in Lee's tales (Lee 2006, 250). For Catherine Clément, the figure of the Virgin Mary is 'monstrous', the 'occcultation of the feminine principle beneath the masculine ideal' (quoted in Pacteau 1986, 70). She is 'a man-made fantasy, the virilization of the woman, a means of oppression and alienation because emanating from a culture where the male principle dominates' (Pacteau 1986, 70). Yet, as 'phallic' mother she represents a source of female power, a potential *femme fatale*. Although in reality the transition from a polymorphous infant sexuality to an adult sexual identity entails surrendering 'the belief in the "phallic" mother', the realms of fantasy allow a regression to that belief, and provide a space within which 'the image of the phallic mother remains intact' (Pacteau 1986, 81–82). For Lee, this androgynous figure seemingly functions as an alternative to the castrato in her supernatural tales allowing, via identification, the simultaneous expression of an androgynous lesbian subjectivity and female power. It also permits both regression to a pre-Oedipal identity and a fusion with the mother that manifests itself in the ostensibly heterosexual adulation and desire for the Virgin who is sometimes implicitly, sometimes explicitly present in the figure of the doll.

Notes

[1] 'The Love Story' (2000, p. 567, ll. 41–44).

[2] This article first appeared as the introduction to *La donna et l'economia sociale* (1902), the Italian version of Charlotte Perkins Stetson's *Women and Economics* (1898), and was repeated in Lee's *Gospels of Anarchy* (1908) (see Ch. 1, note 4), as 'The Economic Parasitism of Women'. Stetson (better known as Gilman) was to correspond with Lee – letters are in Somerville College, Oxford – expressing her admiration for the latter, and a number of annotated copies of Stetson's subsequent publications are to be found in Vernon Lee's library collection at the British Institute in Florence. See Pulham (2003) for further information regarding their relationship.

[3] Quoting a passage from a collection of essays entitled *The Sentimental Traveller* (1908), Gardner alludes to Lee's description of sea shells out of which 'oozed or quivered ... fleshy things, red and sleek like hidden organs, entrails which never see the light and should never be seen' (quoted in Gardner 1987, 409). Gardner writes, 'By the time that Miss Paget experienced the normal changes of puberty, she had pathologically rejected the fact of her femininity. From this circumstance one may suspect that she underwent in childhood a revulsion – almost traumatic in its vehemence – to the appearance of blood' (1987, 407–408). Given Gardner's focus on Lee's latent lesbianism, it is strange that he chooses to ignore the obvious sexual implications of those 'fleshy', 'red' and 'sleek', 'hidden organs'. In a commonplace book entry, 'In Praise of White', dated 27 July from Fladbury Rectory, Lee is disgusted by the red colour of a fellow guest's '*Baudelairian* nightgown [my emphasis]'. Commonplace Books, n.s. 4 (December 1888–1890), Special Collections, Colby College Library, Waterville, Maine, U.S.A.

[4] The term 'new sculpture' is taken from a series of essays written by Edmund Gosse, 'The New Sculpture: 1879–1894', that were published in volume 56 of the *Art Journal* in 1894. According to David Getsy, new innovations and a widespread interest in sculpture began with the exhibition of Frederic Leighton's *Athlete Wrestling with a Python* (1877), (2004, 2–3).

[5] See Chapter 2, note 8.

[6] These models were manufactured in Northern Italy towards the end of the eighteenth century and, as a result of their popularity, were used all over Europe. One of the largest collections was that in La Specola (Royal and Imperial Museum of Physics and Natural History) set up between 1766 and 1780 in Florence. See Jordanova 1989 and Bronfen 1992.

[7] In Ovid's *Metamorphoses*, Pygmalion adorns his statue's fingers with rings and its neck with jewels. It lays on 'a couch that was covered with cloths of Tyrian purple' and its head reclines on 'soft down pillows', as if it could appreciate them (Ovid 1955, 232).

[8] The anatomical perfection of these figures is especially interesting and specific attention is given to the sexual parts, extending to the provision of pubic hair.

[9] The *fort/da* game ('fort' meaning gone and 'da' meaning 'there') played by Freud's grandson in his mother's absence, is referred to in relation to Freud's exploration of the compulsion to repeat in *Beyond the Pleasure Principle* (1920). Freud's analysis of his grandson's actions influenced the development of object-relations theory in the work of Winnicott and Melanie Klein.

[10] 'The Doll' was initially published under the title 'The Image' in the *Cornhill Magazine* in May 1896 (I am indebted to Catherine Maxwell who discovered that 'The Doll' and 'The Image' were in fact the same story). Navarette usefully lists other short stories and articles by Lee that prominently feature dolls, puppets, and stone effigies, although she fails to include 'Marsyas in Flanders' (discussed in the last chapter), and also the short story, 'A Wedding Chest', which I will discuss shortly, in which the body of the doll and the religious relic are implicit.

[11] Lee here refers to the English poet and critic William Cosmo Monkhouse (1840–1901) and to the philosopher Alfred William Benn (1843–1915).

[12] Ironically, 'colour-blindness' is referred to in relation to same-sex desire in Havelock Ellis's analysis of sexual inversion in *Studies of the Psychology of Sex* (1908), (1936, II. 317).

[13] See Psomiades, *Beauty's Body*, 1997, and 'Still Burning from this Strangling Embrace', 1997; Zorn, 2003; Colby, 2003; Brake, 2006; and Evangelista, 2006.

[14] It is worth noting that the educational/sexual nature of the relationship between Hamlin and Anne resonates not only with the relationship between Rossetti and Lizzie Siddall, but also with that of Ford Madox Brown and Emma Matilda Hill, and that of William Holman Hunt and Annie Miller. The latter is particularly suggestive as Walter Hamlin shares Hunt's initials and Annie Miller shares a Christian name with Anne Brown. For further details of Pre-Raphaelite artists' relationships with their models, see Marsh 1985.

[15] The 'clammy thing' that so disturbs Anne Brown is reminiscent of those 'fleshy things, red and sleek like hidden organs' that Lee describes as oozing and quivering out of sea shells in *The Sentimental Traveller* (1908) (see note 3 above).

[16] The word 'Swinburnian' is a reference to the poet, Algernon Charles Swinburne, whose collection, *Poems and Ballads* (1866), drew public outrage as a result of their overtly sexual, content. This vampiric image of Sacha's lesbian desire recalls Bertrand Russell's reference to Vernon Lee as a 'vampire' and a 'bloodsucker' in her relationships with the young women of her acquaintance. Arguably, Sacha's 'vampirism' destabilizes gender boundaries, for the 'Vampire Mouth' is one which, according to Christopher Craft, subverts 'the stable and lucid distinctions of gender, [being] ... the mouth of all vampires male and female' (1989, 218), and those boundaries are blurred still further by the 'androgynous' name 'Sacha' (see Denisoff 1999, 263).

[17] Sacha Elaguine bears a passing resemblance to Toche Bulteau, a one-time friend of Lee's about whom she writes to Kit: 'if she wanted me it was from a sort of passion and habit of beneficent conquest ... . You see she has a way of speaking of the other conquered ones as "mes vampyres," and I couldn't allow myself to be put into that category' (Gardner 1987, 288).

[18] The Smith Museum, Leeds, is Vernon Lee's invention. The translation of the half-effaced Latin inscription would appear to be 'Desiderio from the city of Castiglione del Lago made me'. Such coffers, or *cassone*, were often marriage gifts intended to contain the bride's trousseau. Between the fourteenth and sixteenth centuries they were often heavily decorated.

[19] According to Stefano Infessura (1435–1500) in his *Diarium urbis Romae* (*Diary of the City of Rome*), Julia is the daughter of Claudius, whose body, found well preserved and almost intact in 1485, becomes the object of a cult.

[20] Translated, the Latin inscription means: 'and the child of infamy and wickedness'.

[21] In classical myths, beautiful boys are often loved by the gods: Hyacinthus was the Apollo's beloved, while Ganymede was Zeus's cupbearer.

[22] Lee playfully adopts the persona of the 'boy' in her introduction to *Belcaro* in which she describes the collection as 'not the Sir-Oracle manual of a professor' but 'the copy books of the boy attending a course of lectures' (Lee, 1881, 5). She was also to compare her companion, Clementina Anstruther-Thomson, to 'a very beautiful and modest boy' (quoted in Colby, 1970, 290.

[23] Vernon Lee's opposition to her close friend Mary Robinson's first marriage to James Darmesteter in 1888 is well documented in Gunn 1964, Colby 2003 and in the abridged collection of her letters (Lee 1937).

[24] Writing of Freud's essay 'The "Uncanny"', Samuel Weber points out that Freud's reading of Hoffmann's *Der Sandmann* ('The Sandman') in this text, 'leads Freud to the conclusion

that the uncanny effect of the tale resides in the dread of losing one's eyes, which in turn is for Freud nothing but a substitute manifestation of castration-anxiety' (1973, 1105).

[25]   The doubling between Troilo and Maddalena is implicit in the tale, not only due to the vampiric marks that suggest his penetration and introjection of her, but also as artistic images. Maddalena's face has been employed by Desiderio as a model in paintings of the Virgin Mary and, in death, Troilo, too, becomes the focus of the aesthetic and artistic gaze.

[26]   The name 'Troilo' resonates with 'Troilus' and recalls the love triangle between Troilus, son of the Trojan king, Priam, Cressida and the Greek soldier, Diomedes.

[27]   While Gardner fails to associate the dead Maddalena directly with the corpse-like Anne and neither with the anatomical Venuses, it is evident that there is a subtle link between them that is suggestive in the context of this chapter.

[28]   For Lee's dislike of ornamented madonnas, see note 33 below.

[29]   February comes from the name 'Februarius', which is derived from *februare* (to purify) or from Februa, the Roman festival of expiation and lustration, held in the second half of February (Kuryluk, 1991, 114).

[30]   Lee herself seems to have been the object of worship for some young girls. In her discussion of Lee's 'lesbian tendencies' Smyth says that 'the most a *culte* [adoring fan] could expect was a kiss which one of them, unnamed, described as having been of the sacramental kind' (Maxwell and Pulham 2006, 4).

[31]   The fifteenth-century drawing is probably a copy after a lost painting by Konrad Witz (*c.* 1400–45 or 1446), (see Kuryluk 1991, 195).

[32]   The final image of Benvenuta and the Christ Child functions as an ostensibly 'purified' double to the image of Maddalena and her foetus in 'A Wedding Chest'. In always preserving with him the body of the mother – Maddalena – Desiderio, via his introjection of Troilo, becomes an androgynized double of the figure of Love, and also of Amor in 'Sister Benvenuta and the Christ Child'.

[33]   Lee's distaste for these Spanish madonnas (encountered during her sojourn in Granada early in 1889) is clear in this introduction written in 1927. It would seem that they made a lasting impression on her. The original reference to them, made in her commonplace book demonstrates the intensity of the impression, and includes many of the features that are later incorporated in 'The Virgin of the Seven Daggers'.

[34]   An earlier Don Juan appears in Lee's work in the essay, 'Don Juan (con Stenterello)' in *Juvenilia* and aspects of this early work, including an encounter with a mysterious supernatural woman, and a confrontation with a dead mirror image, remain in the later tale (1887, II. 77–98).

[35]   The Virgin of the Seven Daggers is more commonly known as Our Lady of Sorrows, who is often depicted in Catholic churches with seven daggers plunged in her breast to represent the Seven Sorrows of Mary.

[36]   Vanita argues that fountains function in this manner in works by homosexual writers such as Michael Field and Virginia Woolf. This image occurs in the erotic mermaid who spouts water from her breasts and graces the gardens in which Maddalena is buried in Lee's 'A Wedding Chest'.

[37]   In her discussion of Pater's *La Gioconda*, Vanita notes Lillian Faderman's observation that, since the advent of Coleridge's Christabel, the vampire has been linked to female homosexuality, and this model of same-sex desire is referred to indirectly in *Miss Brown*, and directly in relation to Lee by Bertrand Russell. Vanita suggests that the image of the *Mona Lisa* as 'a diver in deep seas' is also homoerotic, occurring in the works of Oscar Wilde in the figures of Narcissus and Charmides, and in the marine imagery prevalent in lesbian poems such as Renée Vivien's 'Undine' (1996, 66). Navarette points out that Lee described the Spanish-style Madonna as 'the "fair dame in the velvet embroidered gown, with

the long hanging hair"; the sister of "that silly sentimental coquette, the Monna Lisa [*sic*] of Leonardo'": a doubling which, in view of the above, appears to homoeroticize the Virgin in Lee's tale (quoted in Navarette 1998, 168).

[38]   See Chapter One, note 2.

[39]   The colours that characterize the Infanta – red and purple – are also those that Eileen Gregory associates with H.D.'s analysis of Sappho's poetry (Gregory, 1997, 106). These colours also inform Vernon Lee's early desire for Clementina Anstruther-Thomson. In her introduction to *Art and Man*, Lee writes: 'Kit came to stay with us in Florence after leaving Paris at Easter, 1888. The precise date has been fixed in my mind less by the importance it later showed as having in my life than, oddly enough, by the recollection, as vivid as their own colours, of putting scarlet and purple anemones in her room' (1924, 16).

[40]   The Italian word 'desiderio' is defined as a 'desire' or 'longing'; a 'longed-for thing or person' (*Cambridge Italian Dictionary*, 1962).

[41]   While Edison was well known for his work on the phonograph, in 1887 he was also involved in attempting to develop and seek markets for a line of talking dolls, the prototype for which he was reputed to have created for his daughter as early as 1877. The public therefore also associated him with mechanical dolls (Frank 1995, 152).

[42]   In describing Alicia as a *Venus Victorious*, Ewald is comparing her to the *Venus de Milo* which is generally thought to be a representation of *Venus Victrix*, who holds the golden apple given to her by Paris in her hand. Later in the novel, Ewald recalls having taken Alicia to see her sculptural counterpart at the Louvre museum.

[43]   It is worth noting that in *Miss Brown*, Hamlin paints Anne as *Venus Victrix* (the Venus thought to be represented by the *Venus de Milo* (see note 42 above)) whom Alicia Clary resembles (Lee 1884, I. 128–129).

[44]   The main differences between the two versions is that the 1896 tale carries a dedication to 'Mme Louis Ormond', and that, in the final paragraph of the 1927 version, the word 'image' is replaced by 'doll'.

[45]   Pier Desiderio Pasolini (1844–1920), Italian historian and member of the Academy of the Lincei. For details of earlier reference to the doll, see Lee 1904, 144.

[46]   The appearance of these manufactured doll-women in tales by Lee, Hoffmann, and Villiers has a macabre resonance with the doll created by the painter and writer, Oskar Kokoschka, who in 1919 commissioned a Stuttgart toy manufacturer to construct a lifesize doll for him. The doll was made from cloth and sawdust and was meant to be the effigy of Alma Mahler, his former mistress. Although it is uncertain whether Kokoschka wanted the doll as a sex-toy, he did instruct the manufacturer to make her with squeezable breasts and buttocks (Ashley 1999, 16).

[47]   Daniel Dervin argues that when Paul destroys his sister's doll in *Sons and Lovers*, 'we ... see that in the process of one doll's destruction another "doll," namely Paul, hitherto the will-less follower and passive object ... comes alive and begin's consciously to act' (1981, 85). In the light of this, if the narrator's identification with the doll centres (as Navarette suggests) on her own experience of submission and silence in a patriarchal culture, the destruction of the doll functions as a liberating assertion of autonomy. However, there are other implications suggested by the mode of destruction. If the doll and the narrator are 'doubles' (as I suggest), then the flames which destroy the former and serve to liberate the latter are revitalising: the narrator/doll rises from the ashes like a phoenix, which, according to Vanita, is 'one of the most ubiquitous and recurrent images in homoerotic texts since Romanticism' and often 'identified with the narrating voice' (1996, 239).

[48]   The Mother and Maid dyad, symbolized by the Kore, resonates interestingly with the 'kore' or 'doll' referred to by Plato earlier in the chapter. It would seem that the doll's duality,

and its ability to represent both mother and daughter is suggestive for Lee's use of the model in tales that have homoerotic subtexts.

[49]   For an account of Lee's acquaintance with Harrison, and her attack on Harrison's theory of art, see Beard, 2000. Part of Lee's lecture on Harrison's work, originally entitled 'Harrison Unanism Lecture': 'War, Group-Emotion and Art', exists in holograph manuscript in the Special Collections of Colby College Library, Waterville, Maine U.S.A. (Mannocchi 1983, 231–267). Although Lee may have disagreed with Harrison's conception of aesthetics, I would argue that her supernatural tales imply that she shared Harrison's interest in 'mother-cults'.

[50]   Yopie Prins informs us that Harrison refers to her meetings with Walter Pater in *Reminiscences* (1997, 61).

[51]   When abducted, Maddalena is referred to as 'another Proserpina' (Lee 2006, 236). The presence of Orestes in 'The Image' also seems significant. Orestes, whose namesake killed his own mother and 'defeated and repressed' what Paglia calls 'the archaic night world' ruled by 'the Great Mother', here assists in the doll's liberation thus subverting traditional models of male engagement with the maternal body (Paglia, 1992, 230).

Chapter 4

Madonna Portraits and Medusan Mirrors

This is her picture as she was:
It seems a thing to wonder on,
As though mine image in a glass
Should tarry when myself am gone.
Dante Gabriel Rossetti (1881)[1]

The haunting portrait of the Italian Count's deceased wife in 'The Image' resurfaces in a short essay entitled 'The Blame of Portraits' published in *Hortus Vitae: Essays on the Gardening of Life* (1904) in which Vernon Lee writes eloquently of the futility of the portrait form. Our 'humble desire for a likeness' of our loved ones is, she argues, 'one of our most signal cravings after the impossible: an attempt to overcome space and baffle time; to imprison and use at pleasure the most fleeting, intangible, and uncommunicable of all mysterious essences, a human personality' (1904, 140). According to Lee, the impossibility of this desire is particularly acute when the portrait functions as a *memento mori*, and she illustrates her point using as example the macabre copy of the Count's deceased wife in 'The Image'. From the passage below it is clear that her tale is based on a real-life encounter which had a profound effect:

> Perhaps I feel more strongly on this subject because I happen to have seen with my own eyes the *reductio ad absurdum* – to absurdity how lamentable and dreadful! – of this same human craving for literal preservation of that which should not, cannot, be preserved. I wrote a little tale about it; but the main facts were true, and far surpassed the power of invention. ... In a small way, we all of us commit that man's mistake of thinking that the life of our dear ones is in an image, instead of in the heartbeats which the image – like a name, a place, any associated thing – can produce in ourselves. And only changing things can answer to our changing self; only living creatures live with us. Once learned by heart, the portrait, be it never so speaking, ceases to speak, or we to listen to its selfsame message (Lee, *Hortus Vitae* 1904, 144–145).

Whilst Lee's argument is certainly valid, historical evidence suggests that without man's attempts to represent the dead, the world would have been denied an important record of its human, and aesthetic past, for as Eva Kuryluk observes, in ancient Rome 'Deathmasks as *memento mori* for the living played an important role ... and might have contributed to the extreme naturalism of Roman portrait sculpture' (1991, 206). The Romans' artistic preservation of the dead is particularly fascinating and resonates interestingly with the doll in Lee's tale. Kuryluk writes:

> In order to preserve the faces of the dead from corruption, which progressed rapidly in the hot climate, the Romans covered them with wax masks. The masks were later used

as models for wax figures, the *imagines*, which, like the dolls of the contemporary wax cabinets, were painted by a *pollinctor* in natural colors, equipped with hair, and dressed. Pliny ... tells us that wax models of faces were set out on separate sideboards and carried in procession ... . After the funeral the likenesses were exhibited in sarcpohagus-like boxes in the atrium, alea, or vestibulum of their family houses. Portrait-busts and statues as well as portrait-shields of military leaders and heroes were derived from the *imagines* and shown in temples, public places, and private homes (1991, 206–207).

The portrait form, it seems, has always been intimately related to death. Catherine Maxwell specifically associates the birth of portraiture with loss, and comments on two accounts of the development of painting taken from Pliny's *Natural History* (Bk 10). In the first, Pliny argues that although the geographical location of its origin is imprecise, it is generally agreed that the art of painting began 'with tracing an outline round a man's shadow and consequently that pictures were originally done in this way' (quoted in Maxwell 2002, 516). In the second, which discusses the origin of the plastic arts, the origin of portraiture is attributed to a female artist, the daughter of the first sculptor, 'Butades, a potter of Sicyon, at Corinth' who was in love with a young man. When she learned that he was going abroad, she drew 'in outline on the wall the shadow of his face thrown by a lamp' on which her father 'pressed clay' and 'made a relief, which he hardened by exposure to fire with the rest of his pottery' (quoted in Maxwell 2002, 517). From this less than auspicious beginning, the silhouette became 'an important form of eighteenth- and nineteenth-century portraiture, in which the profile view of the subject's head and shoulders is depicted either by a black paper cut-out or in black ink' (Maxwell 2002, 515). Maxwell notes that:

> Most fashionable in the period 1750–1850, these silhouette portraits were also, according to the *OED*, known as 'shades'; a word that ... like its Latin antecedent *umbra*, has the advantage of meaning both 'shadow' and 'ghost'. ... An evocative outline that excludes the particularity of individual features, the silhouette is like a draft or sketch, a ghost of a drawing. Its partial portraiture brings the subject to mind but, repressing the fullness of the person's presence, reminds us that she is not there (2002, 515).

And, as she has written elsewhere, the fully realized portrait is equally elusive in its evocation for, like its ghostly counterpart, the silhouette, it too can be no more than an 'absent presence' (Maxwell 1997, 253).

Although it is clearly the paradoxical nature of the portrait's tangible, yet intangible, nature that is perceived as Lee's concern in 'The Blame of Portraits', her discussion centres on the medium's inability to produce a 'pure' reflection: the 'imperfect likeness[es]' that appear on canvas always being filtered through the artist's consciousness:

> For the image of the sitter on the artist's retina is passed on its way to the canvas through a mind chock full of other images; and is transferred – heaven knows how changed already – by processes of line and curve, of blots of colour, and juxtaposition of light and shade, belonging not merely to the artist himself, but to the artist's whole school ... . The difference due to the individual artist is even greater; and, in truth, a portrait gives

the sitter's temperament merged in the temperament of the painter (*Hortus Vitae* 1904, 141–142).

Evidently, Oscar Wilde would have agreed: in *The Picture of Dorian Gray* (1890– 91), Basil Hallward argues that 'every portrait that is painted with feeling is a portrait of the artist, not of the sitter', and in Arlo Bates's *A Problem in Portraiture* (1889) the portrait is similarly influenced by the artist for it is asserted that 'since every picture must contain something of the personality of the artist, it follows that a portrait-painter is sure to impress the character of his sitters' (Wilde 1988, 10; quoted in Powell 1980, 414). However, for Lee, it is not only the contamination of the portrait that inhibits a 'true' image, but also its very stillness. She warns that during 'the *period of activity* of a portrait – I mean while we still, more or less, look at it – we must beware lest it take, in our memory, the place of the original' and she fears that those 'unchanging features' which have 'the insistence of their definiteness and permanence, ... may insidiously extrude, exclude, the fleeting, vacillating outlines of the remembered reality' (*Hortus Vitae* 1904, 146). Lee was not alone in her concern, for George Eliot feared 'outward images lest they should corrupt the inward' and Robert Browning rejected a memorial bust of Elizabeth Barrett Browning on the grounds that whereas 'the inner light of the soul' could 'fill up all deficiency' and 'transfigure all actually there', the sculptor must 'make all out' – and his facts would be nothing but 'the dead facts' (quoted in Onslow 1995, 456; quoted in Pearsall 1992, 43).

Despite Lee's rejection of the portrait form as inadequate, and of the *memento mori* as a futile attempt to cheat death, a photograph of Annie Meyer, an early object of her desire who died in 1883 (or early 1884), hung over Lee's bed till her death in 1935.[2] In contrast to the view she expresses in 'The Blame of Portraits', in a diary entry relating to Meyer's death, Lee reveals an apparent preference for the commemorative image to the reality. In the death of her friend, she argues, she 'lost nothing or but little' of the real Mme Meyer, 'for does there not remain, unchanged and unchangeable, the imagined one?' (quoted in Gardner 1987, 312).[3] According to Lee, the advantage of the 'imagined' Annie Meyer lies in the fact that 'one cannot lose' the creature 'born of one's fancy and one's desires, the unreal' (quoted in Gardner 1987, 312). This diary entry seems to specifically contradict the crux of her later essay which is that art can never replace the reality. However, her earlier preference for the fantasy may have its basis in insecurity for, as Navarette observes, 'the desires that she voices' in her diary 'are inseparable from those she felt "for artificial beings ... who can never shift the moral light in which we see them, who can never turn round in their frames and say 'see, we are not what you imagined"' (1998 165; quoted in Navarette, 1998, 165). Lee's proprietary gaze allows a control that defies the subject's autonomy and her initial partiality for the inanimate portrait is perhaps a reflection of her own unsatisfactory relationship with Meyer. As she writes in her journal:

It was, to a great extent, still-born, that friendship between her and me. It is sad to have to admit to myself that had she lived, we might not have got much nearer to one another, never perhaps to that point of seeing, of being able to touch and embrace the whole personality, which, in my opinion, is the only complete friendship. Things went quickly with a woman of her ardent, impatient, imperious temper; things usually go quickly with a woman so imaginatively impressionable, as passionate, wayward and vain as myself – perhaps I should add as naked? ... . It is most sad ... that these two years of friendship ... were but a sort of long duel; were spent in vainly trying to tear the mask off each other, to find each other's heart, and in warding off, covering up with artificialities one's real personality (quoted in Gunn 1964, 96–97).

It seems that the primitive fear that one's spirit or soul can be captured in a photographic reproduction, has in some sense been realized in Vernon Lee's fantasy. In possessing Meyer's photograph she appears to possess that entity which so eluded her in the years of their friendship – Meyer herself – who is now at the mercy of Vernon Lee's imagination. One might suggest that instead of allowing a fantasy relationship that can come to a psychic, if not physical, fruition, the stillness of the photographic medium ensures that her 'still-born' friendship with Meyer is preserved forever, suspended in limbo, echoing in its posed artificiality that mask that veiled Annie Meyer's 'real personality'. Yet, as Lee points out, this 'possession' is rooted in fancy: the photograph's inanimate nature allows a static surface for the projection of fantasy and I will discuss the portrait's role in this process in due course.

Lee's rejection of the containing power of the portrait in 'The Blame of Portraits' seems at odds with the opinion she voices with regard to those other arts, music and sculpture. As we have seen, for Lee, music 'exists as an art' only where 'the emotional cry or the spontaneous imitation' is subjected to 'a process of acoustic mensuration' and the sculptural ideal exists only in the perfect lines of ancient Greek statues: those 'silent, motionless people of marble' (Lee 1881, 117; Lee 1894, 92). Given the proclivity for 'form' that characterizes Lee's aesthetics, one cannot but ask why the 'form' of the portrait should be rejected in favour of the fluid reality or the evanescent memory? The answer lies perhaps in the fact that Lee considered portraiture to be 'a curious bastard of art, sprung ... from a desire which is not artistic, nay, if anything, opposed to the whole nature and function of art – the desire for the mere likeness of a person' (Lee 1883, 565). As portraiture is not what Lee considers a 'pure' art, it would appear that it is not subject to the same aesthetic rules, and it is clear that in, her essay, 'The Portrait Art of the Renaissance' (1883) from which this quotation is taken, Lee is at pains to leave the subject of portrait painting behind in order to concentrate on the 'superior' art of portrait sculpture. Yet, the portrait's intimate association with the self may also be a factor.

For Pierre Nicole, a seventeenth-century logician and moralist, the language of painting and portraiture becomes a powerful metaphor for the understanding of self and one's relations to others.[4] He argues: 'We are all with respect to one another like the man who acts as model to pupils in painting academies. Each of those who surround us forms a portrait of us and the different ways in which our actions are regarded permit the formation of an almost infinite variety of portraits' (quoted in Marin 1991, 285). The linguistic ambiguity of the last sentence allows alternative interpretations: if those around us form portraits of us, they may not only create an independent portrait but they may also themselves be 'portraits' *of* us, of our effects on their psyche. Interestingly, Lee's description of Annie Meyer implies a doubling of identity that is suggestive in this context. For Lee, Meyer is 'a woman so imaginatively impressionable, as passionate, wayward and vain as myself' and it is possibly this doubling that leads to Vernon Lee's change of heart regarding portraiture in 'The Blame of Portraits', for it represents perhaps a recognition that her 'captive' beloved's image simultaneously captures her own and prevents that fluidity which is integral to her negotiation of her own identity (quoted in Gunn 1964, 96). However, Nicole offers an alternative process where the self becomes our own artistic construction:

> One must act more or less in this life as if one had a lifelong undertaking to paint one's portrait, that is to say that one must add everyday a few strokes of the brush without blotting out what has already been painted ... . By this means [by this continuous portraiture] we will form little by little a portrait so resembling that we will be able to see at any moment everything which we are (quoted in Marin 1991, 286).

As Louis Marin observes, according to this method, 'The true portrait is not under layers of paint; it is made up of these strokes, these marks and these remarks' (Marin 1991, 286). The true portrait is therefore 'the *figure of an excess* formed by repeated strokes, and not that of a personal essence obtained by rubbing out' (Marin 1991, 286–287). But, as Marin points out, this excess can be problematic for 'at each moment, by the addition of a new stroke, this resemblance becomes unlike itself ... by "amassing" and by "excess"' the 'spectator – painter of his own portrait' runs up 'against the defacement of his own face': the self becomes a 'formless mass' (Marin 1991, 287).

While Marin's philosopher is concerned with the moral development of man, his metaphor provides an interesting model to apply to Lee's relationship with portraiture in her life and in her work. In a letter to her publisher John Lane at The Bodley Head dated the 13 January 1908, Lee makes her own position regarding her image particularly clear. In reply to Lane's request for the use of her photograph on one of her publications Lee writes: 'As I have refused two other publishers, and everyone else the right to use any portrait of mine, Sargent's included, I have to be consistent [and] say no. I hate this hawking about of people's faces. I took a *nom de plume* in order to keep my private personality separate from my literary one'.[5] It is apparent from this quotation that Lee is intent on constructing her own literary identity and, on the surface, her reluctance in agreeing to Lane's request appears perfectly reasonable. The fact remains, however, that, by 1908, it was no longer a secret that 'Vernon Lee' was a woman. Moreover, Lee's androgynous pen-name is itself a reflection of her own sexual ambiguity which is equally evident in John Singer Sargent's 1889 sketch in which she wears mannish clothes and an air of youthful masculine arrogance. One wonders, then, whether it was not in fact the coalescence of her public and private personae in the social arena that Lee feared. Interestingly, portraits of Lee seem to lack a distinct form: Sargent's 1889 sketch of Lee has an unfinished quality; his earlier portrait of her (1881) lacks that clarity of line which generally marks Sargent's portraiture; and a later painting by Mme Berthe Noufflard (1934) is similarly indistinct.[6] Although each of these images displays an indefinable energy, one might argue that the resistance of the sitter is equally in evidence, and it appears significant that the women in the supernatural tales to be discussed in this chapter – Medea da Carpi, Alice Oke, and Dionea – similarly resist being captured and/or remaining captive in art.

Portraits of Lee, then, appear to retain that 'formlessness' which is a feature of Pierre Nicole's subject in process. However, in representing the form in which we see ourselves reflected, portraits also have a primal significance. Not only does the portrait function as a kind of 'mirror', it is also, arguably, linked to its 'precursor' which in 'individual emotional development' is 'the mother's face' (Winnicott 1971, 111). Winnicott claims that, for the sighted infant, the mother's gaze functions as the primary confirmation of self resulting in the formulation: 'When I look I am seen, so I exist' (1971, 114). This initial affirmation of self is, according to Winnicott, crucial to our own reactions to ourselves and others, and those who have an unsatisfactory visual experience of the mother will doubt their own reality and continue to seek the mother's face in the faces of others. In explaining the process with an example taken from his clinical analyses, Winnicott describes the case of a female patient who has been damaged psychologically by the effects of depression on the maternal face. As a result she has 'a marked absence of just that which characterizes so many women, an interest in the face' (1971, 115–116). The severity of her case required that Winnicott displace the mother in order to allow the patient's progression into an independent and acknowledged identity. Towards the end of her seemingly successful treatment, the patient sends Winnicott a portrait of her nurse. He writes:

> I had already had her mother's portrait and I have got to know the rigidity of the mother's defences very intimately. It became obvious that the mother ... had chosen a depressed nurse to act for her so that she might avoid losing touch with the children altogether. A lively nurse would automatically have 'stolen' the children from the depressed mother. ... This same week this patient found a picture of my face on a book cover. She wrote to say she needed a bigger version so that she could see the lines and all the features of this 'ancient landscape'. ... This patient thought that she was quite simply acquiring the portrait of this man who had done so much for her ... . But what she needed to be told was that my lined face had some features that link for her with the rigidity of the faces of her mother and her nurse. I feel sure that it was important that I knew this about the face, and that I could interpret the patient's search for a face that could reflect herself, and at the same time see that, because of the lines, my face in the picture reproduced some of her mother's rigidity (1971, 115–116).

What is particularly interesting about this passage is that it underlines the inevitability of the patient's search for the mother's face, and the need to see it in others even though, or perhaps *because*, it has initially failed to respond to a fundamental childhood need. What is even more important for my own purpose is that Winnicott does not restrict this search to known faces. He argues that the unknown image can be equally suggestive. Referring to portraits by Francis Bacon, he argues:

> From the standpoint of this chapter this Francis Bacon of today's date is seeing himself in his mother's face, but with some twist in him or her that maddens both him and us ... . Bacon's faces seem to me to be removed from perception of the actual; in looking at faces he seems to me to be painfully striving towards being seen, which is at the basis of creative looking (1971, 114).

Winnicott's opinion of Bacon appears to be supported by the detail that he preferred his paintings to be glazed not only because 'the fortuitous play of reflections' would enhance his pictures but also because they gained 'by enabling the spectator to see his own face in the glass' (1971, 117).

For Winnicott, then, the portrait is crucially linked to the mother's face and to one's perception of one's own identity in that face. Given this model, the prevalence of the portrait in Lee's tales takes on an added significance. Not only does it indicate an exploration of the self, it also suggests that this journey is undertaken within the safe 'holding environment' provided by the maternal gaze, and by her simultaneous absence and presence within those portraits which are, according to Winnicott, primary features of the maternal role in the transitional object phase. If one considers those 'portraits' that appear in the preceding chapters: the haunting painting of Rinaldo in 'Winthrop's Adventure'; the engraving of Zaffirino in 'A Wicked Voice'; the sculptural portraits of Marsyas in 'Marsyas in Flanders', and of Venus in 'St. Eudaemon and His Orange Tree'; the 'live picture' that is Anne Brown, and the unsettling portraits of 'blossom-mouthed' women in *Miss Brown*; the madonna paintings that feature Maddalena's face in 'A Wedding Chest'; the portrait of the madonna, and the coloured prints of nuns in 'Sister Benvenuta and the Christ Child'; the 'portrait' statue of the Virgin in 'The Virgin of the Seven Daggers'; and the Count's disturbing doll with her 'Ingres Madonna face' in 'The Image', one can see that all are associated either directly or indirectly with the mother, either via the maternal voice or the maternal body. What, then, may one infer from what Gardner calls Lee's 'most permanent identification' with 'that photograph of Annie Meyer's dead face, which hung at the head of her bed for fifty years'? (1987, 316).

Gardner makes a direct link between Meyer and Vernon Lee's self-image, locating in the former not only another version of the 'Semivir Idol', but the primary one. For Gardner, Meyer is that initial 'feminine counterpart of Miss Paget's own idealized image' who conveniently fulfils the criteria of being both 'static and dead' in order to allow Lee's projection of that 'pure, abstract essence' which he identifies as 'the essence of female superiority' (1987, 316). Furthermore, he suggests that those ghosts that feature in Lee's tales are based on Meyer herself:

> The whole body of Miss Paget's fiction is dominated by the theme of haunting, and, from the basic identity of the haunting images, we may conclude that they all owe something to Miss Paget's personal Madonna, Anne Meyer, full of every 'Vernon Lee' grace and immune to every Violet Paget frailty (1987, 377).

As I argue in Chapter Two, there is little doubt that Gardner's 'Semivir Idol' functions as a form of double for Vernon Lee. Moreover, as I have suggested, the 'Semivir Idol' is also linked to that primary 'idol' of human affection – the mother. Gardner, however, fails to make an explicit connection between Annie Meyer and the mother despite the fact that such an association is implicit in his choice of words, for he describes Meyer as Lee's personal 'Madonna': a figure that functions as the image of universal motherhood. In addition, Meyer's role as the departed object of desire inevitably associates her with the mother who is the primary 'lost' object, and it is perhaps this loss that is implicit in Lee's suggestion that the portrait represents 'one of our most signal cravings after the impossible: an attempt to overcome space and baffle time': elements which characterize the desires of the protagonists in Lee's portrait tales (*Hortus Vitae* 1904, 140). Given the passionate nature of the friendship between Meyer and Lee, it is possible that, for her, the photograph of Meyer stands in place of those Madonna paintings that were to enthral Freud's Dora, and Sister Benvenuta signifying an expression of same-sex desire.

Lee's portrait ghosts may indeed be versions of Annie Meyer but, if we are to agree with Lee's assertion in 'The Blame of Portraits' that all such works are portraits of the artist as well as of the sitter, then the paintings that appear in Lee's tales take on a deeper meaning. Those portraits of Medea da Carpi, Alice Oke, and Dionea are all effectively 'painted' by Lee and must therefore reveal, by her own suggestion, aspects of herself. In the light of Winnicott's thesis, they also indicate her own relationship with the maternal object of desire. Lee's portraits, then, like the voice-object, the sculpture, and the doll, function as 'transitional objects' – objects that are both part of, and external to Lee, which are 'played' with beneath the 'maternal' gaze of the portraits' sitters. It is with these considerations in mind that I wish to look at two of her tales, 'Amour Dure: Passages from the Diary of Spiridion Trepka', and 'Oke of Okehurst; or The Phantom Lover'.

Amour Dure: Passages from the Diary of Spiridion Trepka

The main protagonist in 'Amour Dure', is Spiridion Trepka a young Polish scholar who has come to Italy to write a history of Urbania. This task soon becomes secondary to his fascination with the 'strange figure' of the beautiful Medea da Carpi, a powerful woman from Urbania's past (Lee 2006, 45). For Trepka, 'This woman's history and character remind one of that of Bianca Capello, and at the same time of Lucrezia Borgia' (2006, 45–46).[7] It is a violent history that results in the deaths of five of Medea's lovers and concludes with her assassination at the age of twenty-seven, carried out at the request of Duke Robert, brother to her deceased husband Duke Guidalfonso II. Fearing the political implications of Medea's sexual power over men, Robert ensures that she dies at the hands of two women, both infanticides, over whom she can hold no sway. Such is Robert's horror of Medea whom he sees 'as something almost supernatural', that thoughts of meeting her after death cloud his existence (2006, 58). As a precaution against this, his astrologer concocts a device, a silver image that represents Robert's soul, which is attached to his statue after death that he might sleep, 'awaiting the Day of Judgment, fully convinced that Medea's soul will then be properly tarred and feathered, while his ... will fly straight to Paradise' (2006, 58). Trepka's interest in Medea's history is fuelled by his own erotic fascination with the past for he perceives himself as 'wedded to history, to the Past, to women like Lucrezia Borgia, Vittoria Accoramboni, or that Medea da Carpi' (2006, 54–55).[8] The women of his own day have no attraction for him, and retreat further in his consideration with every portrait of Medea he encounters, of which there are several. The first is a miniature, sent to a prospective lover 'in order to turn his head'; the second is 'a marble bust in the palace lumber-room' and the third is 'a large composition', in which Trepka perceives the figure of Medea in the character of Cleopatra kneeling in an attitude of supplication before Augustus, an 'idealised portrait of Robert II', and 'baring her breast for the victor to strike, but in reality to captivate him,' as 'he turns away with an awkward gesture of loathing' (2006, 51). Yet it is the miniature that initially captures Trepka's imagination. Although, as represented in the portrait, Medea's seems at first 'A curious, ... rather conventional, artificial beauty, voluptuous yet cold', Trepka observes that 'the more it is contemplated, the more it troubles and haunts the mind' (2006, 51–52):

> The face is a perfect oval, the forehead somewhat over-round, with minute curls, like a fleece, of bright auburn hair; the nose a trifle over-aquiline, and the cheek-bones a trifle too low; the eyes gray, large, prominent, beneath exquisitely curved brows and lids just a little too tight at the corners; the mouth also brilliantly red and most delicately designed, is a little too tight, the lips strained a trifle over the teeth. Tight eyelids and tight lips give a strange refinement, and, at the same time, an air of mystery, a somewhat sinister seductiveness ... . The mouth with a kind of childish pout, looks as if it could bite or suck like a leech (2006, 51–52).

Around Medea's neck Trepka notices 'a gold chain with little gold lozenges at intervals, on which is engraved the posy or pun ... "Amour Dure – Dure Amour" [a constant and a cruel Love]' (2006, 52). The haunting quality of the miniature is repeated with redoubled effect in the final portrait of Medea which Trepka discovers unexpectedly. Attracted by 'a very beautiful old mirror-frame' he finds in one of the 'irregular-shaped closets' of the turreted palace, Trepka looks into the glass and is startled by what he sees reflected there:

> I gave a great start, and almost shrieked ... . Behind my own image stood another, a figure close to my shoulder, a face close to mine; and that figure, that face, hers! Medea da Carpi's! ... On the wall opposite the mirror ... hung a portrait and such a portrait! – Bronzino never painted a grander one. Against a background of harsh, dark blue, there stands out the figure of the Duchess (for it is Medea, the real Medea, a thousand times more real, individual, and powerful than in the other portraits), seated stiffly in a high-backed chair, sustained, as it were, almost rigid, by the stiff brocade of skirts and stomacher, stiffer for plaques of embroidered silver flowers and rows of seed pearl. The dress is, with its mixture of silver and pearl, of a strange dull red, a wicked poppy-juice colour, against which the flesh of the long narrow hands with fringe-like fingers; of the long slender neck, and the face with bared forehead, looks white and hard, like alabaster. The face is the same as in the other portraits: the same rounded forehead, with the short fleece-like, yellowish-red curls; the same beautifully curved eyebrows, just barely marked, the same eyelids, a little tight across the eyes; the same lips, a little tight across the mouth; but with a purity of line, a dazzling splendour of skin, and intensity of look immeasurably superior to all the other portraits (2006, 61–62).

As in the miniature, Medea 'looks out of the frame with a cold, level glance', but here her lips smile an enigmatic smile that recalls the *Mona Lisa* (2006, 62). In one hand she 'holds a dull-red rose' while the other 'plays with a thick rope of silk and gold and jewels hanging from the waist' (2006, 62). Around her throat, 'white as marble ... hangs a gold collar with the device on alternate enameled medallions, "AMOUR DURE – DURE AMOUR."' (2006, 62). The portrait has a destabilising effect on Trepka who begins to act erratically: he makes 'a snow-woman' he calls

'Medea'; he composes a song based on an Italian poem which begins 'Medea, mia dea' (Medea, my goddess); and begins to see manifestations of the dead Medea both in person and in print: he spies Medea outside his window, and receives a letter from Medea asking him to meet her at 'the Church of San Giovanni Decollato' (2006, 63–65). Unable to resist the call, Trepka makes his way to the church which displays a marble relief over the door 'showing the grizzly head of the Baptist' and close to which lies an iron cage 'in which were formerly exposed the heads of criminals; the decapitated, or … decollated, John the Baptist, being apparently the patron of axe and block' (2006, 66). Finding the church locked, Trepka fears that a joke has been played on him, but suddenly hearing 'the voice of choristers and the drone of a litany' he retraces his steps and enters the church with ease finding it 'brilliantly illuminated with tapers and garlands of chandeliers' (2006, 66–67). The people he encounters are mysteriously dressed in old-fashioned clothes, and his eye is caught by 'a woman standing in the opposite aisle, close to the altar, and in the full blaze of its lights' (2006, 67). Wrapped in black and holding in her hand an unseasonal red rose, the woman 'loosened her heavy black cloak, displaying a dress of deep red, with gleams of silver and gold embroideries' (2006, 67). As she turns her head toward Trepka, her face caught in 'the full blaze of the chandeliers and tapers' reveals her identity to be that of no other but Medea da Carpi (2006, 67). Raising the leathern curtain, Medea glides out of the church, and Trepka follows to find nothing but the empty street.

This first encounter is followed by others. On the second occasion, Medea leaves a rose, 'a real, living rose, dark red and only just plucked' which the next morning crumbles to dust in Trepka's fingers; the third occasion yields another letter which instructs Trepka to 'cut boldly into the body of the bronze rider who stands in the Corte' (the statue of Robert II), and to take out the silver effigy that protects Robert's soul, promising a reward for this proof of his love (2006, 70–71). On Christmas Eve, determined to gain his reward, Trepka heads for the statue, armed with a hatchet. On the way, he meets the ghostly forms of Medea's former lovers. Ignoring their warnings, he proceeds to meet his fate. Obsessed by his mission, and his love for Medea, Trepka saws the statue open, tears out the silver image, hacks it to pieces, and returns to his lodgings to await Medea. His last diary entry notes a step on the staircase which he interprets as hers and reads: 'It is she! it is she! At last, Medea, Medea! Ah! AMOUR DURE—DURE AMOUR!' (2006, 76). An anonymous supplementary entry tells us that Trepka's body was later discovered, 'dead of a stab in the region of the heart, given by an unknown hand' (2006, 76).

Lee's Medea is evidently a variation of the phallic mother, recalling both the Virgin of the Seven Daggers, with her 'tiny coral mouth', her brocaded skirts of 'silver roses', her body encased in a 'network of seed pearl'; and her dark counterpart, the Infanta, whose 'silver pallor' is broken by a 'mouth most subtly carmined' which rises above a breast 'covered with rows and rows of the largest pearls' (Lee 2006, 250, 268–269). She is also intimately associated with the *Mona Lisa* and 'can be read as an animated version of Pater's portrayal of "La Gioconda" in *The Renaissance*' suggesting that the image of the phallic mother and the fatal woman are here once again conflated, for Medea is also linked to a series of *femmes fatales*: Lucrezia Borgia, Faustine, Cleopatra, the sirens, and to her necromantic namesake, Medea of Colchis (Zorn 1997, 4). With her enigmatic smile and cruel mouth, Medea also bears more than a passing resemblance to the castrato Zaffirino, with his 'odd smile, brazen and cruel': their faces are both, like so many others in Lee's fantastic tales, the 'faces of wicked, vindictive women' (Lee 2006, 162). Medea's church, like that of the Virgin of the Seven Daggers, is steeped in images of castration: it is that of 'San Giovanni Decollato', 'the voice of choristers' (often castrati) herald her appearance, and the altar displays 'a picture of the daughter of Herodias dancing': an allusion to the decapitation/castration of John the Baptist, which symbolically mirrors the incapacitation and intellectual 'castration' that Spiridion Trepka experiences as a result of his erotic obsession with Medea (2006, 66, 69). Moreover, the tale is punctuated by coded references to castration: 'white bullocks' drag Trepka's gig as he enters Urbania; the youths of Urbania are 'like so many young Raphaels, with eyes like the eyes of bullocks'; 'great white bullocks' work in the production of olive oil; and at a cattle-fair, 'hundreds of white bullocks' crowd the piazza under the city walls (2006, 42, 43, 62, 68).[9] Furthermore, Medea's 'brilliantly red' mouth, which looks 'as if it could bite or suck like a leech' in a face framed by snake-like curls recalls the dangerous 'vagina dentata', of Freud's 'Medusa's Head' (2006, 52). But the moment in the text which is perhaps most evocative of castration is Medea's 'unveiling' in full blaze of the blinding tapers that light the church, unwrapping her heavy cloak to reveal that 'dress of deep red', of that 'wicked poppy-juice colour' that mirrors the unveiling of the mother's wound and its 'blinding' effect which Freud associates with the psychic castration of the male (2006, 62, 67). This image is heightened by Medea's association with the Virgin Mary, the universal mother of whom, as Sandro Melani observes, women like Medea are the 'blasphemous and sacrilegious reversal' (1996, 132).[10] Not only does the encounter take place in church but, as Christa Zorn suggests, Medea, on this occasion 'bears a striking resemblance to Piero della Francesca's *Madonna della Misericordia*':

> When she appears to Trepka, she loosens 'her heavy black cloak, displaying a dress of deep red with gleams of silver and gold,' details which echo the open black cloak over a red dress of Piero's frontal Madonna, a massive cylindrical form which towers above the smaller-scale human beings who invoke her. The Madonna della misericordia conveys a sense of power similar to Medea's overbearing magnetism during the imaginary church service (1997, 7).

Moreover, as Zorn goes on to point out, the image of Medea as the threatening mother is implicit throughout the tale and heightened by its violent dénouement:

> Medea's fatal stroke on Christmas Eve and the fulfillment of Spiridion's desire in the moment of death ironically reverse the traditional conception of Christmas as a feast of birth and new life. The 'immaculate' Mother-and-Child myth, eagerly promoted by religious discourses of the nineteenth century, is thus evoked and mocked by the conniving Renaissance Medea, who kills her lovers, and her mythological 'double,' who kills her children. Medea da Carpi's appearance obviously commands traditional Christian iconography: while she appears in the red and black garb of the Compassionate Madonna, she undermines the religious symbolism by the fear she spreads through her pattern of fear and revenge. Like the mythological figure, Medea da Carpi is the 'unfeminine' woman and the 'unmotherly' mother (a female Cronos), who is a latent threat to established order (1997, 7).

Seemingly, from its inception, Medea's impact on Trepka has had a 'castrating' and diminishing effect which receives its symbolic manifestation in the aisles of the haunted church. With each meeting Trepka becomes progressively unhinged, showing evidence of hysteria by which he is necessarily feminized. Spiridion Trepka, then, is arguably a 'castrated' male, a 'castrato'. Given Lee's identification with the castrato figure and his inverted double, the phallic woman, Trepka's desire for Medea is suggestive. Significantly, Trepka and Medea are 'twinned' within the text itself: Trepka's horoscope tallying 'almost exactly with that of Medea da Carpi' (2006, 72). Here, once again, the twinning of characters seems to reveal a negotiation of identity that extends beyond the tale itself: the fluid sexuality made possible by the process of doubling allows an expression of same-sex desire via a model of erotic exchange that is superficially heterosexual. As 'castrated male' and 'phallic woman', Trepka and Medea display an androgyny that is in keeping with the latently homoerotic dyadic and triadic relationships encountered elsewhere in Vernon Lee's fiction.

I suggest that the role played by the portrait, particularly by the final painting of Medea is crucial in this process. This portrait, as a number of critics have noted, owes a great deal to Bronzino's portrait of Lucrezia Panciatichi (fig. 4.1).[11] Bronzino, a second generation Mannerist, is credited with introducing 'a new manner characterized by studied elegance and refined poise' in which a striking contrast is created between 'the detailed treatment given to rich costumes and the aloof, enigmatic faces': in his paintings, 'The sitters look out at us, and yet there seems to be no point of contact between them and the onlooker. Their mysterious melancholy appears as an affectation, a quality emphasized by Bronzino through the extreme formalism of his portraiture' (Mariates 1979, 40–41).

If, as it seems, Medea is inevitably associated with the figure of the mother, then Mariates's comments on Bronzino's portraiture have interesting implications, and if, as Lee states in 'The Blame of Portraits', portraits are always filtered through the artist's consciousness, then her revision of the Bronzino portrait is telling. The portrait form, as we have seen, is intimately associated with our own responses to the mother's face. In conflating the aloofness of the Bronzino portrait with the image of Medea as the dangerous mother, and tracing its impact on Trepka, Lee enacts a process of identification and misidentification which she employs in many of the tales already discussed. Trepka and Medea, like other characters in Lee's fiction, and particularly in her supernatural tales, appear to contain aspects of Vernon Lee herself. Trepka, like Lee, is a scholar, a writer, a male counterpart; and Medea, according to Gardner, bears similar features, Medea's general description tallying with that of Lee in Sargent's 1889 sketch and, one particular detail, her 'fringe-like fingers' linking her directly to a remark made by Sargent regarding Lee's hands which he described as 'ornamental fringes' (Gardner 1987, 326).[12] The process that Lee describes in 'The Blame of Portraits' where the personality of the artist merges with that of the sitter appears to be at work in the figures of Trepka and Medea. Trepka, as writer/scholar, becomes the figure of Lee as 'artist', while Medea, with her physical resemblance to Lee, becomes the 'sitter', the subject displayed in art who simultaneously represents both artist and painted 'object'.

Fig. 4.1   Agnolo Bronzino, *Lucrezia Panciatichi* (*c.* 1540).

Yet, here, Winnicott's theory, which posits the construction of the child's identity in the maternal 'mirror' is also at play. Infantilized by his desire, Trepka becomes the child who seeks himself in his mother's face, and searches for his identity in portraits of Medea: her simultaneous absence and presence providing a fantasy space for its construction. In this context, the portrait functions as both subject and object: it is both the 'mother' that allows the 'child' to explore his individuality in her silent presence, and the transitional object that plays a prominent role in that procedure. However, it is crucial to keep in mind that the portrait also functions as a form of mirror. Significantly, Trepka's encounter with the final portrait of Medea takes place in a framed mirror which makes a 'portrait' of his own reflection. In looking at Medea, Trepka is in some sense looking at himself and the play of reflections recall those that take place between the viewer and the sitter in the reflective glass that seals Francis Bacon's portraits. But her portrait's unresponsiveness suggests that Medea negates Trepka's identity. Not being 'seen', his own reality is in doubt and he retains that formlessness that characterizes the child's pre-Oedipal existence.

As in 'A Wicked Voice' the male 'artist', that counterpart to Lee's public persona, finds his existence called into question as he is engulfed by a powerful feminine entity. Like Zaffirino's, Medea's dangerous magnetism functions as a form of maternal entrapment that recalls Michel Chion's 'umbilical net' which can be simultaneously reassuring and threatening (quoted in Silverman 1988, 74). In this context 'Amour Dure: Dure Amour' (that constant and cruel Love) takes on a sinister significance. Medea's power, the power of the phallic woman, overrides and supersedes Trepka's intellectual power. Here, it appears that Lee's rejected female persona returns with magnified, and insistent, strength. In the tale itself an ambiguous ending cheats us of the knowledge of Trepka's murderer whom we suppose to be Medea. Yet, read symbolically in terms of Lee's negotiation of identity, Trepka's death could be read as a surrender to the phallic woman: an acceptance of aggressive femininity.

Oke of Okehurst; or The Phantom Lover

The latent doublings which take place in 'Amour Dure' are equally present in 'Oke of Okehurst'. Here, however, the double also plays a central part in the development of the tale. The story is narrated by an unnamed artist, possibly based on John Singer Sargent, who arrives at Okehurst, a Jacobean manor in the Kent countryside, in order to paint the portraits of its owners, William and Alice Oke.[13] While William is a 'magnificent specimen of the handsome Englishman', he is still like 'a hundred other young men you can see any day in the Park' (Lee 2006, 137, 107). In contrast, his wife Alice, with her 'exotic' elegance and 'marvellous, fantastic kind of grace'; her 'strange cheeks' and 'exquisite and uncanny' smile, proves a difficult subject (2006, 106). Pre-portrait sketches fill a 'whole sketch-book' yet the painting is 'never finished' and the artist expresses his regret in language that defines her elusiveness:

> I wish, alas! – I wish, I wish, I have wished a hundred thousand times – I could paint her, as I see her now, if I shut my eyes – even if it were only a silhouette ... . But where is the use of talking about her? I don't believe, you know, that even the greatest painter can show what is the real beauty of a very beautiful woman in the ordinary sense: Titian's and Tintoretto's women must have been miles handsomer than they have made them. Something – and that the very essence – always escapes, perhaps because real beauty is as much a thing in time – a thing like music, a succession, a series – as in space. Mind you, I am speaking of a woman beautiful in the conventional sense. Imagine, then, how much more so in the case of a woman like Alice Oke (2006, 106, 114–115).

Nevertheless, a portrait does exist, a portrait which is the uncanny double of Alice Oke. In the hall of Okehurst hang companion portraits of the Okes' ancestors one of whom shares her Christian name with the current Alice, and is 'wonderfully like the present Mrs Oke': 'There were the same strange lines of figure and face, the same dimples in the thin cheeks, the same wide-opened eyes, the same vague eccentricity of expression ... . One could fancy that this woman had the same walk, the same beautiful line of nape of the neck and stooping head as her descendant' (2006, 118–119). Moreover, the resemblance is heightened by the fact that the present Alice Oke often makes herself up to look like her ancestress, 'dressing in garments that had a seventeenth-century look ... that were sometimes absolutely copied from this portrait' (2006, 119). The reasons for Alice Oke's strange interest in her ancestor soon become clear. In the 'heady and oppressive' atmosphere of the yellow drawing-room, a room supposedly haunted by Christopher Lovelock, a seventeenth-century poet reputed to be the earlier Alice's adulterous love, the current Alice Oke seemingly communes with the past, and conducts a ghostly flirtation with her ancestor's former lover. This 'communion' is signalled by a 'distant look in her grey eyes' and an 'absent-looking smile in her thin cheeks' (2006, 130).

From William Oke, who recoils from entering the room, the artist learns the bare bones of Lovelock's story. Riding home alone one evening, Lovelock had been 'attacked and murdered, ostensibly by highwaymen, but as was afterwards rumoured, by Nicholas Oke, accompanied by his wife dressed as a groom' (2006, 121). Alice, however, is only too happy to fill in the details and, intrigued by what he perceives to be her 'caprice' or 'mania' to 'resemble the Alice Oke of the year 1626', the artist indulges her fantasies and requests that he might paint her in the yellow drawing-room (2006, 122). Here, Alice Oke reads him Lovelock's poems in 'a delicate, shadowy,' voice which has 'a curious throbbing cadence, as if she were reading the words of a melody, and restraining herself with difficulty from singing it' (2006, 127). She also shows him that, on her writing-table in the yellow room, she keeps a portrait of Christopher Lovelock which stands 'as on an altar' behind 'a silk curtain ... the sort of thing behind which you would have expected to find a head of Christ or the Virgin Mary' (2006, 128). Drawn back, the curtain reveals 'a large-sized miniature, representing a young man, with auburn curls and a peaked auburn beard, dressed in black, but with lace about his neck, and large pear-shaped pearls in his ears' (2006, 128).

In the heavy ambience of the room, Alice Oke takes on an almost sinister demeanour. For the artist, this 'exquisite woman' becomes 'something ... almost repulsive,' something, 'perverse and dangerous' (2006, 128). Slowly he becomes aware of the intensity of her 'mania': her Vandyck dress, which he had considered to be 'a modern copy' is the 'original dress of Alice Oke, the daughter of Virgil Pomfret – the dress in which, perhaps, Christopher Lovelock had seen her in that very room', and when she talks of the former Alice, she enters so 'completely and passionately' into her feelings that she speaks of her as if she were 'not another woman, but herself' (2006, 130–131). For William Oke, Alice becomes increasingly disturbing. In and out of the yellow drawing-room she torments his jealousy with sightings of the ghostly Lovelock, and at an impromptu masquerade she appears as 'a boy, slight and tall' in the costume in which her namesake 'used to go out riding with her husband in the days of Charles I': the groom's outfit which Alice Oke had worn to murder Christopher Lovelock (2006, 138). Provoked mercilessly, William Oke, grows 'perfectly unstrung, like a hysterical woman', and finally murders his wife in the yellow drawing-room. Too late to prevent the tragedy, the artist enters only to find:

Oke ... standing in the middle of the room, with a faint smoke around him; and at his feet, sunk down from the sofa, with her blond head resting on its seat, lay Mrs Oke, a pool of blood forming in her white dress. Her mouth was convulsed, as if in that automatic shriek, but her wide-open white eyes seemed to smile vaguely and distantly (2006, 144, 152).

According to Burdett Gardner, Alice Oke, like Medea, can be identified as a double of Lee herself. 'Tall and slender' and 'straight ... as a bamboo', her figure has 'a suppleness and a stateliness' that reminds the artist of a 'peacock' or a 'stag', and Gardner 'of numerous snapshot poses of Miss Paget herself in many of which she struck "picturesque" attitudes – as though seeking for striking, weird and recherché effects' (Lee 2006, 114; Gardner 1987, 335). Yet I suggest that here, as in 'Amour Dure', Lee's processes of identification are far more complex than Gardner's comments indicate, and that the unnamed artist is also a facet of Vernon Lee. Like Spiridion Trepka who believes he understands Medea 'so well; so much better than ... [his] facts warrant', the artist feels that he instinctively understands Alice's character 'so well' and argues that 'to understand it well seemed to imply ... a comfortable acquiescence' to her eccentricities (Lee 2006, 56, 140). Moreover, like Trepka, the artist experiences a psychic 'castration' and is unable to complete his task after his encounter with an enigmatic woman.

Like Medea, Alice is another version of the *femme fatale*: her 'uncanny' smile, her 'exotic' elegance and 'marvellous, fantastic kind of grace' recall the figure of Pater's *La Gioconda*, and her indefinable beauty so strangely reminiscent of 'a peacock' or 'a stag' displays an androgynous quality which we also associate with the phallic mother (Lee, 2006, 106, 114). The moment in which Alice 'unveils' arguably takes place in the final scene where, according to Diana Basham, the 'pool of red forming in her white dress' functions as a 'menstrual configuration' that mirrors Medea's symbolic exposure of woman's wound in 'Amour Dure' (1992, 176). While the artist's 'castration' seemingly takes place after this incident, his psychic castration is prefigured by that of William Oke who is progressively feminized by his mounting hysteria, and I would suggest that the recurrent and forlorn bleating of 'lambs separated from their mothers' which punctuate the tale, perform a dual function: they are both a prediction and reminder of their mutual maternal loss. Like the artist in 'A Wicked Voice', the artist in 'Oke of Okehurst' appears to double for Lee's literary persona, he is 'a rather unusual kind of man', a counterpart to Alice Oke, 'a very unusual kind of woman' (Lee 2006, 113). Yet, unlike Magnus and Trepka, the artist in this tale does not fall in love with Alice Oke, although he does experience a strange attraction to Alice that forges his sympathy for William Oke. Instead, the erotic focus of the tale is the triangular relationship between the nineteenth-century and the seventeenth-century versions of Alice Oke, and the poet, Christopher Lovelock.

Although Lovelock is ostensibly the object of desire, Dennis Denisoff argues otherwise. In 'Oke of Okehurst', Denisoff detects a manifestation of same-sex desire:

> The force of the same-sex bond in 'Oke of Okehurst' arises from the heroine's devotion to her namesake surpassing not only the portraitist's interest in the living Alice but also the dead Alice's dubious attachment to a lover who may have never existed and, if he did, whom she then helped to murder. The incommensurability of Alice's main attraction, on the one hand, and generic and cultural conventions, on the other, causes a disjuncture that established social and textual narratives appear unable to reconcile without killing off the heroine. More precisely, Alice's murder is the result of her society's inability or unwillingness to accept her attachment to this woman from the past. William kills his wife not for her interest in another man but for her undying devotion to another woman (1999, 256).

I agree with Denisoff that there is an implicit eroticism in the relationship between the two Alices, and would add that the relationship between these women has other interesting implications. If Winnicott's psychoanalytic model holds true, then when the nineteenth-century Alice looks at the portrait of the seventeenth-century Alice, what she sees is a satisfying 'maternal' reflection that affirms her existence and her identity. If, as Gardner suggests, Alice Oke is a fictional version of Vernon Lee, then that identification also applies to Lee herself. Yet what kind of an identity is it? Not only does Alice Oke display the androgynous qualities of the phallic mother, she also masquerades as a groom, a 'beautiful boy' which has, as Vicinus observes, a particular role to play in the expression of homosexuality. Moreover, her 'diaphanous' 'incorporealness', suggests a ghostliness that identifies her with Medea, and both with the 'apparitional lesbian', that ghostly manifestation which Terry Castle identifies as haunting both overt and covert expressions of lesbian desire in literature and in film (Lee 2006, 123, 151; Castle 1993).

Her Sphinx-like nature also links her to another of Lee's ghosts, the castrato Zaffirino, for the Sphinx, like the castrato, is a hybrid figure. Furthermore, like the castrato, the Sphinx was in the past 'characterized by her song', and Alice Oke, as we have seen, speaks in a 'throbbing cadence' that borders on song (Schneider 1988, 194; Lee 2006, 127). According to Monique Schneider, the Sphinx is transformed by Sophocles from 'The bitch [who] has bewitched us with her songs' into a reassuring image of the Freudian phallic mother: 'an examiner who asks questions' not a singer who sings songs (Schneider 1988, 195). For Schneider, this process functions as an imposition of the 'phallic, authoritative superego ... by force on the voice of the woman': in this way, 'The man doesn't have to listen to the voice of the woman, just as he doesn't have to listen to the voice of the sirens' (Schneider 1988, 195). Yet, it is worth noting that in Lee's tales, the phallic mother – that inverted counterpart of the castrato – can be both reassuring and dangerous, and often wields a power that castrates even as it seems to protect the men with whom she comes into contact. Interestingly, in 'Oke of Okehurst' the Sphinx's song is seemingly restored and wreaks its castrating revenge on the artist who listens. Although the 'artist' identifies with Alice Oke through his instinctive understanding, he is nevertheless ultimately disempowered, and left unable to recreate her image. In the narcissistic engagement between the two Alices we also find an implied return to a pre-Oedipal plenitude that allows Lee to suggest same-sex desire, and Alice, like Medea, functions simultaneously as an expression of a powerful femininity that is denied to Lee, and which Lee denies her professional persona.

The Alice of 1626 may be the covert object of the nineteenth-century Alice's lesbian attraction, but the ostensible object of her desire in the text is Christopher Lovelock. However, in Lee's tale, Alice's erotic interests are not necessarily mutually exclusive. If one returns to Lee's description of Lovelock's miniature, one finds that it lies hidden behind a silk curtain, 'the sort of thing behind which you would have expected to find a head of Christ or of the Virgin Mary' (2006, 128). Lovelock also shares part of his name with Christ, and the lace and pearls that adorn him recall those ornately decorated madonnas encountered in tales discussed above. Given the link between Christ and the castrato traced in Chapter Two, Lovelock becomes increasingly intriguing. Linked to this androgynous figure, the image in the miniature with its 'peaked auburn beard' and 'auburn curls', its lace and its pearls, is feminized (2006, 128). Moreover, like Christ, and the Virgin Mary, the miniature image of Lovelock's disembodied head recalls that other – the head of Medusa – the mythical woman who, as I suggest in Chapter One, is herself implicitly identified with the castrato. Kuryluk traces a more explicit link between the two figures:

> The 'true' faces of Christ were preceded by the masks of Medusa. It is certain that her omnipresence in Graeco-Roman antiquity contributed to the popularity of Jesus' and the Baptist's disembodied heads which, like those of Medusa, were depicted as either dark or light, and often with serpentine hair. Medusa's heads – horrible as well as beautiful, and occasionally furnished with beards – persisted throughout the Byzantine period, and at the beginning of the second millennium they could still be found on Russian amulets called *zmeeviki* (images with snakes) (1991, 153).

It seems that even bearing a peaked beard, Lovelock can represent a Medusan figure, a phallic Madonna, who is strangely worshipped with an intensity akin to that of Dora or of Sister Benvenuta enthralled by their Madonna paintings. In the light of these coded associations, the name 'Lovelock' becomes particularly significant: 'love-lock' figures as a word that characterizes the autoerotic quality of Alice Oke's obsession with her ancestor, and the nature of same-sex desire which is implicit in the seemingly heterosexual eroticism of Alice's love for the ghostly Caroline poet.

Portrait of a Vampire

The magic portrait motif, employed in Lee's tales, has been a staple of Gothic fiction since the eighteenth century, playing a prominent part in such works as Horace Walpole's *The Castle of Otranto* (1764), and Ann Radcliffe's *The Mysteries of Udolpho* (1794). In the nineteenth century, the theme proliferated, appearing in the works of a wide range of writers. While most of these might be usefully considered in relation to Lee, I will focus on three: Henry James's 'The Story of a Masterpiece' (1868), Edgar Allan Poe's 'The Oval Portrait' (1845), and Oscar Wilde's *The Picture of Dorian Gray* (1890–91) in order to compare the treatment of the artist in these works with that he receives in Lee's. While James was also to employ the magic portrait motif in recognizable form in his later unfinished novel, *The Sense of the Past* (1917), 'The Story of a Masterpiece', which offers a more subtle use of the theme, has been chosen because its female protagonist, Marian Everett, bears an interesting resemblance to Lee's Medea.

When James wrote to Lee in 1890 to thank her for sending him a copy of *Hauntings: Fantastic Stories*, which includes tales that play in subtle ways with the theme of magic portraiture, he is somewhat dismissive of the genre even as he compliments Lee on her work:

> The supernatural story, the subject wrought in fantasy, is not the class of fiction I myself most cherish (prejudiced as you may have perceived me in favour of a close connotation, or close observation, of the real, or whatever one may call it – the familiar, the inevitable). But that only makes my enjoyment of your artistry more of a subjection (1980, III. 277).

It is perhaps surprising then that in 'The Story of a Masterpiece' James should describe 'a portrait in many ways indebted to the magic-picture tradition' (Powell 1983, 153). The portrait in question is in fact one of two paintings which appear in the text. The first is encountered by James's male protagonist, John Lennox, who finds in the portrait a resemblance to his bride-to-be:

> It bore a representation of a half-length female figure, in a costume and with an expression so ambiguous that Lennox remained uncertain whether it was a portrait or a work of fancy: a fair-haired young woman, clad in a rich medieval dress, and looking like a countess of the Renaissance. Her figure was relieved against a sombre tapestry, her arms loosely folded, her head erect and her eyes on the spectator, toward whom she seemed to move – '*Dans un flot de velours trainant ses petits pieds.*' As Lennox inspected her face it seemed to reveal a hidden likeness to a face he knew well – the face of Marian Everett (James 1962, 263).

Intrigued by the portrait, Lennox learns from the artist, Stephen Baxter, that it is entitled 'My Last Duchess' after Robert Browning's poem.[14] Despite the poem's sinister subtext in which the portrait can be understood as a substitute for a woman killed by her possessive husband for suspected sexual misdemeanours, Lennox finds that the longer he looks at Baxter's painting, 'the more he liked it, and the deeper seemed to be the correspondence between the lady's expression and that with which he had invested the heroine of Browning's lines' and the 'less accidental ... seemed that element which Marian's face and the face on the canvas possessed in common.' (1962, 264). Impressed by Baxter's artistry, Lennox asks him to paint a portrait of his beloved not knowing that Baxter and Marian were once involved in a romantic liaison that ended as a result of Marian's flirtatious behaviour. When the painting is completed, Lennox examines it to find that:

> It was Marian, in very truth, and Marian most patiently measured and observed. Her beauty was there, her sweetness, and her young loveliness and her aerial grace, imprisoned forever, made inviolable and perpetual ... . The figure sat peacefully, looking slightly to the right, with the head erect and the hands – the virginal hands, without rings or bracelets – lying idle on its knees. The blond hair was gathered into a little knot of braids on the top of the head ... and left free the almost childish contour of the ears and cheeks. The eyes were full of color, contentment and light; the lips were faintly parted. Of color in the picture, there was, in strictness, very little; but the dark draperies told of reflected sunshine, and the flesh spaces of human blushes and pallors, of throbbing life and health' (1962, 283–84).

Although Lennox recognizes the portrait as 'his Marian' he finds that it discloses a superficiality of character which he had hitherto failed to notice, displaying a coldness that leads him to formulate the question, 'Marian, where is your heart?' and to Lennox it seems 'that some strange potent agency had won from his mistress the confession of her inmost soul, and had written it there upon the canvas' (1962, 284–285). Doubt sets in and Lennox cannot help but ask: 'Was she a creature without faith and without conscience? What else was the meaning of that horrible blankness and deadness that quenched the light in her eyes and stole away the smile from her lips?' (1962, 285). Later, seeing the painting exhibited alongside the portrait of 'My last Duchess' only confirms, for Lennox, Marian's cynicism and heartlessness. Struck by the dreadful prospect of a loveless marriage, Lennox sees no honourable escape and decides to go ahead regardless. However, when the portrait is delivered to his home on the eve of his wedding, he destroys it, stabbing it with 'a long keen poinard', thrusting it 'with barbarous glee, straight into the lovely face of the image', dragging it downward and making 'a long fissure in the living canvas' before wantonly hacking it across with 'half a dozen strokes' (1962, 295–96).

James's tale functions as an interesting revision of Browning's 'My Last Duchess'. It carries a similar theme of jealousy and possession: Marian's grace, like the Duchess's beauty which is held captive in the curtained frame, is 'imprisoned forever, made inviolable and perpetual' in the painting Lennox has commissioned (1962, 283). As in Browning's poem, the portrait supposedly captures the reality. Like the coquettish Duchess whose 'looks went everywhere', Marian is revealed to have a 'levity' of soul, that marks her as 'a creature without faith and without conscience' (Browning 1989, 25, l.24; James 1962, 285). Yet there is a fundamental difference between the two texts. Browning's own rejection of his wife's image in sculpted form on the grounds that it would capture only the 'dead facts', is belied by the portrait in his poem; here, the life of the subject exceeds the frame: the Duchess looks 'as if she were alive' (quoted in Pearsall 1992, 43; Browning 1989, 25, l.2).

In contrast, Baxter's portrait of Marian which draws its tints from life, reveals a 'horrible blankness' and a 'deadness that quenched the light in her eyes and stole away the smile from her lips' (James 1962, 285). Whereas Browning's portrait shows a dead woman who, like Medea, seems very much alive, James's portrait of Marian shows a living woman who seems to be 'dead'. This difference is confirmed by the fact that Lennox, on seeing the painting of Marian exhibited alongside that of Baxter's 'My Last Duchess', stands amazed and is prompted to ask, 'Was this the face and figure that, a month ago, had reminded him of his mistress? Where was the likeness now? It was utterly absent as if it had never existed' (1962, 294). The 'deadness' that shadows the picture of Marian, seems to infect other portraits that appear in James's work. In *The Wings of the Dove* (1902), the Bronzino portrait which resembles the dying Milly Theale is, as Adeline Tintner has noted, no other than that which arguably also inspired Lee's Medea: the painting of Lucrezia Panciatichi. Yet, as Maxwell points out, whereas 'Lee's Bronzino has a peculiar animation ... in James' description the picture is sepulchral and epitaphic: the lady is very much dead' (1997, 267).

James's tale resonates interestingly with that of Poe's 'The Oval Portrait'. In Poe's tale, a young girl is depicted in a 'vignette' in which her arms, bosom 'and even the ends of her radiant hair' melt 'imperceptibly into the vague yet deep shadow which formed the background of the whole' and which holds the spectator spellbound with the 'absolute *life-likeness*' of its expression (Poe 1986, 251). The sitter is the artist's wife who sits 'meekly for many weeks in the dark high turret-chamber where the light dripped upon the pale canvas only from overhead' and who resents the attention her husband gives to Art, considering it to be her 'rival' and his 'bride' (1986, 252). The artist's commitment to his art leads to the neglect of his young wife and he turns 'his eyes from the canvas rarely, even to regard the countenance of his wife', not seeing that 'the tints which he spread on the canvas were drawn from the pallid cheeks of her who sat beside him', and when the last brushstroke is done, and he stands 'entranced' before his work, proclaiming it to be 'Life itself', he turns to his wife only to find her dead (1986, 252–53).

In both James's and Poe's texts the woman is 'killed' into art. Marian's moral deficiencies, which escape notice in the live model, are literally and figuratively drawn from Marian and stilled in her portrait that Lennox might see them. Sylvia Richards notes that, in Poe's tale, 'The subject becomes the artist's palette from which he takes the colors to create the *life-likeness* of the canvas ... so that the representation of the woman becomes more real than the reality' (1983, 309). According to Richards, 'This transference of life from the lady to the painting is termed *vampirism*' (1983, 309). While James's tale reads as a revision of Browning's poem, Poe's tale prefigures Christina Rossetti's 1856 poem, 'In an Artist's Studio' in which the portrait model, like Poe's, is the victim of the artist's act of vampirism:

> He feeds upon her face by day and night,
>   And she with true kind eyes looks back on him
> Fair as the moon and joyful as the light:
>   Not wan with waiting, nor with sorrow dim;
> Not as she is, but was when hope shone bright;
>   Not as she is, but as she fills his dream
> (1994, 52, ll. 9–14)

Yet, as I point out in Chapter Three, the act of vampirism is self-perpetuating, and it is therefore perhaps fitting that the women 'killed' into art in the tales discussed in this chapter, all seem to exist in an intermediary space between life and death. Portraiture, as Hawthorne observes, is that art which, like vampirism, can create a living death and 'keep the form of the dead among the living' (quoted in Richards 1983, 310). Marian, whose portrait tells of 'human blushes and pallors, of throbbing life and health' nevertheless conveys a 'blankness' and 'deadness'; Poe's portrait displays an uncanny '*life-likeness*' despite being almost literally a 'death-mask' of the artist's wife; Lee's Medea looks as if she 'could bite or suck like a leech' although dead for hundreds of years; and the Alice Oke of 1626 is both 'dead' and 'undead': reincarnated in her descendant, the Alice Oke of the nineteenth century (James 1962, 284–285; Poe 1986, 251; Lee 2006, 52). What distinguishes Lee's 'vampires' from those of James and Poe, is that Lee's women, although seemingly equally dead, succeed in escaping the frame. In James's and Poe's tales it is the artist who is in control. It is the artist who succeeds in transposing the inner life of the woman onto the canvas. In Lee's stories, the women not only elude the constraints of the frame, they also sap the power of the artist: Trepka is unable to complete his history, and the artist's portrait of Alice Oke remains unfinished. That 'purity of line' that constructs the 'glazed armouring' of Bronzino's Mannerist figures is not strong enough to contain Medea's chthonian power, and, like Medea, Alice Oke, who for the artist is merely 'a wonderful series of lines', refuses the restraint of Apollonian form (Paglia 1992, 150; Lee 2006, 62, 114).

The vampire, as indicated in Chapter Three, is often associated with homoeroticism, particularly via the androgynous vampire mouth with which it feeds on its own as well as on the opposite sex. However, vampirism might also serve as a model for that embryonic fusion with the mother that informs Lee's negotiation of sexual identity: in the womb, the baby feeds vampirically on the mother's blood-enriched placenta, taking nutrients and oxygen from her body. In the tales of James and Poe, the artist/vampire is protected from the vampire woman he creates by the containing presence of the frame. Although Lee's artists are not the painters of the original portraits that inhabit her tales, they are identified with them by implication: the unnamed artist in 'Oke of Okehurst' wants to capture (or re-capture) Alice's image, and Trepka wishes to 'frame' Medea in his history of Urbania. Yet, Lee's fatal women elude or escape those frames that their artists attempt to impose, and feed in turn on the artists themselves. In this context, the vampiric actions of the sitters echo the child's vampiric feeding on the mother: the created feed on their creators.

If one recalls Helene Deutsch's psychoanalytic model of lesbian desire in which the relationship between two women is described as 'a perfectly conscious mother and child situation, in which sometimes one and sometimes the other played the part of the mother', this vampiric model of pre-Oedipal union sheds new light on Bertrand Russell's view of Lee as a 'vampire' and a 'bloodsucker' (quoted in O'Connor and Ryan 1993, 63; quoted in Gardner 1987, 60). It suggests that the relationship between Lee's vampiric women and the 'artists' in 'Amour Dure' and 'Oke of Okehurst' function as alternative identities that allow an expression, however coded, of homoerotic interaction.

According to Camille Paglia, the vampire is also at large in Oscar Wilde's *The Picture of Dorian Gray.* She writes:

> Basil and Dorian's first meeting ... invokes one of the primary Romantic principles, vampirism. In the middle of a party, Basil senses someone looking at him. Dorian's gaze is palpable ... . When their eyes meet, Basil feels Dorian is 'so fascinating' as to 'absorb' him. At this moment of visual fixation, Dorian, like a vampire, dominates the plane of eye-contact. Basil, mesmerized, actually grows 'pale,' like the vampire's bled victim (1992, 519).

And, like the vampire, Dorian corrupts all those who fall under his spell: his friends 'lose all sense of honour, of goodness, of purity' (Wilde 1988, 118) and like the painting of Marian in 'The Story of a Masterpiece', Dorian's picture mirrors those moral deficiencies: just as her portrait betrays her absent 'heart', so to Dorian his portrait reveals 'A face without a heart' (James 1962, 284; Wilde 1988, 163). As in all the paintings encountered so far, the painting of Dorian is both 'dead' and 'undead', for though it is ostensibly the static representation of Dorian Gray, it secretly metamorphoses behind its purple cloth. The static quality of the artwork is transferred to Dorian himself who remains as young, and as free from the signs of debauchery, as the day on which the portrait was painted – therefore Dorian, too, exists in a borderland between 'life' and 'death'. Wilde's story has more in common with Lee's tales than with those of James and Poe. In Wilde's text, as in Lee's, it is the artist who is sucked dry. Describing his first meeting with Dorian to Lord Henry Wotton, Basil Hallward explains, 'I knew that I had come face to face with someone whose mere personality was so fascinating that, if I allowed it to do so, it would absorb my whole nature, my whole soul, my very art itself (1988, 13).

Of Dorian's portrait he argues that it is not the sitter who is revealed by the painting, but the artist who 'on the coloured canvas reveals himself', and informs Wotton, 'The reason I will not exhibit this picture is that I am afraid that I have shown in it the secret of my own soul' (1988, 10). For Hallward, Dorian is 'the visible incarnation of that unseen ideal whose memory haunts us artists like an exquisite dream' and as he works on Dorian's portrait, it appears to him that 'every flake and film of colour' reveals his 'secret' (1988, 89–90). It seems only fitting then that Hallward should die at the hands of his own inspiration. The 'dream' that sapped his talent also saps his life. Yet, in *The Picture of Dorian Gray* the sitter is inexorably linked with the artist. Looking at his actions reflected in the portrait, Dorian muses, 'Was there some subtle affinity between the chemical atoms, that shaped themselves into form and colour on the canvas, and the soul that was within him?' (1988, 76). His 'absorption' of Basil Hallward seems to have had an unexpected effect: not only does Dorian Gray literalize Pierre Nicole's metaphorical artist whose moral actions paint his likeness, but the merging of his soul with that of Hallward also ensures that, like Hallward, the portrait will function as his conscience.

In the light of the vampiric relationship between mother and child described earlier, it seems significant that this uncanny symbiosis between Dorian and his portrait is described by Paglia as an 'umbilical link' (1992, 526). Although for Paglia this 'umbilical link' functions as a form of 'incestuous bond between Romantic twins', one might suggest that, in view of Winnicott's understanding of the mirror-role played by the mother's face, this 'umbilical link' may revert to its maternal root. It is intriguing that the portrait of Dorian's beautiful mother, dressed as a Bacchante, with 'vine leaves in her hair' and eyes that followed him 'wherever he went', also forms 'a double to his own' (Wilde 1988, 112–113; Psomiades, *Beauty's Body* 1997, 187). Moreover, Dorian's narcissistic response to the portrait (he at one point feigns to kiss 'those painted lips that now smiled so cruelly at him' (1988, 83)) implies a return to a pre-Oedipal androgyny which, as in Lee's texts, permits an expression of same-sex desire which is one subtext of Wilde's novel.

Like Lee's fantastic tales, Wilde's novel suggests a negotiation of homosexual identity within a liminal supernatural space and also, like Lee, Wilde's adherence to 'form' as the principle of aesthetic understanding is undermined within the supernatural text. As Paglia points out:

> In *The Critic as Artist* [Wilde] says: 'Form is everything. It is the secret of life ... . Start with the worship of form, and there is no secret in art that will not be revealed to you.' ... [Yet] What is odd about the picture of Dorian Gray is that it is in Dionysian metamorphosis. The changing painting insults beauty and form: Dorian calls it 'the misshapen shadow,' 'the hideous painted thing,' 'this monstrous soul-life.' ... Painting is invaded by a daemonic form-altering power, because Wilde has tried to make nature surrender her authority (1992, 528–529).

While Paglia's point may be valid, the metamorphic properties of Dorian's portrait may be read quite differently. They may function, as in Lee's tales, as a process of exploring alternative identities. According to Martha Vicinus, in the nineteenth century the 'beautiful boy' – to which category Dorian most certainly belongs – encodes 'the defining, free agent' who best expressed homosexuality, and Psomiades argues that 'Aestheticism's beautiful masculine figures signify an erotic/aesthetic realm' in which the idea of the beautiful functions as a 'form of resistance to the medico-legal view of same-sex desire as ugly and perverse' (Vicinus 1994, 92; Psomiades, *Beauty's Body* 1997, 181). In this context Dorian's 'misshapen' portrait is suggestive and expresses perhaps Wilde's struggles with his own demons, and with his sexual orientation, perceived in the constraining 'frame' of late-Victorian society. Yet there is a fundamental difference between Wilde's story and those of Lee. In Wilde's text, Dorian's attempt to destroy the portrait leads only to his own destruction. As he stabs the picture, in a manner reminiscent of Lennox's destruction of Marian's portrait in 'The Story of a Masterpiece', an uncanny exchange takes place:

> When they [Dorian's servants] entered, they found, hanging on the wall, a splendid portrait of their master as they had last seen him, in all the wonder of his exquisite youth and beauty. Lying on the floor was a dead man, in evening dress, with a knife in his heart. He was withered, wrinkled, and loathsome of visage. It was not till they had examined the rings that they recognised who it was (Wilde 1988, 170).[15]

In *The Picture of Dorian Gray* it seems that the beautiful boy must be trapped within art, within the constraints of a socially acceptable 'frame'. In contrast, Lee's portrait tales feature dangerous, androgynous women who escape that frame, who refuse to be constrained. The ambiguity surrounding Medea ensures that she 'lives' on in our imaginations whether or not she was merely a figment of Trepka's disordered mind, and Alice Oke, despite being shot, lives on in another world, 'her wide-open white eyes' smiling 'vaguely and distantly', her ghostly reunion with Lovelock signalled by that 'distant look in her grey eyes' and 'absent-looking smile in her thin cheeks' (Lee 2006, 152, 130). Transgressing the boundary of the picture frame, Lee's portrait-women succeed in doing what, according to Lee, the portrait cannot do: they 'overcome space and baffle time' (Lee, *Hortus Vitae* 1904, 140).

Dionea

Unlike Medea and Alice Oke, who are initially contained within portrait frames from which they 'escape', Lee's Dionea refuses the frame entirely. When she is chosen to model for the sculptor Waldemar, a strange phenomenon occurs. In a letter to Dionea's benefactress, the Lady Evelyn Savelli, Princess of Sabina, Lee's narrator Dr. Alessandro de Rosis writes:

> How strange is the power of art! Has Waldemar's statue shown me the real Dionea, or has Dionea really grown more strangely beautiful than before? ... . Do you remember – you, who have read everything – all the bosh of our writers about the Ideal in Art? Why, here is a girl who disproves all this nonsense in a minute; she is far, far more beautiful than Waldemar's statue of her (Lee 2006, 100).

Waldemar's sculpture, destined to be a statue of Venus, becomes instead a poor portrait-statue of Dionea with whose beauty it cannot compete. Dionea, it seems, not only refuses the 'frame' of art, she exceeds it so completely that she cannot be captured at all. Yet, it is not only her superior beauty that enables this escape but also a Dionysian excess, a chthonian power, that defies the constricting lines of Apollonian artistry. As Maxwell observes:

'Dionea' is another name for Aphrodite or Venus, Goddess of Love, who in some mythological genealogies is the daughter of Dione. Lee's choice of this particular name for Aphrodite with its evident echo of Dionysus seems deliberate: Dione, rather than Semele, is also said by some ancient commentators to be the mother of Dionysus as well as that of Venus (1997, 262–263).

Like the strange Dionysian effigy in 'Marsyas in Flanders', Dionea is washed ashore, and being a young orphan, is placed in a convent where she is cared for by the Sisters of the Stigmata under the watchful eye of Dr. Alessandro de Rosis, the village doctor, who, periodically, reports her progress to her patron, the Lady Evelyn Savelli. It is these reports that construct the narrative of Lee's tale. Concerned that the young girl's name is not fitting for a convent resident, the nuns seek to christen her anew, but are prevented from doing so by one of their number who discovers that a 'Saint Dionea, Virgin and Martyr' exists and consequently sanctifies the pagan name (2006, 80). Dionea soon proves an unusual, and not altogether welcome, addition to the convent. Beautiful but unruly, she shows no aptitude for those traditional skills that are cherished by the sisters, and in her early teens is caught in the process of committing sacrilegious offences. On one occasion, she is discovered 'handling in a suspicious manner the Madonna's gala frock and her best veil of *pizzo di Cantù*' and is reputed to have been surprised 'as she was about to adorn her wicked little person with these sacred garments' (2006, 84). On another occasion she is found in the chapel, 'seated on the edge of the altar, in the very place of the Most Holy Sacrament' (2006, 84). When confronted by the ecclesiastical council concerning these events, Dionea cuts an incongruous figure among the plaster images of St. Francis and the Virgin Mary.

Wild and dark, she has 'an odd, ferocious gleam in her eyes,' and sports 'a still odder smile, tortuous, serpentine, like that of Leonardo da Vinci's women' (2006, 84). Dionea's strange reputation precedes her entry into the outside world, and though acutely aware of her beauty, the village boys view her with feelings 'rather of fear than of love' (2006, 85). A 'glance from her' is considered 'too much' for their peace of mind, and she is regarded as 'possessing the evil eye' (2006, 85). Dionea's strange influence manifests itself in a series of unusual events. Her presence acts as a malevolent love-potion that leads to unhappy liaisons, 'wherever she goes the young people must needs fall in love with each other, and usually where it is far from desirable' (2006, 85). The convent succumbs to a form of love-sickness: 'an extraordinary love epidemic' smites its schoolgirls; 'Unknown things' spring up 'in these good Sisters' hearts'; one of their number elopes with a young sailor; and a young priest, the convent confessor, dies suddenly, having battled an unknown temptation (2006, 86–87).

As soon as she becomes old enough to leave the convent, de Rosis is faced with the difficulty of finding Dionea a welcoming household. Her reputation ensures that no one in the village will have her and he is forced to place her with a rich patriarch,

Sor Agostino, who is soon mysteriously struck by lightning: an act attributed indirectly to Dionea who had warned him that if he did not leave her alone 'Heaven would send him an accident' (2006, 90). Dionea returns to the village where she lives alone, surrounded only by the white pigeons that follow her, surviving ostensibly on Lady Evelyn's charity and by performing a number of 'miscellaneous jobs' but 'her real status' as de Rosis points out, 'is that of village sorceress' (2006, 93).[16]

When the sculptor Waldemar, a friend of Lady Evelyn's, arrives for a stay in the village he is welcomed by de Rosis who takes a particular liking to Waldemar's wife, Gertrude, who reminds him of 'a Memling Madonna finished by some Tuscan sculptor' (2006, 95).[17] It is to the sculptor's love for his 'pale, demure, diaphanous' wife that de Rosis attributes the Waldemar's lack of interest in the female form as a subject for artistic representation:

> I think that hereby hangs the explanation of his never doing any but male figures: the female figure, he says ... is almost inevitably inferior in strength and beauty; woman is not form, but expression, and therefore suits painting, but not sculpture. The point of a woman is not her body, but (and here his eyes rested very tenderly upon the thin white profile of his wife) her soul (2006, 96–97).

It would seem that for Waldemar, as for Winckelmann and for Pater, the Ideal in sculpture is male. Gertrude, however, sets her heart on Waldemar sculpting a female figure and, to the Lady Evelyn, de Rosis voices his disapproval that 'such a snow-white saint' should be on the lookout for a model for her husband and 'should wish another woman to part with all instincts of modesty' so that Waldemar might create (2006, 97). Gertrude's eyes light on Dionea who becomes the model for Waldemar's statue of Venus which he sculpts in 'the long-desecrated chapel' of an old Genoese fort that, according to popular legend, lies on the site of 'the temple of Venus' (2006, 100). As Waldemar becomes increasingly obsessed with Dionea's superior beauty, Gertrude's jealousy grows, and when one night he decides to pose her before the statue of Venus, 'by an artificial light' in the way in which 'the ancients lit up the statues in their temples', Gertrude follows him with disastrous consequences. De Rosis explains:

> He had placed Dionea on the big marble block behind the altar, a great curtain of dull red brocade ... behind her, like a Madonna of Van Eyck's. He showed her to me once before like this, the whiteness of her neck and breast, the whiteness of the drapery round her flanks, toned to the colour of old marble by the light of the resin burning in pans all around ... . Before Dionea was the altar – the altar of Venus which he had borrowed from me. He must have collected all the roses about it, and thrown the incense upon the embers when Gertrude suddenly entered (2006, 103–104).[18]

We can only guess what followed, but the remnants of the pyre, constructed from 'faggots of dry myrtle and heather', 'pine-cones' and 'resin' remain, and the body of Gertrude is found slumped across the altar, 'her pale hair among the ashes of the incense, her blood ... trickling among the carved garlands and rams' heads, blackening the heaped-up roses' (2006, 103–104). Waldemar's corpse is found 'at the foot of the castle cliff' (2006, 104). Dionea mysteriously disappears, but de Rosis logs a last sighting of her:

> a sailor-boy assures me, by all the holy things, that the day after the burning of the Castle chapel ... he met at dawn, off the island of Palmaria, beyond the strait of Porto Venere, a Greek boat, with eyes painted on the prow, going full sail to sea, the men singing as she went and against the mast, a robe of purple and gold about her, and a myrtle-wreath on her head, leaned Dionea, singing words in an unknown tongue, the white pigeons circling around her (2006, 104).

Dionea, as Maxwell has noted, is a 'god in exile' who is clearly linked to Pater's Denys L'Auxerrois and Apollo in Picardy and to his description of the *La Gioconda* in *The Renaissance*.[19] Interestingly, Maxwell also associates Dionea with Medea, and with Alice Oke and traces their comparable characteristics, arguing that, 'The strange, beautiful and demanding women who figure in these stories insist on crossing the boundaries of historical time; they require the performance of ritual and the sacrifice, most importantly of male devotees' and notes that there is also 'something about them that eludes a fixed representation, and certainly possession' (1997, 265). Dionea, then, is another of Lee's fatal women and, like Pater's *Mona Lisa*, and her counterparts, Medea, and Alice Oke, she, too, is 'a blasphemous and sacrilegious reversal' of the Virgin Mary (Melani 1996, 132). Like those pagan gods in exile who sometimes return 'in the stolen garb of the Madonna or the saints' (2006, 91), Dionea is seen adorning herself in the Virgin's sacred garments; her name is taken from Saint Dionea, a 'Virgin and Martyr'; and for de Rosis, Dionea's pose behind the altar is reminiscent of 'a Madonna of Van Eyck's' (2006, 80, 103). Yet de Rosis's comment has interesting implications for it posits Dionea as a double, not only of the Virgin, but also of the artist's wife Gertrude who is herself like a 'Memling Madonna' and this duplication is echoed elsewhere in the text, for just as Dionea is 'as cold as ice, as pure as snow', Gertrude is a 'a snow-white saint' (2006, 95, 87, 94). The twinning of these two women is suggestive for, as Kristeva points out, it is the 'passion between two women' which creates 'one of the most intense figures of doubling' (quoted in Weir 1993, 86).

Although Lee's tale explores Dionea's ability to cause people to fall in love with each other 'where it is far from desirable' the examples given are purely heterosexual. However, one might argue that there is a lesbian subtext to Lee's tale. It is not made clear what 'Unknown things' sprang up in the hearts of the good Sisters of the Stigmata, but if, as Vanita suggests, these same-sex communities carry those connotations of autoeroticism and homosexuality outlined in Diderot's *La Réligieuse*, then Lee's use of 'Stigmata' in this context is evocative for, as we have seen, in her supernatural tales Lee's 'stained' and bloodied women are seemingly linked to expressions of lesbian sexuality (Lee 2006, 86). The blood that trickles from Gertrude's dead and naked body therefore takes on an added significance – she becomes yet another of Lee's 'dolls' stained by the 'impurities' of a transgressive desire. In the light of this, Gertrude's jealousy, interpreted by de Rosis to be directed at Dionea, may in fact be directed at Waldemar, envying his time with Dionea, for if one returns to the text it is worth noting that it is Gertrude who identifies Dionea as the model for Venus. This suggests an attraction to Dionea and a recognition of her sexual power. Moreover, Dionea herself is symbolically associated with lesbian love for her great desire 'to get to the sea' employs marine imagery which is prevalent in lesbian poetry (Lee 2006, 81; Vanita 1996, 66). Furthermore, as de Rosis points out, Dionea's wish is to '*get back to the sea*' implying that the sea is her home rather than a desired destination (Lee 2006, 81).

The sexual fluidity which marks many of Lee's tales is equally in evidence in Dionea. When Gertrude offers Dionea to Waldemar as his model for Venus, he initially rejects her, preferring to sculpt male figures, and argues, 'I have found a model – a fisher-boy, whom I much prefer to any woman' (2006, 97). Waldemar's affirmation of the male body as the sculptural ideal resonates interestingly with the works of Winckelmann, Symonds, and Pater discussed in preceding chapters and suggests that homoerotic desire underlies his artistic preferences. Moreover, Gertrude, despite being pregnant, has that incorporeal 'diaphanous' presence which is also used to describe the boyish Alice Oke and this suggests that their ostensibly heterosexual marriage encodes homoerotic desires (2006, 97). Although, reputed by de Rosis to be obsessed with Dionea, Waldemar's passion is the infatuation of the artist with the living work of art, for Dionea exceeds his own creation, and has, from the beginning, been 'a thing fit for ... Burne Jones or Tadema' to paint (2006, 82).[20] In addition, as god in exile, it is clear that Dionea herself can be identified as an androgynous entity for she is linked to 'the Phidian Pallas' and the 'Venus de Milo', both of which Waldemar posits as fitting subjects for sculpture, arguing that 'those are not women' (2006, 96).[21] It appears significant, then, that Waldemar's final desire is to pose Dionea in the flickering light of 'the resin burning in pans all round', recalling that phenomenon which, captured in the Greek term *poikilos*, encodes homoerotic love (2006, 104).

In this tale, as in 'Amour Dure' and 'Oke of Okehurst', the artist, that counterpart to Lee's public persona, is thwarted, his control defied and exceeded by the mirror-image he seeks in his art. In his place we are left with a vision of a powerful androgynous figure, whose image, like his own, shifts with multiple identifications. It is perhaps only fitting that, like the sacrificial pyre in 'The Image', Waldemar's kindling should include the 'pine cone' for as Navarette observes, the pine cone is 'sacred to Dionysus' and Dionysus is the god of transformation, who 'enables you for a short time to *stop being yourself*, and thereby set you free' (Navarette 1998, 171; Paglia 1992, 97).

Notes

[1]   'The Portrait' (1991, 53, ll.1–4).
[2]   Annie Meyer was the aunt of one of Lee's friends, Alice Callendar. Lee became passionately attached to Meyer and the friendship lasted for two years. When the rupture came, Lee was deeply hurt and she was to look for Meyer's likeness in future friendships: when she met Kit Anstruther-Thomson in 1887, she described her as having 'the face of Annie Meyer' (Gunn 1964, 119).
[3]   Although the quotation does not refer explicitly to Meyer's photograph, it seems implicit in the rhetorical questions that immediately follow in which Lee asks: 'Do I not know that

one? Have I not lived by her side, leaned upon her in my trouble, looked into her face in my isolation …?' (Gardner 1987, 312).

[4]   Pierre Nicole (1625–1695) taught in the schools of Port-Royal where Racine was one of his pupils, and was important in the formation of French prose. The quotations used here are taken from his essay 'Traité de la connaissance de soi-même' which appeared in *Essais de Morale* (1725), vol. III.

[5]   John Lane Company Records, Series A: Correspondence 1856–1933, Harry Ransom Humanities Research Centre at the University of Texas at Austin, USA.

[6]   The Sargent sketch can be found on the cover of the Maxwell and Pulham collection 2006; the Sargent portrait is used as the frontispiece of Colby 2003 and the Noufflard portrait is reproduced in Gunn 1964.

[7]   Bianca Capello (1548–1547), grand Duchess of Tuscany, and member of one of the noblest Venetian families. Famed for her beauty, she eloped and married a young Florentine clerk, and later became the mistress, and then wife, of Francesco de' Medici, grand Duke of Tuscany. She was hated by her brother-in-law Cardinal Ferdinand. Lucrezia Borgia (1480–1519), illegitimate daughter of the Spanish Cardinal, Rodrigo Borgia, later Pope Alexander VI. Although commonly known for her beauty and depravity, recent scholarship suggests that her reputation may be based more on rumour than historical truth. Vittoria Accoramboni (1557–1585), famous for her beauty, accomplishments, and tragic history involving murder and imprisonment.

[8]   Vittoria Accoramboni (1557–1585), accomplished Italian beauty who, due to family jealousies and political intrigue, Accoramboni was imprisoned and later assassinated. Her life inspired John Webster's play, *The White Devil* (1612).

[9]   A bullock is a castrated bull, a steer.

[10]   Thanks to Franca Basta for translating Melani's essay.

[11]   See Maxwell 1997, Tintner 1993, and Zorn 1997.

[12]   Gardner notes that Berthe Noufflard, who painted a portrait of Lee in 1934, reported this remark, and in her own painting she also emphasized Lee's 'long, narrow hands' (1987, 326).

[13]   In the story, the artist has been involved in some professional scandal. Sargent experienced similar difficulties after his provocative portrait of Madame Pierre Gautreau (Madame X) caused an outrage when exhibited in the Paris Salon of 1884.

[14]   Browning's poem was first published under the title 'Italy' and appeared in *Bells and Pomegranates*, III, under *Dramatic Lyrics* in 1842.

[15]   The similarity between the ending of James's tale and Wilde's own prompts a reexamination of the significance of 'Marian' in James's text. As we have seen in Chapter Three, in the nineteenth century, homosexual men were referred to as 'Maryannes'. It seems possible that in his portrait of Marian, James, as literary artist, reveals something of himself, something that, like Dorian, must be destroyed, or contained within a social 'frame'. It is also interesting that in Lee's short story 'Lady Tal' published in Vanitas. Polite Stories (1892) the male protagonist, who bears more than a passing resemblance to Henry James, is called 'Jervase Marion', who is referred to as 'Mary Anne' by Lady Tal's cousin (Lee 1892, 70). See also Schabert 1999.

[16]   White pigeons and doves are birds associated with Aphrodite.

[17]   Hans Memling (c. 1430/40–1494), German-born painter who lived in Bruges. Gertrude is intended to represent the type of virtuous Madonnas found in Memling's devotional paintings.

[18]   Jan van Eyck (d. 1441), major artist of the Netherlandish school who often painted Madonnas against rich brocade backgrounds; roses are flowers associated with the goddess Aphrodite.

[19]   Dionea also functions as a female counterpart to Lee's Marsyas. At her baptism, 'she kicked and plunged and yelled like twenty little devils, and positively would not let the holy water touch her', recalling Marsyas's rejection of the consecrated cross (Lee 2006, 79).

[20]   Sir Edward Coley Burne Jones (1833–1898), English painter associated with the Pre-Raphaelites; Sir Lawrence Alma Tadema (1836–1912), Dutch painter who lived in England and painted exotic scenes featuring Hellenic women.

[21]   The statue known as the Phidian Pallas was a gigantic image of Pallas Athena by the famous Greek sculptor Phidias that was originally erected in The Parthenon, but no longer survives.

Coda

Dionea, as discussed in Chapter Four, has much in common with those other *femmes fatales* Medea da Carpi and Alice Oke. Like Medea, and her namesake, Medea of Colchis, Dionea is witch-like, privy to arcane knowledge that is specifically linked to the idea of cruel love. Like Alice, she projects an autoerotic plenitude that defies all interference, and, like both Medea and Alice, the desires she inspires lead to death and/or figurative castration. Interestingly, according to Rebecca Stott, the *femme fatale* is related to 'another familiar type' in turn-of-the-century literature – the New Woman. However, Stott argues that there is a fundamental difference:

> Unlike the New Woman, the *femme fatale* is mythically rooted and derives power from her association with figures such as Cleopatra, Salome, Judith, Helen, mermaids and sirens ... . The New Woman, in contrast, comes to refer to a new type of woman emerging from the changing social and economic conditions of the late nineteenth century: she is a woman who challenges dominant sexual morality, and who begins to enter new areas of employment and education. While she is often threatening, and sometimes sexually threatening, in her challenging of sexual norms, she does not carry the sexual fatalism of the *femme fatale* type (1992, viii–ix).

Although, one may seek in vain for Lee's name in most of the New Woman debates of the *fin de siècle*, she nevertheless fulfills the image of this independent, outspoken 'mannish' figure, and in 1993 Elaine Showalter included her work amongst that of New Woman writers in the collection *Daughters of Decadence: Women Writers of the Fin-de-Siècle*. It is perhaps unsurprising, then, that the *femme fatale*, to whom, as Stott, suggests, the New Woman is related, should appear as a transgressive figure in Lee's supernatural tales. I suggest that, in Lee's work, the New Woman can openly claim kin with those dangerous female figures which Stott identifies exclusively with the *femme fatale*.

As established in Chapter One, the New Woman's strident vocality is mythologically linked to the Medusan cry, and it is this cry which is aestheticized by Lee's 'Athenian' public persona in the flute-like voice of the 'castrato': a voice which is simultaneously male and female and 'embodied' in the pseudonym 'Vernon Lee'. However, Athena and Medusa are permanently bonded: Athena wears the head of Medusa on her breast-plate and on her shield, and, interestingly, in Lee's tales the castrato is endowed with that dangerous and paralyzing power that is attributed to his dark Medusan counterpart. Perhaps it is only to be expected, then, that Lee's portrait-women, those *femmes fatales* who also exhibit the independence, self-sufficiency, and the androgynous features of the New Woman, should similarly display Medusan characteristics. Medea, whose 'intensity of look' 'looks out of the frame with a cold level glance' wears her hair in snake-like curls; in his miniature, the disembodied head of Christopher Lovelock, who functions as a 'double' for Alice Oke, is reminiscent of the head of Medusa; and Dionea who has 'an odd, ferocious gleam in her eyes,' is said, like Medusa, to carry a fatal glance and is thought to possess 'the evil eye' (Lee 2006, 62, 84–85). Moreover, those Paterian adjectives: 'strange', 'uncanny', 'exquisite', 'weird' used in descriptions of the three women, recall those Lee and Sargent used to describe the portrait of Farinelli: a castrato, whose voice is associated, as I have shown, with Medusa's gorgonian cry.

If one reconsiders Winnicott's concept of the portrait as the mother's face in which one seeks one's own reflection, and affirms one's own existence, Lee's Medusan portrait-women become intriguingly suggestive. They imply that what Lee sees when she looks at her supernatural portraits is Medusa, a figure who challenges and paralyzes her Athenian persona, that sexless figure which upholds the constraints of Apollonian art in her aestheticism. In effect, as Kuryluk contends, Athena and Medusa are doubles: Medusa is 'the other self of Athena', she represents the sexualized Athena, symbolizing 'the staining and corruption of the virginal membrane' which, in Athena must remain intact (1991, 154).

As goddess of heaven and culture, Athena must retain that purity that allows her to partake of Olympian power. Yet, Athena, like Lee, is 'threatened from within by her own Medusan nature' that wishes to yield to transgressive desires (Kuryluk 1991, 156). Interestingly, one of the items with which Athena arms Perseus in order to execute the gorgon, is 'her own aegis, a solar shield-mirror-weapon, which saves Perseus from being killed by Medusa's terrible sight' (Kuryluk 1991, 154). Kuryluk argues that although it is Perseus who executes Medusa, 'the moving spirit behind the act' is Minerva [Athena], 'the honorary male of the Greek Olympus' and suggests that by murdering Medusa, 'she shed off her female physiology, sexuality, and destiny which would have collided with her power as the virgin-goddess of heaven' (1991, 154). 'Medusa's death', as Kuryluk observes, 'transformed Minerva into an artist' (1991, 158). Yet Medusa leaves an indelible mark that Athena cannot erase: as Medusa bleeds to death 'her dreadful likeness' is 'caught again by Minerva's [Athena's] mirror – to stay there forever' (Kuryluk 1991, 154).

It seems that Lee uses her Athenian mirror-shield, the shield of Apollonian art, to deflect Medusa's power, and on that shield, as on the goddess's, the gorgon's head remains; her snaky locks resurfacing in the borderlands of Lee's supernatural tales. In these liminal spaces, her formidable strength is regained. For Athena/Minerva, the gorgon's 'fluid, serpentine reflection' not only tarnishes 'the immaculate goddess,' it also shields her; as Kuryluk points out:

> The aegis confronts us not with a public front, but with a private back, not with a god's face or head, but with a goddess's 'underface' – emblematic of a menstruating vagina, decapitation, and castration. The *vera icon* ['true' image] of Medusa does not cure. Flashed at the beholder, it petrifies him with terror, offering Minerva [Athena] the best protection from male assault (1991, 158).

The 'true' image of 'Vernon Lee', that Medusan image which admits transgressive desires, and permits the negotiation of a fluid identity may also have been her best defence in the male-dominated literary world in which she became an honorary 'Victorian "man-of-letters"'; like Athena, 'an honorary male' amongst 'Olympians' such as Pater, Symonds, Wilde, and Henry James (Zorn 2003, xvi; Kuryluk 1991,

154). It is perhaps a likeness that James glimpsed through a chink in her Athenian armour for he warned his brother William against an acquaintance with Lee on the grounds that 'she is as dangerous and uncanny as she is intelligent, which is saying a great deal' (quoted in Mannocchi 1983, 231). In Lee's tales, Medusa functions as both subject and object. Her unsettling maternal presence provides that 'holding environment' which allows Lee to play with her image, while her myriad manifestations in the art objects that litter Lee's texts act as 'transitional objects'. These objects, these grown-up toys, assist Lee's search for alternative female subjectivities in the intermediary space of the supernatural. Medusa represents not only Vernon Lee's engagement with her darker self, but also with her own creative power.[1]

Note

[1]   Susan R. Bowers argues that 'women achieve greater creativity by braving an encounter with their own creative power, their own Medusa' (1990, 233).

Select Bibliography

Archives

John Lane Company Records, Harry Ransom Humanities Research Center, University of Texas, Austin, Texas.
Vernon Lee Papers, Colby College, Maine, Manuscript Collections.

Primary Texts

Balzac, Honoré de. 'Sarrasine'. In Roland Barthes, *S/Z*. Trans. Richard Miller. Oxford: Blackwell, 1992. 221–254.
Hardy, Thomas. 'Barbara of the House of Grebe'. In Susan Hill, ed., *The Distracted Preacher and Other Tales*. London: Penguin, 1979. 211–243.
Hoffmann, E.T.A. 'The Sandman'. In *Tales of Hoffmann*. Trans. R.J. Hollingdale et al. London: Penguin, 1982. 85–125.
James, Henry. 'The Story of a Masterpiece'. In Leon Edel, ed., *The Complete Tales of Henry James*. 12 volumes, Vol. 1, 1864–1868. London: Rupert Hart-Davis, 1962. 259–296.
———. 'The Last of the Valerii'. In Michael Swann, ed., *Daisy Miller and Other Stories*. London: Penguin, 1983. 13–42.
Lee, Vernon, *Miss Brown: A Novel in Three Volumes*. Edinburgh and London: William Blackwood and Sons, 1884.
———. 'Amour Dure: Passages from the Diary of Spiridion Trepka'. In *Hauntings: Fantastic Stories*. London: William Heinemann, 1890. 3–37. Rpt. in Catherine Maxwell and Patricia Pulham, eds, *Hauntings and Other Fantastic Tales*. Ontario: Broadview Press, 2006. 41–76.
———. 'A Wicked Voice'. In *Hauntings: Fantastic Stories*. London: William Heinemann, 1890. 195–237. Rpt. in Catherine Maxwell and Patricia Pulham, eds, *Hauntings and Other Fantastic Tales*. Ontario: Broadview Press, 2006. 154–181.
———. 'Dionea'. In *Hauntings: Fantastic Stories*. London: William Heinemann, 1890. 61–103. Rpt. in Catherine Maxwell and Patricia Pulham, eds, *Hauntings and Other Fantastic Tales*. Ontario: Broadview Press, 2006. 77–104.
———. 'Oke of Okehurst; or The Phantom Lover'. In *Hauntings: Fantastic Stories*. London: William Heinemann, 1890. 109–191. Rpt. in Catherine Maxwell and Patricia Pulham, eds, *Hauntings and Other Fantastic Tales*. Ontario: Broadview Press, 2006. 105–153.
———. 'The Image'. *Cornhill Magazine*, o.s. 73, n.s. 26 (1896): 516–523.
———. *Ariadne in Mantua*. Oxford: Blackwell, 1903.
———. 'St Eudaemon and His Orange Tree'. In *Pope Jacynth and Other Fantastic Tales*. London: Grant Richards, 1904. 171–191.

————. 'The Featureless Wisdom'. In *Pope Jacynth and Other Fantastic Tales.* London: Grant Richards, 1904. 195–200.

————. 'Sister Benvenuta and the Christ Child'. *Fortnightly Review*, o.s. 84, n.s. 78 (1905): 1–16.

————. 'Winthrop's Adventure'. In *For Maurice: Five Unlikely Stories.* London: John Lane, The Bodley Head, 1927. 143–205.

————. 'The Virgin of the Seven Daggers'. In *For Maurice: Five Unlikely Stories.* London: John Lane, The Bodley Head, 1927. 95–140. Rpt. in Maxwell and Pulham, eds, *Hauntings and Other Fantastic Tales.* Ontario: Broadview Press, 2006. 249–278.

Poe, Edgar Allan, 'The Oval Portrait'. In David Galloway, ed., *The Fall of the House of Usher and Other Writings.* London: Penguin, 1986. 250–53.

Villiers de L'Isle Adam. *Tomorrow's Eve.* Trans. Robert Martin Adams. Chicago: University of Illinois Press, 2001.

Wilde, Oscar. *The Picture of Dorian Gray.* Ed. Donald L. Lawler. New York: Norton, 1988.

Secondary Texts

Agnew, Lois. 'Vernon Lee and the Victorian Aesthetic Movement: "Feminine Souls" and Shifting Sites of Contest'. *Nineteenth-Century Prose*, 26: 2 (Fall 1999): 127–42.

Anstruther-Thomson, Clementina. *Art and Man:Essays and Fragments.* London: John Lane, The Bodley Head, 1924.

Ashley, Tim. 'The Old Man and the Doll'. *Opera House: The Magazine of the Royal Ballet and the Royal Opera*, 10 (Winter 1999): 16–22.

Astern, Linda Phyllis. '"No women are indeed": The Boy Actor as Vocal Seductress in Late Sixteenth- and Early Seventeenth-Century Drama'. In Leslie C. Dunn and Nancy A. Jones, eds, *Embodied Voices: Representing Female Vocality in Western Culture.* Cambridge: Cambridge University Press, 1994. 83–102.

Barbier, Patrick. *The World of the Castrati: The History of an Extraordinary Operatic Phenomenon.* Trans. Margaret Crossland. London: Souvenir Press, 1996.

Barkan, Leonard. '"Living Sculptures": Ovid, Michelangelo, and *The Winter's Tale'.* *English Literary History*, 48 (1981): 639–67.

Basham, Diana. *The Trial of Woman: Feminism and the Occult Sciences in Victorian Literature and Society.* London: Macmillan, 1992.

Bashant, Wendy. 'Singing in Greek Drag: Gluck, Berlioz, George Eliot'. In Corinne E. Blackmer and Patricia Juliana Smith, eds, *En Travesti: Women, Gender, Subversion, Opera.* New York: Columbia University Press, 1995. 216–241.

Baudelaire, Charles. 'Morale du JouJou'. In Charles Pichois, ed., *Oeuvres complètes de Baudelaire.* Paris: Gallimard, 1963. 523–529.

Beard, Mary. *The Invention of Jane Harrison.* Cambridge, Massachusetts and London: Harvard University Press, 2000.

Beattie, Susan. *The New Sculpture.* New Haven and London: Yale U.P., 1983.

Beazley, J.D. and Ashmole, B. *Greek Sculpture and Painting to the End of the Hellenistic Period.* Cambridge: Cambridge University Press, 1966.

Bloom, Michelle E. Pygmalionesque Delusions and Illusions of Movement: Animation from Hoffmann to Truffaut. *Comparative Literature*, 52: 4 (Autumn 2000): 291–320.

Bowers, Susan R. 'Medusa and the Female Gaze'. *National Women's Studies Association Journal* 2 (1990): 217–235.

Braddon, Mary E. *Lady Audley's Secret*. Ed. David Skilton. Oxford: World's Classics, 1987.

Brake, Laurel. 'Vernon Lee and the Pater Circle'. In Catherine Maxwell and Patricia Pulham, eds, *Vernon Lee: Decadence, Ethics, Aesthetics*. Basingstoke: Palgrave Macmillan, 2006. 40–57.

Bronfen, Elisabeth. *Over Her Dead Body: Death, Femininity and the Aesthetic*. Manchester: Manchester University Press, 1992.

Browning, Robert. 'My Last Duchess'. In Daniel Karlin, ed., *Selected Poetry*. London: Penguin, 1989). 25–26.

Busst, A.J.L. 'The Image of the Androgyne in the Nineteenth Century'. In Ian Fletcher, ed., *Romantic Mythologies*. London: Routledge, 1967. 1–95.

Caballero, Carlo. '"A Wicked Voice": On Vernon Lee and Wagner, and the Effects of Music', *Victorian Studies*, 35 (1992): 385–408.

Cambridge Italian Dictionary. Italian–English. Cambridge: Cambridge University Press, 1962.

Carriker, Kitti. *Created in Our Image: The Miniature Body of the Doll as Subject and Object*. London: Associated University Presses, 1998.

Castle, Terry. *The Apparitional Lesbian: Female Homosexuality and Modern Culture*. New York: Columbia University Press, 1993.

Christ, Carol T. '"The Hero as Man of Letters": Masculinity and Victorian Nonfiction Prose'. In Thais E. Morgan, ed., *Victorian Sages and Cultural Discourse*. New Brunswick: Rutgers University Press, 1990. 19–31.

———. 'Browning's Corpses'. *Victorian Poetry,* 33: 3–4, (Autumn-Winter, 1995): 391–401.

Cixous, Hélène. 'Fiction and its Phantoms: A Reading of Freud's Das Unheimliche', *New Literary History* (1976): 534–48.

Clapton, Nicholas. *Handel and the Castrati: The Story Behind the Eighteenth-Century Superstar Singers*. London: Handel House Museum, 2006.

Colby, Vineta. *The Singular Anomaly: Women Novelists of the Nineteenth Century*. New York: New York University Press, 1970.

———. *Vernon Lee: A Literary Biography*. Charlottesville and London: University of Virginia Press, 2003.

Comparetti, Ermanno F. 'A Note on the Origin of *Ariadne in Mantua*'. *Colby Library Quarterly*, 3 (1954). 226–229.

Craft, Christopher. 'Kiss Me with those Red Lips'. In Elaine Showalter, ed., *Speaking of Gender*. New York and London: Routledge, 1989: 216–242.

Davies, Catherine Glyn. *Conscience as Consciousness: The Idea of Self-Awareness in French Philosophical Writing from Descartes to Diderot*. Oxford: The Voltaire Foundation, 1990.

Denisoff, Dennis, 'The Forest beyond the Frame: Picturing Women's Desires in Vernon Lee and Virginia Woolf'. In Talia Schaffer and Kathy Alexis Psomiades, eds, *Women and British Aestheticism*. Charlottesville: University Press of Virginia, 1999. 251–269.

Dervin, Daniel. 'Play, Creativity and Matricide: The Implications of Lawrence's "Smashed Doll" Episode'. *Mosaic: A Journal for the Interdisciplinary Study of Literature*, 14:3 (Summer 1981): 81–94.

Donoghue, Emma. 'Imagined More than Women: Lesbians as Hermaphrodites, 1671–1766'. *Women's History Review*, 2 (1993). 199–216

Dowling, Linda. 'Ruskin's Pied Beauty and the Constitution of a "Homosexual Code"'. *The Victorian Newsletter* (1989). 1–8.

Ellis, Havelock. *Studies in the Psychology of Sex*. 8 vols. New York: Random House, 1936. Vol. 2, Part 2.

Engh, Barbara. 'Adorno and the Sirens'. In Leslie C. Dunn and Nancy A. Jones, eds, *Embodied Voices: Representing Female Vocality in Western Culture*. Cambridge: Cambridge University Press, 1994. 120–135.

Evangelista, Stefano. 'Vernon Lee and the Gender of Aestheticism'. In Catherine Maxwell and Patricia Pulham, eds, *Vernon Lee: Decadence, Ethics, Aesthetics*. Basingstoke: Palgrave Macmillan, 2006. 91–111.

Fitzlyon, April. *The Price of Genius: A Life of Pauline Viardot*. London: Calder, 1964.

Forrest, Jennifer. 'The Lord of Hadaly's Rings: Regulating the Female Body in Villiers de L'Isle Adam's *L'Eve future*'. *South Central Review*, 13:4 (Winter, 1996): 18–37.

Frank, Felicia Miller. *The Mechanical Song: Women, Voice, and the Artificial in Nineteenth-Century French Narrative*. Stanford: Stanford University Press, 1995.

Fraser, Hilary. 'Women and the Ends of Art History: Vision and Corporeality in Nineteenth-Century Critical Discourse'. *Victorian Studies*, 42:1 (Autumn 1998–99): 77–100.

Freud, Sigmund. 'Dora'. In *The Pelican Freud Library*. 24 vols. Trans. and ed. Angela Richards. London: Penguin, 1977. Volume 8. 31–164.

———. 'The "Uncanny"'. In *The Standard Edition of the Complete Psychological Works of Sigmund Freud*. 24 vols. Trans. and ed. James Strachey, Anna Freud et al. London: The Hogarth Press and the Institute of Psychoanalysis, 1955. Volume 22. 219–252.

———. 'The Psychogenesis of a Case of Homosexuality in a Woman'. In *The Penguin Freud Library*. 24 vols. Trans. James Strachey. Ed. Angela Richards. London: Penguin, 1979. Volume 10. 367–400.

———. 'Medusa's Head'. In *The Standard Edition of the Complete Psychological Works of Sigmund Freud*. 24 vols. Trans. and ed. James Strachey, Anna Freud et al. London: The Hogarth Press and the Institute of Psychoanalysis, 1955. Volume 18. 273–274.

Gardner, Burdett. *The Lesbian Imagination (Victorian Style): A Psychological and Critical Study of 'Vernon Lee'*. New York: Garland, 1987.

Gautier, Théophile. 'Contralto'. In *The Works of Théophile Gautier*, 24 vols. 1900–1903. Trans. P.J.T. Sumichrast. London: Harrap. Volume 24 *Emaux et Camées*. Trans. Agnes Lee (1903). 70–73.

Getsy, David J. *Body Doubles: Sculpture in Britain, 1877–1905*. New Haven and London: Yale University Press, 2004.

Ginsberg, Ruth. 'A Primal Scene of Reading: Freud and Hoffmann.' *Literature and Psychology*, 38: 3 (1992): 24–46.

Goeffroy-Menoux, Sophie. 'L'enfant dans les textes de Vernon Lee'. *Cahiers Victoriens et Edouardiens*, 47 (1998): 251–63.

Goodwin, Sarah Webster, and Bronfen, Elisabeth, eds, *Death and Representation*. Baltimore and London: The Johns Hopkins University Press, 1993.

Graves, Robert. *The Greek Myths*. London: Penguin, 1992.

Gregory, Brian. 'Sexual Serpents: Ruskin's *The Queen of the Air*'. *Nineteenth-Century Prose* 26: 2 (1999). 73–85.

Gregory, Eileen. *H.D. and Hellenism: Classic Lines*. Cambridge: Cambridge University Press, 1997.

Gronberg, Tag. 'Beware Beautiful Women: The 1920s Shopwindow Mannequin and a Physiognomy of Effacement'. *Art History*, 20:3 (September 1997): 375–396.

Gunn, Peter. *Vernon Lee: Violet Paget, 1856–1935*. London: Oxford University Press, 1964.

Gubar, Susan. '"The Blank Page" and the Issues of Female Creativity'. In Elaine Showalter, ed., *The New Feminist Criticism: Essays on Women, Literature and Theory*. London: Virago Press, 1986. 292–313.

Harrington, Emily. 'The Strain of Sympathy: A. Mary F. Robinson, *The New Arcadia*, and Vernon Lee'. *Nineteenth-Century Literature*, 61:1 (June 2006): 66–98.

Hartman, Mary S. *Victorian Murderesses*. London: Robson, 1977.

Hawthorne, Nathaniel. *The Marble Faun*. Ed. Richard H. Brodhead. London: Penguin, 1990.

Hollander, Anne. *Seeing Through Clothes*. London: University of California Press, 1993.

Holliday, Peter J. 'John Addington Symonds and the Ideal of Beauty in Greek Sculpture: An Introduction'. *Journal of Pre-Raphaelite and Aesthetic Studies*, 2:1 (Spring 1989): 89–107.

Hotchkiss, Jane. '(P)revising Freud: Vernon Lee's Castration Phantasy'. In Carola M. Kaplan and Anne B. Simpson, eds, *Seeing Double: Revisioning Edwardian and Modernist Literature*. London: Macmillan, 1996. 21–38.

Irigaray, Luce. 'The Bodily Encounter with the Mother'. In *The Irigaray Reader*. Ed. Margaret Whitford. Oxford: Blackwell, 1991. 34–46.

———. *The Sex Which is Not One*. Trans. Catherine Porter and Carolyn Burke. Ithaca: Cornell University Press, 1993.

James, Henry. Letter to Vernon Lee, 27 April 1890. In Leon Edel, ed., *Henry James, Letters*. 4 vols. London: Macmillan, 1980. Vol. 3. 1883–1895.

Jeffreys, Sheila. *The Spinster and Her Enemies: Feminism and Sexuality 1880–1930*. London: Pandora Press, 1985.

Jordanova, Ludmilla. *Sexual Visions: Images of Gender in Science Between the 18th Century and 20th Century*. London: Harvester Wheatsheaf, 1989.

Kahane, Claire. *Passions of the Voice: Hysteria, Narrative, and the Figure of the Speaking Woman, 1850–1915*. Baltimore: Johns Hopkins University Press, 1995.

Kane, Mary Patricia. *Spurious Ghosts: The Fantastic Tales of Vernon Lee.* Rome: Carocci, 2004.

Kaplan, Cora, 'Language and Gender'. In Dennis Walder, ed., *Literature in the Modern World.* Oxford: Oxford University Press, 1992. 310–16.

Koestenbaum, Wayne. *The Queen's Throat: Opera, Homosexuality and the Mystery of Desire.* New York: Penguin, 1994.

Kord, Susanne T. 'Eternal Love or Sentimental Discourse? Gender Dissonance and Women's Passionate Friendships'. In Alice A.K. Kuzniar, ed., *Outing Goethe and His Age.* Stanford: Stanford University Press, 1996. 228–249.

Kristeva, Julia. 'Motherhood According to Giovanni Bellini'. In Leon S. Roudiez, ed., *Desire in Language.* Trans. Thomas Gora et al. Oxford: Basil Blackwell, 1980. 237–270.

———. *Polylogue.* Paris: Editions du Seuil, 1977.

———. 'Revolution in Poetic Language'. In Toril Moi, ed., *The Kristeva Reader.* New York: Columbia University Press, 1986. 89–136.

———. 'The Pain of Sorrow in the Modern World: The Works of Marguerite Duras'. Trans. Katharine A. Jensen. *PMLA*, 102: 2 (March, 1987): 138–152.

Kuryluk, Ewa. *Veronica and Her Cloth: History, Symbolism, and Structure of a 'True' Image.* Oxford: Blackwell, 1991.

Laity, Cassandra. *H.D. and the Victorian Fin de Siècle: Gender, Modernism, Decadence.* Oxford: Oxford University Press, 1996.

Lathers, Marie. *Bodies of Art: French Literary Realism and the Artist's Model.* Lincoln and London: University of Nebraska Press, 2001.

Lee, Vernon. 'The Art of Singing, Past and Present'. *British Quarterly Review*, 72 (1880): 322–342.

———. *Belcaro: Being Essays on Sundry Aesthetical Questions.* London: Satchell,1881.

———. 'Faustus and Helena: Notes on the Supernatural in Art'. In *Belcaro: Being Essays on Sundry Aesthetical Questions.* London: W. Satchell, 1881. 70–105. Rpt. in Maxwell and Pulham, eds, *Hauntings and Other Fantastic Tales.* Ontario: Broadview Press, 2006. 291–319.

———. 'The Portrait Art of the Renaissance'. *Cornhill Magazine*, 47 (May 1883): 564–581.

———. *Juvenilia: Being a Second Series of Essays on Sundry Aesthetical Questions.* 2 vols. London: Fisher Unwin, 1887. Vol. 2.

———. *Commonplace Book*, n.s. 4 (Dec 1888–Dec 1890). Special Collections, Colby College Library, Waterville, Maine.

———. Preface. *Hauntings: Fantastic Stories.* London: Heinemann, 1890. viii–xi. Rpt. in Catherine Maxwell and Patricia Pulham, eds, *Hauntings and Other Fantastic Tales.* Ontario: Broadview Press, 2006. 37–40.

———. 'An Eighteenth-Century Singer: An Imaginary Portrait'. *Fortnightly Review*, o.s. 56, n.s. 50 (1891): 842–80.

———. 'Lady Tal'. In *Vanitas: Polite Stories.* London: William Heinemann, 1892, 7–19. Rpt. in Elaine Showalter, ed., *Daughters of Decadence: Women Writers of the Fin de Siècle.* London: Virago, 1993. 192–261.

————. *Althea: A Second Book of Dialogues on Aspirations and Duties*. London: Osgood McIlvaine, 1894.

————. *Renaissance Fancies and Studies*. London: Smith & Elder, 1895.

————. 'Prince Alberic and the Snake Lady'. *Yellow Book*, 10 (July 1896): 289–344. Rpt. in Maxwell and Pulham, eds, *Hauntings and Other Fantastic Tales*. Ontario: Broadview Press, 2006. 182–228.

————. Preface. *Ariadne in Mantua*. Oxford: Blackwell, 1903. vii–x.

————. *Hortus Vitae: Essays on the Gardening of Life*. London: John Lane, The Bodley Head, 1904. 139–147.

————. 'The Riddle of Music'. *Quarterly Review* 204 (1906): 207–27.

————. Letter to John Lane at The Bodley Head, 13th of January, 1908. John Lane Company Records, Series A: Correspondence 1856–1933. Harry Ransom Humanities Research Center at the University of Texas at Austin, USA.

————. *Gospels of Anarchy and Other Contemporary Studies*. London: Fisher Unwin, 1908.

————. *Laurus Nobilis: Chapters on Art and Life*. London: John Lane, The Bodley Head, 1909.

————. 'The Religious and Moral Status of Wagner'. *Fortnightly Review* (1911), 868–885.

————. *The Tower of Mirrors*. London: John Lane, The Bodley Head, 1914.

————. Introduction. *Art and Man: Essays and Fragments*. By Clementina Anstruther-Thomson. With Twenty Illustrations. London: John Lane, The Bodley Head, 1924. 3–112.

————. Introduction. *For Maurice: Five Unlikely Stories*. London: John Lane, The Bodley Head, 1927. ix–li.

————. *The Handling of Words and other Studies in Literary Psychology*. London: John Lane, The Bodley Head Ltd., 1927.

————. Preface to 'The Virgin of the Seven Daggers'. Introduction. *For Maurice: Five Unlikely Stories*. London: John Lane, The Bodley Head, 1927. xvi–xxii. Rpt. in Maxwell and Pulham, eds, *Hauntings and Other Fantastic Tales*. Ontario: Broadview Press, 2006. 243–248.

————. *Vernon Lee's Letters*, with a preface by her executor, Irene Cooper Willis. Privately Printed, 1937.

Leighton, Angela. 'Ghosts, Aestheticism, and "Vernon Lee"'. *Victorian Literature and Culture* (2000): 1–14.

Macleod, Catriona. 'The "Third Sex" in an Age of Difference: Androgyny and Homosexuality in Winckelmann, Friedrich Schlegel, and Kleist'. In Alice A.K. Kuzniar, ed., *Outing Goethe and His Age*. Stanford: Stanford University Press, 1996. 194–214.

Maltz, Diana. 'Engaging "Delicate Brains": From Working Class Enculturation to Upper-Class Lesbian Liberation in Vernon Lee and Kit Anstruther-Thomson's Psychological Aesthetics'. In Talia Schaffer and Kathey Alexis Psomiades, eds, *Women and British Aestheticism*. Charlottesville: University of Virginia Press, 1999.

Mannocchi, Phyllis F. '"Vernon Lee": A Reintroduction and Primary Bibliography'. *English Literature in Transition 1880–1920*, 26 (1983): 231–267.

Mannocchi, Phyllis F. 'Vernon Lee and Kit Anstruther-Thomson: A Study of Love and Collaboration between Romantic Friends'. *Women's Studies*, 12 (1986): 129–148.

Mariates, Maria Rika. *Mannerism in Italian Music and Culture 1530–1630*. Manchester: Manchester University Press, 1979.

Marin, Louis. 'The Figurability of the Visual: 'The Veronica or the Question of the Portrait at Port-Royal'. *New Literary History*, 22 (1991): 281–296.

Marsh, Jan. *The Pre-Raphaelite Sisterhood*. London: Quartet, 1985.

Maxwell, Catherine. 'Browning's Pygmalion and the Revenge of Galatea'. *English Literary History*, 60 (1993): 989–1013.

———. 'From Dionysus to "Dionea": Vernon Lee's Portraits'. *Word & Image*, 13: 3 (July–September, 1997): 253–69.

———. Vision and Visuality. In Alison Chapman and Anthony H. Harrison, eds, *A Companion to Victorian Poetry*. Oxford: Blackwell, 2002. 510–525.

———. 'Vernon Lee and Eugene Lee-Hamilton'. In Catherine Maxwell and Patricia Pulham, eds, *Vernon Lee: Decadence, Ethics, Aesthetics*. Basingstoke: Palgrave Macmillan, 2006. 21–39.

Maxwell, Catherine, and Patricia Pulham. Introduction. *Vernon Lee: Decadence, Ethics, Aesthetics*. Basingstoke: Palgrave Macmillan, 2006. 1–20.

McNeillie, Andrew. *The Essays of Virginia Woolf*. 4 vols. London: The Hogarth Press, 1986–1994. Vol. 1.

Meisel, Perry. *The Myth of the Modern: A Study in British Literature and Criticism after 1850*. New Haven and London: Yale University Press, 1987.

Melani, Sandro. 'I ritratti fatali di Vernon Lee'. *Rivista di Studi Vittoriani*, 1: 2 (July, 1996): 125–141.

Mérimée, Prosper. 'The Venus of Ille'. In *Carmen and Other Stories*. Trans. Nicholas Jotcham. Oxford: Oxford University Press, 1898. 132–61.

Michelson, Annette. 'On the Eve of the Future: The Reasonable Facsimile and the Philosophical Toy'. *October*, 29 (Summer, 1984): 3–20.

Miller, Felicia. 'Farinelli's Electronic Hermaphrodite and the Contralto Tradition'. In Richard Dellamora and Daniel Fischlin, eds, *The Work of Opera: Genre, Nationhood, and Sexual Difference*. New York: Columbia University Press, 1997. 73–92.

Mulvey, Laura. 'Visual Pleasure and Narrative Cinema'. *Screen*, 16: 3 (1975): 6–18.

Navarette, Susan. *The Shape of Fear: Horror and the Fin de Siècle Culture of Decadence* Kentucky: Kentucky University Press, 1998.

Newman, Sally. 'The Archival Traces of Desire: Vernon Lee's Failed Sexuality and the Interpretation of Letters in Lesbian History'. *Journal of the History of Sexuality*, 14: 1/2 (January/April, 2005): 51–75.

Nietzsche, Friedrich. *The Birth of Tragedy*. Ed. Michael Tanner. Trans. Shaun Whiteside. London: Penguin, 2003.

O'Connor, Noreen, and Joanna Ryan, eds, *Wild Desires and Mistaken Identities: Lesbianism and Psychoanalysis*. London: Virago, 1993.

Onslow, Barbara. 'Deceiving Images, Revealing Images: The Portrait in Victorian Women's Writing'. *Victorian Poetry*, 33: 3–4 (Autumn-Winter, 1995): 450–475.

Ovid. *Metamorphoses*. Trans. Mary M. Innes. London: Penguin, 1955.

Oxford English Dictionary, 2ⁿᵈ edn (Oxford: Clarendon Press, 1989).

Pacteau, Francette. 'The Impossible Referent: Representations of the Androgyne'. In Victor Burgin et al., *Formations of Fantasy*. London: Methuen, 1986. 62–84.

Paglia, Camille. *Sexual Personae: Art and Decadence from Nefertiti to Emily Dickinson*. London: Penguin, 1992.

Pater, Walter. 'Denys L'Auxerrois'. In *Imaginary Portraits*. London: Macmillan, 1910. 47–77.

Pater, Walter. 'A Study of Dionysus: The Spiritual Form of Fire and Dew'. *In Greek Studies: A Series of Essays*. London: Macmillan, 1928. 1–41.

———. *The Renaissance: Studies in Art and Poetry*. Oxford: Oxford University Press, 1986.

Pearsall, Cornelia, D.J. 'Browning and the Poetics of the Sepulchral Body'. In *Victorian Poetry*, 30: 1 (Spring 1992): 43–61.

Plato. *Charmides, Alcibiades 1&2, Hipparchus, The Lovers, Theages, Minos, Epinomis*. Ed. E. Capps et al. Trans. W. R. M. Lamb. London: Heinemann, 1927.

Plato. *Symposium*. Ed. and trans. Robin Waterfield. Oxford: Oxford University Press, 1994.

Poizat, Michel. '"The Blue Note" and "The Objectified Voice and the Vocal Object"'. *Cambridge Opera Journal*, 3 (1991): 195–211.

Pope, Rebecca A. 'The Diva doesn't Die: George Eliot's *Armgart*'. In Leslie C. Dunn and Nancy A. Jones, eds, *Embodied Voices: Representing Female Vocality in Western Culture*. Cambridge: Cambridge University Press, 1994. 139–151.

Potts, Alex. 'Male Phantasy and Modern Sculpture'. *Oxford Art Journal*, 15: 2 (1992): 38–47.

———. 'Dolls and Things: The Reification and Disintegration of Sculpture in Rodin and Rilke'. In John Onians, ed., *Sight and Insight: Essays on Art and Culture in Honour of E. H. Gombrich at 85*. London: Phaidon Press, 1994. 335–78.

———. *Flesh and the Ideal: Winckelmann and the Origins of Art History*. New Haven: Yale University Press, 1994.

Powell, Kerry. 'Hawthorne, Arlo Bates, and *The Picture of Dorian Gray*'. *Papers on Language and Literature: A Journal for Scholars and Critics of Language and Literature*, 16 (1980): 403–16.

Powell, Kerry. 'Tom, Dick, and Dorian Gray: Magic Picture Mania in Late Victorian Fiction'. *Psychological Quarterly*, 62: 2, (Spring 1983): 147–170.

Praz, Mario. Review. Vernon Lee: Violet Paget, 1856–1935 by Peter Gunn. *English Studies*, 47 (1966): 310–314.

Prins, Yopie. 'Greek Maenads, Victorian Spinsters'. In Richard Dellamora, ed., *Victorian Sexual Dissidence*. Chicago: The University of Chicago Press, 1997. 44–81.

Psomiades, Kathy Alexis. *Beauty's Body: Femininity and Representation in British Aestheticism*. Stanford: Stanford University Press, 1997.

———. '"Still Burning from This Strangling Embrace": Vernon Lee on Desire and Aesthetics'. In Richard Dellamora, ed., *Victorian Sexual Dissidence*. Chicago: The University of Chicago Press, 1997. 21–41.

Pulham, Patricia, 'Duality and Desire in Louis Norbert'. In Catherine Maxwell and Patricia Pulham, eds, *Vernon Lee: Decadence, Ethics, Aesthetics*. Basingstoke: Palgrave Macmillan, 2006. 123–142.

———. 'A Transatlantic Alliance: Charlotte Perkins Gilman and Vernon Lee'. In Ann Heilmann, ed., *Feminist Forerunners (New) Womanism and Feminism in the Early Twentieth Century.* London Pandora Press, 2003. 34–43.

Rands, William Brighty. 'The Love Story'. In Valentine Cunningham, ed., *The Victorians: An Anthology of Poetry and Prose*. Oxford: Blackwell, 2000. 56–67.

Reynolds, Margaret. 'Ruggiero's Deceptions, Cherubino's Distractions'. In Corinne E. Blackmer and Patricia Juliana Smith, eds, *En Travesti: Women, Gender, Subversion, Opera*. New York: Columbia University Press, 1995.

Richards, Sylvia L.F. 'The Eye and the Portrait: The Fantastic in Poe, Hawthorne and Gogol'. *Studies in Short Fiction*, 20: 4 (Fall, 1983): 307–315.

Richter, Simon. *Laocoön's Body and the Aesthetics of Pain: Winckelmann, Lessing, Herder, Moritz, Goethe*. Detroit: Wayne State University Press, 1992.

Rilke, Rainer Maria. 'Dolls: On the Wax Dolls of Lotte Pritzel'. In *Essays on Dolls: Kleist, Baudelaire, Rilke*. Ed and trans. Idris Parry and Paul Kegan. London: Penguin, 1994. 26–39.

———. 'The Rodin-Book: Second Part'. In *Rodin and Other Prose Pieces*. Trans. G. Craig Houston. London: Quartet Books, 1986. 44–71.

———. 'Some Reflections on Dolls (occasioned by the wax dolls of Lotte Pritzel)'. In *Rodin and Other Prose Pieces*. Trans. G. Craig Houston. London: Quartet Books, 1986. 119–126.

Rossetti, Christina. *Poems and Prose*. Ed. Jan Marsh. London: Everyman, 1994.

Rossetti, Dante Gabriel. *Selected Poems & Translations*. Ed. Clive Wilmer. Manchester: Carcanet, 1991.

Rudnytsky, Peter. Introduction. *Transitional Objects and Potential Spaces: Literary Uses of D. W. Winnicott*. New York: Columbia University Press, 1993. xi–xxii.

Schabert, Ina. 'An Amazon in Venice: Vernon Lee's "Lady Tal"'. In Manfred Pfister and Barbara Rodopi, eds. *Venetian Views, Venetian Blinds: English Fantasies of Venice*. Amsterdam: Scatt, 1999. 155–167.

Schiller, Friedrich. *On the Aesthetic Education of Man: In a Series of Letters*. Ed. and Trans. Elizabeth M. Wilkinson and L.A. Willoughby. Oxford: Clarendon Press, 1967.

Schneider, Monique. 'Paris, Summers 1985 and 1986'. In Elaine Hoffman Barach and Lucienne J. Serrano, eds, *Women Analyze Women*. New York: Harvester Wheatsheaf, 1988. 167–203.

Segal, Charles. 'The Gorgon and the Nightingale: The Voice of Female Lament and Pindar's Twelfth Pythian Ode'. In Leslie C. Dunn and Nancy A. Jones, eds, *Embodied Voices: Representing Female Vocality in Western Culture*. Cambridge: Cambridge University Press, 1994. 17–33.

Severi, Rita. Introduction. *Ariadne in Mantua*. By Vernon Lee. Mantova: Fondazione Marcegaglia, Gazoldo degli Ippoliti, 1996. 10–39.

Shelley, Percy Bysshe. 'On Love'. In Donald H. Reiman, and Sharon B. Powers, eds, *Shelley's Poetry and Prose*. New York: Norton, 1977. 473–474.

————. 'Alastor'. In Harold Bloom and Lionel Trilling, eds, *The Oxford Anthology of English Literature*. New York and London: Oxford University Press, 1973. 402–408.

Showalter, Elaine. *Sexual Anarchy: Gender and Culture at the Fin de Siècle*. London: Virago Press, 1992.

————. Introduction. *Daughters of Decadence: Women Writers of the Fin de Siècle*. London: Virago, 1995. vii–viii.

Silverman, Kaja. *The Acoustic Mirror: The Female Voice in Psychoanalysis and Cinema*. Bloomington: Indiana University Press, 1988.

Simms, Eva-Maria. 'Uncanny Dolls: Images of Death in Rilke and Freud'. *New Literary History*, 27 (1996): 633–77.

Smyth, Ethel. *Maurice Baring*. London: Heinemann, 1938.

Spencer, Herbert. *The Principles of Psychology*. 2 vols. 2nd edn, Vol. 2. London: Williams and Norgate, 1872.

Sprengnether, Madelon. 'Ghost Writing: A Meditation on Literary Criticism as Narrative'. In Peter L. Rudnytsky, ed., *Transitional Objects and Potential Spaces: Literary Uses of D. W. Winnicott*. New York: Columbia University Press, 1993. 87–98.

Stanton, Domna. 'Difference on Trial: A Critique of the Maternal Metaphor in Cixous, Irigaray, and Kristeva'. In Carolyn G. Heilbrun and Nancy K. Miller, eds, *The Poetics of Gender*. New York: Columbia University Press, 1986. 157–182.

Stewart, Susan. *On Longing: Narratives of the Miniature, the Gigantic, the Souvenir, the Collection*. Baltimore: Johns Hopkins University Press, 1984.

Stott, Rebecca. *The Fabrication of the Late-Victorian Femme Fatale: The Kiss of Death*. London:Macmillan, 1992.

Swinburne, Algernon Charles. 'Hermaphroditus'. In Catherine Maxwell, ed., *Algernon Charles Swinburne*. London: Everyman, 1997. 33–35.

Symonds, John Addington. *A Problem in Greek Ethics: Being An Inquiry into the Phenomenon of Sexual Inversion Addressed Especially to Medical Psychologists and Jurists*. London: Privately Printed, 1908.

————. *Studies of the Greek Poets*. 2 vols. London: Black. 1902.

Tintner, Adeline. *Henry James and the Lust of the Eyes: Thirteen Artists in His Work*. Baton Rouge: Louisiana State University Press, 1993. 95–104.

Vanita, Ruth. *Sappho and the Virgin Mary: Same-Sex Love and the English Literary Imagination*. New York: Columbia University Press, 1996.

Vicinus, Martha. 'The Adolescent Boy: Fin de Siècle Femme Fatale?' *Journal of the History of Sexuality*, 5 (1994): 90–114.

Waterfield, Robin. Introduction. *Symposium*. Oxford: Oxford University Press, 1994. xi–xl.

Watson, Jay. 'Guys and Dolls: Exploratory Repetition and Maternal Subjectivity in the Fort/Da Game'. *American Imago*, 52 (1995): 463–503.

Weber, Samuel. 'The Sideshow, or: Remarks on a Canny Moment'. *Modern Language Notes*, 88 (1973): 1102–1133.

Weil, Kari. *Androgyny and the Denial of Difference*. Charlottesville: University Press of Virginia, 1992.

Weir, Allison. 'Identification with the Divided Mother: Kristeva's Ambivalence'. In Kelly Oliver, ed., *Ethics, Politics, and Difference in Julia Kristeva's Writing*. New York: Routledge, 1993. 79–91.

Weissberg, Liliane. 'Language's Wound: Herder, Philoctestes, and the Origins of Speech'. *Modern Language Notes*, 104 (1989): 548–579.

Wilde, Oscar. *The Picture of Dorian Gray*. Ed. Donald L. Lawler. New York: Norton, 1988.

Wiley, Catherine. '"Waming Me Like a Cordial": The Ethos of the Body in Vernon Lee's Aesthetics'. In Catherine Maxwell and Patricia Pulham, eds, *Vernon Lee: Decadence, Ethics, Aesthetics*. Basingstoke: Palgrave Macmillan, 2006. 58–740.

Wilkinson, Elizabeth M. and Willloughby, L.A. Introduction. Friedrich Schiller, *On the Aesthetic Education of Man: In a Series of Letters*. Oxford: Clarendon Press, 1967. xi–cxcvi.

Winnicott, D.W. *Playing and Reality*. London and New York: Tavistock/Routledge, 1971.

Woolf, Virginia. *A Room of One's Own*. London: Penguin, 1965.

Ziolkowski, Theodore. *Disenchanted Images: A Literary Iconology*. Princeton: Princeton University Press, 1977.

Zorn, Christa. 'Aesthetic Intertextuality as Cultural Critique: Vernon Lee Rewrites History through Walter Pater's "La Gioconda"'. *Victorian Newsletter* (Spring 1997): 4–10.

Zorn, Christa. *Vernon Lee: Aesthetics, History, and the Victorian Female Intellectual*. Athens, Ohio: Ohio University Press, 2003.

Index